A probing exploration of the temporal dimensions of education. This book is an intellectual masterpiece that will set the standard for a long time to come.

Gert Biesta, Brunel University, London, UK

Questioning common assumptions regarding temporal rhythms is inherently transgressive. In this fascinating and groundbreaking theoretical analysis, Michel Alhadeff-Jones explores the intersection of temporal rhythms, learning processes and the dynamics of emancipatory education.

Stephen Brookfield, University of St. Thomas, USA

Unlike the scientist who quests for the instant of understanding, the educator has to make an ally of the full stretch of time. He or she needs to develop an appreciation of time's heterogeneous and contradictory nature rather than seeing it simply as the foe of speed and efficiency. Michel Alhadeff-Jones's study constitutes the richest examination of educational temporality I have ever encountered. It is immensely learned, assembling and responding to a body of literature that crosses multiple scholarly fields; it is penetratingly insightful, particularly in the way it explains how emancipation is, literally, a matter of rhythm; and it is utterly original. Educational theorists will find ample food for thought and debate in this book, and educators a groundbreaking way of reconceiving of their practice.

Rene V. Arcilla, New York University Steinhardt School of Culture, Education, and Human Development, USA

This deeply thoughtful book merits our attention so as to appreciate time's complexity, the subtlety of the analysis and its emancipatory intent. We often experience time as tyranny, at work, in classrooms, in families or as a general aspect of 'hyper-modernity'. Time may never seem our own. But there are routes to emancipation by taking time out to recognize tyrannies and how to transgress them. This compelling book combines interdisciplinary understanding with biographical sensibility to consider temporal constraints and resistance to them. So take time to read it, and consider time's biological, psychological, cultural and emancipatory rhythms. Giving time to the book will in fact be a good, transgressive act in its own right!

Linden West, Canterbury Christ Church University, UK

A very rich narrative on how diverse experiences of time structure our educational and learning experiences and vice-versa. Drawing on both continental and Anglo-American multidisciplinary sources, Michel Alhadeff-Jones constructs a framework that enables researchers and practitioners to explore new ways of considering how 'life rhythms' and institutional practices of work and learning often contradict each other, yet, how these conflicts can also be the source of emancipatory trajectories of both individuals and collectivities. A groundbreaking work that takes the reader step by step on an inspiring journey, from reductionist approaches to complexity-inspired views on human learning and education, whilst transgressing the boundaries between diverse practices such as formal and non-formal education, social work, vocational education and training and human resource development. This work opens new perspectives on how to conceive of emancipation in connection with the rhythms of life of individuals, institutions and societies.

Danny Wildemeersch, University of Leuven, Belgium

Time and the Rhythms of Emancipatory Education

Time and the Rhythms of Emancipatory Education argues that by rethinking the way we relate to time, we can fundamentally rethink the way we conceive education. Beyond the contemporary rhetoric of acceleration, speed, urgency or slowness, this book provides an epistemological, historical and theoretical framework that will serve as a comprehensive resource for critical reflection on the relationship between the experience of time and emancipatory education.

Drawing upon time and rhythm studies, complexity theories and educational research, Alhadeff-Jones reflects upon the temporal and rhythmic dimensions of education to (re)theorize and address current societal and educational challenges. The book is divided into three parts. The first begins by discussing the specificities inherent to the study of time in educational sciences. The second contextualizes the evolution of temporal constraints that determine the ways education is institutionalized, organized and experienced. The third and final part questions the meanings of emancipatory education in a context of temporal alienation.

This is the first book to provide a broad overview of European and North American theories that inform both the ideas of time and rhythm in educational sciences, from school instruction, curriculum design and arts education to vocational training, lifelong learning and educational policies. It will be of key interest to academics, researchers and postgraduate students in the fields of philosophy of education, sociology of education, history of education, psychology, curriculum and learning theory and adult education.

Michel Alhadeff-Jones is a psychosociologist and a philosopher of education. He works as an adjunct associate professor in the Adult Learning and Leadership Program at Teachers College, Columbia University. In Europe, he teaches at the universities of Fribourg and Geneva (Switzerland) and is associated with the French Laboratory of Research EXPERICE (Experience, Cultural Resources and Education) at the University of Paris 8. He is the founder of the Sunkhronos Institute located in Geneva.

Theorizing Education Series

Series Editors
Gert Biesta, *Brunel University, UK*
Julie Allan, *University of Birmingham, UK*
Richard Edwards, *University of Stirling, UK*

For a full list of titles in this series, please visit www.routledge.com

Theorizing Education brings together innovative work from a wide range of contexts and traditions which explicitly focus on the roles of theory in educational research and educational practice. The series includes contextual and sociohistorical analyses of existing traditions of theory and theorizing, exemplary use of theory and empirical work where theory has been used in innovative ways. The distinctive focus for the series is the engagement with educational questions, articulating what explicitly educational function the work of particular forms of theorizing supports.

Books in this series:

Forgotten Connections
On culture and upbringing
Klaus Mollenhauer
Translated by Norm Friesen

Psychopathology at School
Theorizing mental disorders in education
Valerie Harwood and Julie Allan

Curriculum Theorizing and Teacher Education
Complicating conjunctions
Anne M. Phelan

Filmed School
Desire, transgression and the filmic fantasy of pedagogy
James Stillwaggon and David Jelinek

On the Politics of Educational Theory
Rhetoric, theoretical ambiguity and the construction of society
Tomasz Szkudlarek

Time and the Rhythms of Emancipatory Education
Rethinking the temporal complexity of self and society
Michel Alhadeff-Jones

Time and the Rhythms of Emancipatory Education

Rethinking the temporal complexity of self and society

Michel Alhadeff-Jones

LONDON AND NEW YORK

First published 2017
by Routledge
2 Park Square, Milton Park, Abingdon, Oxon OX14 4RN

and by Routledge
711 Third Avenue, New York, NY 10017

First issued in paperback 2018

Routledge is an imprint of the Taylor & Francis Group, an informa business

© 2017 Michel Alhadeff-Jones

The right of Michel Alhadeff-Jones to be identified as author of this work has been asserted by him in accordance with sections 77 and 78 of the Copyright, Designs and Patents Act 1988.

All rights reserved. No part of this book may be reprinted or reproduced or utilised in any form or by any electronic, mechanical, or other means, now known or hereafter invented, including photocopying and recording, or in any information storage or retrieval system, without permission in writing from the publishers.

Trademark notice: Product or corporate names may be trademarks or registered trademarks, and are used only for identification and explanation without intent to infringe.

British Library Cataloguing in Publication Data
A catalogue record for this book is available from the British Library.

Library of Congress Cataloging in Publication Data
Names: Alhadeff-Jones, Michel, author.
Title: Time and the rhythms of emancipatory education : rethinking the temporal complexity of self and society / Michel Alhadeff-Jones.
Description: New York, NY : Routledge, 2016. | Includes bibliographical references and index.
Identifiers: LCCN 2016022877 | ISBN 9781138845848 (hardcover) | ISBN 9781315727899 (electronic)
Subjects: LCSH: Transformative learning. | Time.
Classification: LCC LC1100 .A55 2016 | DDC 370.11/5—dc23
LC record available at https://lccn.loc.gov/2016022877

ISBN 13: 978-1-138-60219-9 (pbk)
ISBN 13: 978-1-138-84584-8 (hbk)

Typeset in Bembo
by Apex CoVantage, LLC

In memoriam
Benjamin Wilson Alhadeff (1919–2010)
Jacques Ardoino (1927–2015)

Contents

Acknowledgements xi

Introduction: How to establish the educational values of time? 1

PART I
The study of time in educational sciences 13

1 The study of time and its epistemological challenges 15
2 Theorizing educational temporalities 32
3 The functions and meanings of temporal constraints in education 50

PART II
The evolution of temporal constraints and the rhythms of education 67

4 The evolution of temporal discipline in education, from antiquity to the Early Modern period 69
5 Temporal efficiency and rhythmic harmony, two competing educational ideals at the turn of the 20th century 86
6 The rise of temporal double binds in formal education throughout the second half of the 20th century 104
7 The rhythms of lifelong learning, between continuity and discontinuity 121

PART III
Theorizing the rhythms of emancipation in education 139

8 The meanings of emancipation within a context
of temporal alienation 141

9 Toward a rhythmic theory of emancipation in education 158

10 Facilitating emancipatory education, from critical pedagogy
to rhythmanalysis 172

11 The moment of emancipation and the rhythmic patterns
of transgression 191

12 The emergence of a rhythmological critique and
the moment of theory in education 209

Index 219

Acknowledgements

A book emerges from the succession and the organization of heterogeneous rhythms, among them the rhythms of research, exchanges and discussions; the rhythms of reflection, reading, writing and resting; and the rhythms of edition, production and distribution. Some of those rhythms involve slowness and maturation; others reveal spontaneity or speed. All require to be adjusted and regulated. I would like to express my deep gratitude to those who stimulated, supported and nurtured the rhythms required for this book to come to existence. I am grateful to my wife, Natasha, for her ongoing support and the sacrifices she made so that I could stay committed to this project on a daily basis. With the concomitant births of our two children, Noemie and Nathaniel, I also owe my family a fair amount of attention. The reflection developed in this book would have probably never emerged if I did not have the opportunity to elaborate and confront my ideas with the colleagues and the students I have been working with. I am much appreciative for the steady support Victoria Marsick and Lyle York provide to the life history seminars I have been facilitating for the last 12 years as they are respectively coordinating the Adult Learning and Leadership Program, and the Adult Education Guided Intensive Study Doctoral Program at Teachers College. I am also particularly grateful to John Broughton, who encouraged me to design and develop an original interdisciplinary course on time and education in the Arts and Humanities Department. Through my teachings at Columbia University, and the Universities of Geneva and Fribourg, I have the opportunity to meet outstanding people who feed my reflections around time, rhythms and emancipation. My appreciation goes to all the students who trusted me by sharing their life histories and allow me to learn from their experiences. My thankfulness goes especially to Ruth, who accepted her narrative to be featured in this book. Among the colleagues who helped me envisioning and building up the relevance of this project over time, I would particularly like to thank Rene Arcilla, Francis Lesourd, Pascal Michon and Megan Laverty for their inspiring advice, their intellectual stimulation and their friendly support. I am also deeply grateful to Gert Biesta, who invited me to submit the project of this manuscript and recognized the value of my contribution. Doing so, he provided me with the *kairos* – the opportune time – to grow my reflection into a shared narrative. Finally, I would like to acknowledge the editorial team at Routledge, as well as Sadegh Nashat, my friend and colleague at the Sunkhronos Institute, for their support, feedback and assistance throughout this process.

Introduction
How to establish the educational values of time?

When I started working at the University of Geneva in 2000, courses were still provided on a yearly basis over a period of eight months.[1] In 2004, when I moved to New York City and designed my first life history seminar at Columbia University,[2] I had to adjust a process that used to be facilitated over 30 sessions to fit within a five-week period. It required me to divide the number of class hours by two. The compression – some would call it an acceleration – was not only concerning the amount of time spent with students; it was also affecting the frequency of our encounters and the learning process that was occurring between each session. Such an experience triggered in me what I would call today a 'rhythmic dissonance', that is, a conflict inherent to the tensions between the temporal standards that were defining my practice in higher education in Switzerland and the temporal constraints that characterized the academic environment I was getting accustomed to. Some would argue that it may have been the opportunity for me to increase the efficiency of my teaching. There is no doubt that adjustments could be made; after all my American colleagues were used to teaching in such a temporal setting, and students were displaying preferences for fast-paced curricula. Questions remained however: what would be the impact on the learning dynamics? Would it be possible to accelerate any aspects of the learning process? How to negotiate the rhythms involved in critical and complex processes, such as introspection, self-reflection or the establishment of a trustful group dynamic? Beyond the efficiency associated with a specific class format, what would be communicated to participants regarding the value of a slower pace of learning?

The experience of temporal pressures is not new in education. Since the end of the 14th century, it was documented by humanist scholars who were confronted with a significant increase of books to study (Dohrn-van Rossum, 1997, p. 262). Temporal pressures eventually increased through the Early Modern period as the ideal of improving school efficiency became more prominent. With the Industrial Revolution, such an ideal became ubiquitous in Western countries. More recently, accelerated learning programs emerged during the 1970s in higher education to provide working adult students with opportunities to take less time than conventional curricula to attain university certification

(Wlodkowski, 2003). Nowadays, acceleration and standardization trigger critical reactions. For the proponents of the slow school movement (e.g., Domènech Francesch, 2009), the increased pace imposed on formal education appears as another consequence of its commodification. Because of the limitations they impose on the exercise of reflexivity and the conception of the future they favor (e.g., Clegg, 2010), the perverse effects produced by the temporal logics inherent to neoliberalism are also denounced in higher and adult education. However, critics denouncing the alienating consequences of the increased tempo of education are not new either. At its origins, the Greek *scholè* literally referred to the ideas of free time, rest and delay, suggesting that school's critical function was to provide an environment detached from the time and space of both society and the household (Masschelein & Simons, 2013, p.28). Twenty-five centuries ago in *Republic*, Plato was already theorizing the connection that may exist between the development of a 'good soul' and learners' exposition to 'good rhythm'. In *Emile*, Rousseau (1762/1966) suggested that 'losing one's time' may be the most valuable rule for education. Later, at the turn of the century, emerging dissents got a significant momentum in Europe, with the formulation of rhythmic theories of education privileging students' inner rhythms over those imposed by the rise of industrialization and capitalism (Hanse, 2007). Nowadays, considering time as a central aspect of education is a truism. Determining how to establish its value constitutes, however, a much more problematic issue. There is indeed no single way to proceed.

The complexity of educational time

Time represents both a crucial concept to interpret one's own experience and a taken-for-granted dimension of everyday life. It is inherent to the most profound aspects of one's existence (e.g., one's own finitude) as much as it allows one to regulate the most superficial daily routines (e.g., being on time). It can be conceived as universal (e.g., seasons), providing one with a resource to measure local changes (e.g., organization); its appreciation remains however contingent, depending on factors such as history, place and activity. It is thus collectively defined (e.g., calendars or ages of life), but its perception varies according to individual experiences (e.g., one's mood or life history). When it enables the planning and the synchronization of numerous operations (e.g., at work or with friends), it provides one with a feeling of coherence and predictability that constitutes a source of order; but when it is lived through conflicting temporal demands (e.g., work vs. family or long-term planning vs. spontaneous actions), it appears as a disabling cause of stress, confusion and suffering. Time is often considered as neutral (e.g., the clock); however, the meanings it takes (e.g., being fast/slow, early/late, retarded/advanced, or mature/immature) remains socially constructed. And because such meanings impact individual and collective actions, time remains fundamentally a locus of power dynamics. If the idea of time suggests some form of singularity, temporalities are always plural. The multiple changes they refer to (e.g., individual, organizational, institutional, and environmental) all contribute to the definition of who we are, how we behave and what we learn. Education is therefore shaped by the heterogeneous, complementary, antagonistic and contradictory temporalities that rhythm the activity and the life of learners, educators, institutions, society and knowledge itself. Education also determines the way we learn to relate to time and the heterogeneous rhythms of existence (e.g., school temporal discipline or family routines). Whether it is grasped through everyday experience, philosophical inquiry, artistic expressions, religious meanings or through scientific theories, time is therefore neither a simple idea waiting to be explained nor a complicated phenomenon ready to be decomposed and analyzed. It should rather be envisioned as a complex phenomenon. As such, it relates to heterogeneous forms of change, occurring at the different levels of one's existence (e.g., physical, biological, psychological, social, esthetic, and spiritual), plaited together, interwoven in a way that is hardly apprehended by the mind, not easily analyzed or disentangled. Time appears thus as a truly complex topic of investigation. But what does it mean to make such complexity intelligible? How does it impact the way we conceive educational theories and practices? And more fundamentally, how does it relate to transformation and emancipation?

Time and critique

In 2009, when I designed and implemented at Teachers College a course titled *Time and Learning: Developing the Rhythms of Empowerment*, my drive was to explore with students the connections between the development of critical reflection, lifelong learning, and an experience of time, often lived as a source of tensions, stress or even suffering. Inspired, among others, by the innovative work of my French colleague Gaston Pineau (2000), I was intrigued by the idea that the experience of rhythms could become a matter of *formation*. Assuming that Late Modernity may be characterized by specific struggles and conflicts associated with a more intense feeling of acceleration and urgency (e.g., Bouton, 2013; Rosa, 2005/2013), it was clear that such phenomena should constitute a matter of concern from an educational and scholarly point of view as well. Whether the mechanisms explaining their emergence are new or belong to ongoing social dynamics still remains up for debate (Archer, 2014). However, there was no doubt that people's experience of temporal alienation, expressed through emerging forms of discrimination and struggle, had to be questioned from an educational perspective. It seemed therefore crucial to explore further how people may learn to develop a new form of critical sensibility toward their own experience of time and the way it is shaped by society. Beyond the instrumental aspects of time management strategies, what seemed critical was to question how to challenge the deeply held assumptions that limit the way people experience time. Four years later, such questions led to the elaboration of this book and the formulation of the three main postulates that ground the reflection conducted.

The necessity of organizing heterogeneous temporal influences

The complexity inherent to the idea of time appears through both everyday experience and scholarly research. In Western societies, the experience of time has probably never been as ordered, controlled and disciplined than it is today. At the same time, individual lives may also be more often experienced as discontinuous, troubled and chaotic than before. Between the increased pressure of temporal orders and the daily experience of disorganized temporalities, people have to learn how to negotiate the heterogeneous rhythms that compose their lives. To some extent, the same is true at the epistemic level. In many disciplines (e.g., physics, biology, psychology, and sociology), conceptions of time are more formalized nowadays than ever before in the history of human thought; at the same time, they still remain fragmented and unrelated to each other (Adam, 1994). Theoretical confusion emerges whenever one tries to interpret how heterogeneous temporalities (e.g., cosmological, embodied, cultural, and social) influence each other, as it is the case in education. The complexity of temporal matters thus constitutes an existential as much as a practical and theoretical issue. It requires the development of interdisciplinary approaches (e.g., Fraser, 1966) that distinguish and articulate the relationships between heterogeneous knowledge and experiences. Research on time should provide scholars and practitioners with a privileged field of study to explore the connections and influences between heterogeneous phenomena that may be simultaneously perceived or experienced as complementary, antagonistic and contradictory (Morin, 1990/2008).

The importance of enriching temporal imagination

A second assumption framing the reflection conducted in this book is that to grasp the complexity of time, our temporal imagination has to be enriched, and a new language has to be established. Following Castoriadis's (1975/1997) contribution, it seems thus critical to challenge the representations that frame the ways time is conceived in everyday life (e.g., time as the quantitative measure of changes) and through scholarly discourses (e.g., time as an abstract concept or as a social construct). Part of the processes through which the experience of time becomes a source of alienation relates to the fact that the ways it is represented, depicted and imagined nowadays does not allow one to envision it as a complex fabric of experiences. The vocabulary may already exist (e.g., temporality, rhythm, moment, pattern, periodicity, movement, *kairos*, etc.), but the meanings associated to the semantics of time still have to be further reflected, nuanced and enriched to discriminate, interpret, evaluate, argue, judge and challenge more critically one's experience. If "[t]he essence of any tyranny resides in the fierce refusal of complexity" (Burckhardt, as cited in Ardoino & Lourau, 1994, p. 57, my translation), then the contemporary experiences of temporal alienation may be perpetuated by the persistent difficulty to imagine and negotiate the complexity of time beyond reductionist conceptions, including those found in common, everyday language and tight academic contributions, as elaborated as they may be.

The relevance of renewing rhythmic theories in education

The necessity of elaborating a framework to critically organize heterogeneous temporal conceptions and the need to further refine the way time is thought, imagined and conceptualized in education, lead to a third assumption. To proceed, it seems particularly meaningful to adopt a perspective focusing on the rhythmic aspects that characterize temporal experiences. From this angle, the reflection conducted in this book benefits from the pioneering work of philosophers such as Whitehead and Bachelard, anthropologists and sociologists such as Mauss and Lefebvre, or semiologists and linguists such as Benveniste, Barthes and Meschonnic, who all explored throughout the 20th century the critical aspects associated with the analysis of rhythmic phenomena. More specifically, the framework developed in this book relies on the recent contribution of scholars such as Michon (2005, 2007) and Sauvanet (2000a, 2000b), who have both developed systematic and synthetic theories that privilege complex and transdisciplinary understanding of rhythms as constitutive of the fabric of temporal experience. Beyond their specific inputs, the value of those models – and the intent of this book – has therefore to be understood through the positions they occupy in the contemporary renewal of a long tradition of research around human rhythms and their political dimensions (Michon, 2012a, 2012b), a tradition that crossed many times the history of educational theory itself. It is strongly believed that such an approach may open up a path toward the development of innovative educational methods, revisiting fruitful and well-established intuitions and focusing on the in-depth analysis of everyday rhythms.

Rethinking educational rhythms

Based on those three assumptions, the aim of this book is to renew the way time can be envisioned, and therefore experienced, in education and beyond. Referring to the concept of rhythm, it challenges how the complex organization of heterogeneous temporalities may be conceived in practice and in theory. More specifically, it explores how the rhythms that regulate the lifelong dynamics of emancipation may be envisioned and theorized from an educational perspective. Doing so, the reflection conducted also participates to broader intellectual efforts. Claiming that educational sciences occupy a specific position in the scientific arena, due to the cross-pollination of the disciplinary backgrounds they mobilize and the relevance of education as a ubiquitous human phenomenon

(Charlot, 1995), this reflection may also contribute to existing debates around the specificities of educational theory (Biesta, Allan, & Edwards, 2014; Charlot, 1995). In addition, it is also carried on by the desire to fill the gap existing between different linguistic areas as they express heterogeneous cultural sensibilities around the notions of time, rhythm, critique and complexity and the way they are interpreted in educational theory (Alhadeff-Jones, 2010). At the core, the reflection conducted in this book claims that by rethinking the way we relate to time, we can fundamentally rethink the way we conceive education. Inspired by complexivist scholarship, informed by time and rhythm studies, and committing to systematically explore the evolution of educational praxis and theory, the reflection conducted provides the reader with a resource that should serve as a comprehensive introduction to critically reflect on the matter of time and education, privileging questions raised by the development of autonomy and the promotion of emancipation. This book should therefore provide graduate students, practitioners, researchers, and policy makers with an epistemological, historical and theoretical framework to conceive and challenge both the heterogeneous rhythms that frame their activities and what is at stake in the process of theorizing the critical role they play in education.

Book organization

The study of time in educational sciences

To start envisioning the complexity inherent to the idea of time, the first chapter of this book explores some of the main contributions that inform its understanding in philosophy, physics, biology and human sciences. It provides the reader with a multidisciplinary background to better understand the origins and the evolution of the representations and the discourses on time found in educational theory. Inspired by Morin's (1990/2008) paradigm of complexity, this first chapter also introduces principles of thought that provide an epistemological framework to interpret complementary, antagonistic and contradictory time theories and temporal phenomena.

A lot has been written about time and education; however, the contribution of this literature remains relatively marginal and clearly disparate. The second chapter discusses the specificity of studying time in educational sciences. It provides a theoretical lens to organize and question the fragmented literature informing the ideas of time and rhythm in educational research and praxis. Educational temporalities relate to multiple forms of change (e.g., physical, biological, psychological, and social) that affect every level of existence from the most material to the most spiritual. The hybridity of educational time appears as a key feature that translates one of the specificities of educational theory. Some educational phenomena require slowness and maturation (e.g., development); others may involve speed and efficiency (e.g., classroom management). Thus, whenever multiple temporalities need to be articulated and organized, there is a necessity to think about how they are conceived and how they relate with each other: how are they envisioned, measured, or valorized? Which one is privileged or takes over the others? Theorizing educational temporalities requires the development of both an epistemology and a research method that privilege the articulation of heterogeneous points of view grounded in multiple disciplines and revealing conflicting finalities. It requires one to conceive jointly the epistemological, cultural and political dimensions involved.

This is particularly true when the aim of education is apprehended through the lens of autonomy and emancipation. The assumption that frames the third chapter is that to theorize what is at stake in a process of emancipation from a temporal and educational perspective, one must first understand the dynamics through which autonomy evolves and may be regulated. Such dynamics suggest the interplay between physical, biological and social influences that occur through time and that determine how time itself is experienced. The notion of temporal constraint is introduced to refer to the heterogeneous forms of temporal influence that impact the development of individual and collective autonomy. Privileging a sociological perspective, temporal constraints are first conceived through the prism of social history: the genealogy of the temporal norms, standards and influences among institutions (e.g., religion and economy) that impact the evolution of education. Temporal constraints are also conceived from an institutionalist perspective stressing how, as a social construct, time carries both functional and symbolic effects that shape human activity. Temporal constraints may appear thus through the organizational functions they fulfill (e.g., regulating social order). Symbolically, they are tight to the bounded representations of time instituted through education (e.g., age norms). Considering the critical role played by the representations and the discourses through which time is envisioned, the concept of rhythm is finally introduced as a way to question and enrich the interpretation of temporal experiences theorized in education.

The evolution of temporal constraints and the rhythms of education

Based on the assumptions developed in the three first chapters, the second part of the book explores and contextualizes how temporal constraints have evolved through the history of education and what they may reveal about the relationships among time, rhythms, autonomy and education. Accordingly, the fourth chapter analyzes the history of the relationships among temporal constraints, education and society, considering the increasing formalization of educational time and the implementation of rhythmic discipline. The rhythmic features of early Jewish education, musical education during Spartan and Hellenic periods, monastic education throughout medieval times, and the introduction of new school regulations during the Early Modern period are discussed. Those examples illustrate how the rhythms that shape education also participate to the reproduction of the social and political order of a community through the preservation of tradition, culture, language, the control of habits and routines and the spreading of specific temporal standards.

The fifth chapter contextualizes and describes the twofold movement that characterizes educational research and theory from a temporal and rhythmic perspective at the turn of the 20th century. On the one hand, the scientific study of instructional time appears then as a means to further refine the temporal discipline previously introduced in school organization to fulfill the ideal of efficiency promoted by the Industrial Revolution. On the other hand, the emergence of educational methods privileging artistic and embodied rhythmic experiences (e.g., Jaques-Dalcroze's eurhythmics, Bode's rhythmic gymnastics and Steiner's anthroposophy) participates to a countermovement invested by people who were driven by a social ideal of rhythmic harmony.

Since the 1950s, a significant shift occurred in the conception of the relationship between time and the politics of education. The emancipatory aim expressed through the development of rhythmic education faded away, replaced by the micropolitics of temporal autonomy. Analyzing the development of studies related to instructional and didactic time, the implementation of nongraded curricula or learning cycles, and the contribution of chronobiological and chronopsychological research to educational policy, the sixth chapter discusses how, throughout the second half of the 20th century, the requirement to accommodate conflicting temporal demands (e.g., managing time efficiently vs. respecting each pupil's own rhythm) appears as an emerging feature within formal education. The internalization of temporal double binds constitutes, since then, a shift in the way time and autonomy are conceived and experienced by educators. Professionals are now confronted with a new form of temporal constraint, potentially leading to inner tensions and conflicts within the institution.

Such a movement has also been reinforced by the social and cultural transformations that led to the emergence of lifelong learning policy, the defragmentation of formal education and the increased need to embrace the discontinuities characterizing formal, nonformal and informal education. The experience of discontinuity has been progressively recognized throughout the 20th century as a constraining feature of education. The seventh chapter analyzes this phenomenon through four lenses: the rhythms that characterize the learner's activity, alternating between freedom and constraint; the effects associated with the *alternance* between work and study in the dual organization of vocational education; the relationship between formal and informal education throughout lifelong learning; and the formative dimension associated with the heterogeneous temporalities that constitute adult learners' life history (e.g., family vs. work time). As they illustrate the way continuities and discontinuities may be experienced, such contributions further reveal the educational power associated with the capacity to elaborate temporal cohesion through the organization of educational rhythms.

Theorizing the rhythms of emancipation in education

What emerges from the previous chapters is that the relationship between temporal constraints and autonomy is shaped by multiple logics (e.g., temporal norms, temporal discipline, increased confusion inherent to conflicting temporal demands and discontinuities that punctuate the course of one's life). In the contemporary societal context – at least in Western countries – the effects of such dynamics have become more intense, influenced by the increased preponderance of 'speed' within our society. Such phenomena have brought scholars to focus more specifically on how people experience and eventually suffer from a greater sense of urgency, a more intense pace of life, and a sustained feeling of acceleration of their everyday lives. In this temporal environment, what does it mean to be emancipated, and what does a process of emancipation involve? Those questions are located at the core of the third part of the book.

Thus, the eighth chapter discusses the rhythmicity of a process of emancipation and the forms of temporal alienation that characterize today's social environment. Emancipation is conceived through the fluidity that defines both its aim (between autonomy and dependence) and the nature of the changes it may carry (between ongoing process and steady state). Furthermore, emancipation requires the capacity to articulate the complementary, contradictory and antagonistic rhythms that shape the ways temporal constraints are experienced in everyday life.

Beyond the rhetoric of accelerated and slow education, a theory of educational rhythms appears as a necessary contribution to nuance and interpret the relationships among the experience of temporal constraints, autonomy and dependence. Based on the historical examples developed through the second part of the book, and inspired by contemporary rhythm theories (Lefebvre, Michon and Sauvanet), the ninth chapter sketches what may be at stake in such a framework. The exploration of rhythmic 'patterns' leads to focus on how people's social, discursive and corporeal activities display forms of temporal organization that affect autonomy and agency. Studying the 'periodicity' of educational rhythms brings one to interrogate the relationships between the qualities of repetitive behaviors and the experience of alienation. Investigating the 'movement' of educational rhythms questions the singularity of one's rhythms and the transformative role played by the experience of discontinuity in the process of emancipation.

The tenth chapter explores the rhythmic dimensions of pedagogical approaches whose aim is to promote emancipation. Focusing on Freire, Rancière and Mezirow's contributions as illustrations, it discusses some of the assumptions and limitations inherent to contemporary critical pedagogies from a temporal perspective. The development of rhythm-centered pedagogical approaches is then considered. Bachelard and Lefebvre's considerations around the idea of rhythmanalysis are introduced. Their influence on educational theory is illustrated through the contributions of two generations of contemporary French scholars who explicitly refer to rhythmanalysis in the field of adult and higher education.

The eleventh chapter explores further the relevance of the theoretical framework previously conceived to interpret how the biographical movement through which someone increases one's autonomy is organized around patterns and periodicities that reveal the rhythmicity of emancipation. The rhythmic features of emancipation and alienation are first theorized through Lefebvre's theory of moments. As a moment of existence, emancipation is then conceived in relation to experiences of transgression that open up a time of rupture. The life narrative of a young adult is then interpreted to illustrate three rhythmic features of emancipation: the singular biographical movement through which one learns to relate to transgression; the periodicity of activities experienced, either as alienating or liberating; and the patterns of transgression and the strategies developed to accommodate the temporal constraints that rhythm one's life.

To open up the reflection initiated throughout this book, the last chapter suggests six core issues that should be considered to develop further the elaboration of a rhythmological theory of emancipatory education and the praxis it may involve. Adopting a recursive position, it concludes with a reflection around the specific rhythms of educational theory and some of their critical functions.

Notes

1 At that time, the Bologna process, whose aim was to increase the standardization of higher education in Europe, was initiated, but not yet implemented.
2 The format of this course requires not only theoretical readings, but also the individual writing of one's own life history, the sharing of oral narratives with classmates, the reading of each other's written narrative, and group discussions centered on each narrative, as well.

References

Adam, B. (1994). *Time and social theory*. Cambridge: Polity Press.
Alhadeff-Jones, M. (2010). Challenging the limits of critique in education through Morin's paradigm of complexity. *Studies in Philosophy and Education*, 29(5), 477–490.
Archer, M.S. (Ed.). (2014). *Late modernity, trajectories towards morphogenic society*. London: Springer.
Ardoino, J., & Lourau, R. (1994). *Les pédagogies institutionnelles*. Paris: Presses Universitaires de France.
Biesta, G., Allan, J., & Edwards, R. (Eds.). (2014). *Making a difference in theory: The theory question in education and the education question in theory*. London: Routledge.
Bouton, C. (2013). *Le temps de l'urgence*. Lormont, France: Le Bord de l'eau.
Castoriadis, C. (1997). *The imaginary institution of society* (K. Blamey, Trans.). Malden, MA: Polity Press. (Original work published 1975)
Charlot, B. (1995). *Les sciences de l'éducation: Un enjeu, un défi*. Paris: ESF.
Clegg, S. (2010). Time future: The dominant discourse of higher education. *Time & Society*, 19(3), 345–364.
Dohrn-van Rossum, G. (1997). *L'histoire de l'heure: L'horlogerie et l'organisation moderne du temps*. Paris: Maison des Sciences de l'Homme.

Domènech Francesch, J. (2009). *Elogio de la educación lenta*. Barcelona: Grao.
Fraser, J.T. (1966). *The voices of time*. New York: George Braziller.
Hanse, O. (2007). *Rythme et civilisation dans la pensée allemande autour de 1900*. [Electronic version]. Doctoral dissertation, Université Rennes 2, France. Retrieved January 15, 2014, from https://tel.archives-ouvertes.fr/tel-00204429
Masschelein, J., & Simons, M. (2013). *In defence of the school: A public issue* (J. McMartin, Trans.). Leuwen, Belgium: E-ducation, Culture & Society Publishers.
Michon, P. (2005). *Rythmes, pouvoir, mondialisation*. Paris: Presses Universitaires de France.
Michon, P. (2007). *Les rythmes du politique*. Paris: Les Prairies Ordinaires.
Michon, P. (2012a). *Notes éparses sur le rythme comme enjeu artistique, scientifique et philosophique depuis la fin du XVIIIème siècle*. Retrieved December 12, 2013, from http://rhuthmos.eu/spip.php?article540
Michon, P. (2012b). *Une brève histoire de la théorie du rythme depuis les années 1970*. Retrieved December 12, 2013, from http://rhuthmos.eu/spip.php?article608
Morin, E. (2008). *On complexity* (S.M. Kelly, Trans.). Cresskill, NJ: Hampton Press. (Original work published 1990)
Pineau, G. (2000). *Temporalités en formation: Vers de nouveaux synchroniseurs*. Paris: Anthropos.
Rosa, H. (2013). *Social acceleration: A new theory of modernity* (J. Trejo-Mathys, Trans.). New York: Columbia University Press. (Original work published 2005)
Rousseau, J.-J. (1966). *Emile ou de l'éducation*. Paris: Flammarion. (Original work published 1762)
Sauvanet, P. (2000a). *Le rythme et la raison (vol. 1): Rythmologiques*. Paris: Kimé.
Sauvanet, P. (2000b). *Le rythme et la raison (vol. 2): Rythmanalyses*. Paris: Kimé.
Wlodkowski, R.J. (2003). Accelerated learning in colleges and universities. *New Directions for Adult and Continuing Education, 97*, 93–97.

Part I
The study of time in educational sciences

Chapter 1

The study of time and its epistemological challenges

Time and complexity

The way time is conceived in education translates influences that encompass a broad range of perspectives. Philosophical inquiry, physics, biology or sociology provide us with key contributions to describe and interpret the temporalities shaping educational phenomena. As it will also appear in the following chapters, contributions from the history of religions, economy, linguistics and the arts also provide significant insights that have to be considered to understand how the representation and the experience of time evolve in education. From a cultural perspective, the analysis conducted in this book is purposefully limited to conceptions mainly developed throughout the history of the Western world. The choice has thus been made to discuss issues related to the epistemology of time, based on the diversity of perspectives developed within European and North American scholarship, rather than through a broader comparative inquiry. This is a significant limitation and a debatable choice that resulted from the necessity to set boundaries, considering the richness of the topic, the space available to discuss it and the cultural background surrounding the production of this book.

Such a limitation is only one among other reductions operated.[1] It reveals one of the major issues inherent to the study of time: the challenge inherent to the understanding of the complexity of the discourses and logics that shape how time is conceived and experienced. When considering the history of thought, a double movement seems indeed to emerge. On the one hand, it is characterized by the multiplication and the increased sophistication of representations, produced within human societies to describe, interpret and measure the experience of change, through various languages, mythologies, arts, doctrines or theories. On the other hand, to be conceived by people, including artists, philosophers, scientists or scholars, the idea of time appears systematically fragmented, compartmentalized and reduced according to the logics shaping social practices or disciplines. The way the idea of time is envisioned nowadays in academia, in education, and in society at large is therefore caught in intertwined processes of knowledge production that increase and reduce at the same time the complexity associated with this notion (e.g., Adam, 1994; Fraser, 1966, 1987; Pomian, 1984).

Taking seriously the complexity of time in education requires one to be aware of, and to question, such a fragmentation. Thus, formulating a nontrivial description and interpretation of the ways intertwined aspects of time shape educational phenomena raises the challenges of articulating knowledge coming from a heterogeneous range of sources. It leads one to reflect on the assumptions and logics that rule the organization of knowledge production, especially in academia (Morin, 1982) and through education more broadly (e.g., Morin, 2014). It requires one to adopt what Morin (1990/2008) has described as a 'complex thought' (*pensée complexe*). Referring to the notion of complexity does not however provide any straight answers to deal with the heterogeneity of theories of time. Indeed, if a Cartesian epistemology reduces complex phenomena to an analysis of their components – understood as simple, absolute and objective – a complexivist epistemology favors understanding phenomena as part of a fabric of relations: "There is no simple idea, because a simple idea . . . is always inserted, to be understood, in a complex system of thoughts and experiences" (Bachelard, 1934/2003, p. 152, my translation). The recognition of complexity appears thus at the origins of a specific kind of scientific explanation that perceives simplicity as a specific provisional phenomenon. If complication refers to the idea of an intricate situation waiting to be disentangled, complexity supposes then the fundamental non-simplicity of studied phenomena (Ardoino, 2000).

Accordingly, the reflection developed in this book assumes that time is neither a simple idea waiting to be explained nor a complicated phenomenon ready to be decomposed and analyzed. Interpreting the study of time as a complex phenomenon means – according to the etymology of the term – that it embraces or comprehends heterogeneous elements plaited together, interwoven in a way that is hardly apprehended by the mind, not easily analyzed or disentangled (Alhadeff-Jones, 2008; Ardoino, 2000). The idea of time, and the phenomena it refers to, raise questions that are fundamentally complex, and as such, their study in education requires not only theoretical considerations but also the development of an epistemology that defines principles according to which it can be conducted (Alhadeff-Jones, 2010).

Inspired by the pioneering work of Morin in anthropology of knowledge and his epistemological contribution to the definition of a "paradigm of complexity" (1973, 1977/1992, 1977–2004/2008, 1982, 1990/2008), the primary aim of this chapter is to identify principles that may provide us with an epistemological ground to navigate theories that appear simultaneously as complementary, antagonistic and contradictory with each other. Doing so, this chapter also provides the reader with a broad (but necessarily superficial) overview of some of the main ideas that inform the contemporary understanding of time in philosophy, physics, biology and human sciences to better understand the origins and the roots of the discourses on time found in educational sciences.

The study of time in philosophy

The question how to conceive time is at the core of Western philosophical inquiry. Most philosophical problems find their roots in the fact that life only exists through time. Since Plato and Aristotle, it has been thought following four leading issues: the questions associated with the reality – or the level of reality – of time, its nature, its origin and its independence toward the soul, the mind or the spirit (Chenet, 2000). References dealing with the difficulties to define or tell time are as numerous as the attempts to understand this notion. The challenges inherent to the formulation of what time is are constitutive of the history of philosophy (Gonord, 2001). To express time, to explain what it may be, language remains limited, as exemplified by Augustine's famous quote in the *Confessions* (Book XI, chap. 14, transl. A.C. Outler): "What, then, is time? If no one asks me, I know what it is. If I wish to explain it to him who asks, I do not know." The fact that this quote appears in almost every contemporary book related to this topic expresses the fact that contemporary reflections on time – this "familiar stranger" (Fraser, 1987) – still remain embedded in fundamental and irreducible tensions. From a philosophical perspective, as suggested by Gonord (2001), the limitations of language and the challenges they raise have brought philosophers to establish some form of 'invariant' (e.g., number, soul, eternity, nature or subjectivity) to consolidate their arguments about time. Throughout the centuries, the multitude of philosophical projects and their heterogeneous variations display therefore an ongoing, repeated and renewed 'effort' to establish some form of temporal order (Gonord, 2001). To identify some of the key aspects of such an evolution, we will follow the logics developed by Ricoeur's (1985) analysis, focusing in particular on three aporias he identified as characterizing the philosophical study of time.

External versus internal time

As discussed by Ricoeur (1985), two main perspectives emerge from the evolution of philosophical thought. First, according to a cosmological and physical view, time must be apprehended objectively through the observation and measurement of external natural phenomena. Unlike Plato's conception of time as eternal, Aristotle conceives it in Book IV of *Physics* as intrinsically related to change, in particular to the regular movement of celestial bodies, as observed through the alternance of day and night, seasons' cycles, and moon phases (Lurçat, 1995). What is located 'in' time can then be understood through a succession (before and after) that can be measured through a number. The second perspective locates time at the level of consciousness; what matters is the intimate relationship between time and subjectivity. Such an internal conception of time relies on the capacity to order one's experience according to an internal notion of time grounded in the present and linked to past and future (Chenet, 2000, pp. 18–19). In the *Confessions* (Book XI, chap. 28), Augustine distinguishes thus three temporal modalities constitutive of the human mind: the time of the past (memory), the time of the present (consideration) and the time of the future (expectation). For him, memory, consideration and expectation appear to be three expressions of the present located at the core of a subjective, psychological, lived time. The formulation of those two conceptions of time remains problematic (Dubar, 2008; Ricoeur, 1985). If one cannot think about time without change, time is not however reducible to it. It requires a 'psyche' (i.e., a rational soul) to measure it. If such cosmological time is 'external', it still requires some form of intelligence able to establish a connection between time and movements. Therefore, there cannot be objective time without a subject able to perceive a 'before' and an 'after'. For Ricoeur, the same aporia characterizes Augustine's position but in a reverse way. It is indeed impossible to perceive 'internal' time independently of 'external' movements. Subjective time is based on the perception of something that goes beyond the subject itself. Centuries later, the critique of Aristotle's cosmological approach contributed to the development of Kant's criticism in the 18th century, and Augustine's phenomenological approach led to the emergence of Husserl's phenomenology in the early 20th century (Dubar, 2008, para. 6).

Oneness versus plural expressions of time

Kant only recognizes as legitimate knowledge what comes from the phenomenal world, as conveyed by our senses and processed by reason. For him (Kant, 1783/1963), time is a form a priori of sensibility; it is not a property of the object. It is revealed to the subject as a priori only through the experience of the external world. Phenomena occur in time, as well as time is elaborated within the self. Permanence, succession and simultaneity are temporal schemes produced by the transcendental imagination of the Kantian subject who relates sensibility and understanding to conceive past, present and future. Kant's temporal schemes refer to a structure of order that organizes one's thinking about time and reality itself. As highlighted by Ricoeur (1985), the temporal order suggested by Kant leads to another aporia: the dissociation among past, present and future – which denotes plural categories – conflicts indeed with the unavoidable notion of time imagined as a single totality (singular collective) (Dubar, 2008, para. 9). Coming back to Augustine's phenomenology, Husserl (1916/2007) considers the "intimate consciousness of time" as an act of "creation of time" (Ricoeur, 1985, p. 64). For him, time is constitutive of the subject rather than the primary parameter within which life takes place. Like Bergson (1922/1968), who differentiates between *temps* and *durée*, Husserl privileges 'experienced duration' rather than 'perceived time'. He conceptualizes past and future as "horizons" constituted by and integrated in a present as well as constituting through it. Doing so, his attempt raises a third aporia related to the way time is figured: time as such remains inscrutable since we cannot escape our cultural figurations of it. It requires using contradictory metaphors (e.g., flow, emergence, impregnation and creation) to symbolize it (Dubar, 2008, para. 11). The tension remains: how can we indeed be surrounded by the vastness of an 'external' time, be 'in' it and simultaneously experience it intimately through one's own consciousness? The confrontation of Husserl and Kant leads to an impasse comparable to the one revealed by the confrontation of Augustine and Aristotle: neither the phenomenological approach nor the transcendental one is sufficient unto itself (Ricoeur, 1985, p. 106) to produce a unified theory of time.

The languages of time

Heidegger's (1927/1964) contribution goes beyond the distinctions established previously to bring them together into a coherent whole. In *Being and Time*, he distinguishes three ways to define, think and live time. Those 'levels' are differentiated and constitute a hierarchy from the deepest to the more superficial; they segment conceptions more or less true and lived experiences of time more or less authentic (Dubar, 2008). At the core, the 'existential' level (*Zeitlichkeit*) refers to the most elaborated definition of time and the most authentic lived experience; it touches the ultimate philosophical question, the identity of the being beyond empirical beings. Heidegger's *Dasein* (being-in-the-world) is not 'in time'; it is time. The *Dasein* is not an ego or a substantial subject; it is temporal, and its temporality can be apprehended through the awareness of one's own death. The prevalence of one's own finitude is what gives time its fundamental meaning (Gonord, 2001). The second level refers to historical time (*Geschichtlichkeit*); this intermediary level concerns phenomena – studied by social sciences through theories located and contextualized in a present that offers a particular perspective on time (Dubar, 2008, para. 14). The last level (*Innerzeitlichkeit*) refers to inner time, as the ordinary and 'vulgar' conception of time. As the most superficial level, it concerns what is mundane, the behaviors determined by institutions (e.g., the time of media, clocks, calendars and habits) characterized by inauthenticity, insignificance and the non-consciousness of one's own finitude. To renew the problematic of time, Heidegger invents a new vocabulary. Doing so, he implicitly demonstrates the fact that time is a matter of language (Dubar, 2008, para. 18). As summarized by Dubar (2008, para. 18), if there are many languages that figure time, there must be many modes of temporalization and therefore many temporalities. The existential temporality of the *Dasein*, the historical time of generations and the ordinary time of the clocks are heterogeneous. They refer to different languages: poetic or metaphoric language is used to express personal lived time; conceptual and empirical languages are constitutive of the historical time studied by social sciences; and mathematics describes the time of the world as a physical variable (Dubar, 2008, para. 18). For Ricoeur (1985), Heidegger's contribution does not solve the aporetics of time; it rather demonstrates the limitations of a purely philosophical and unitary conception of time, opening the way to conceive it according to a layered approach that reveals tensions between different levels and forms of temporalization. For Dubar (2008, para. 18), one of Heidegger's key contribution is to open the possibility to shift from the single temporality of abstract philosophy toward the temporalities of human concrete languages and in particular those that serve as sources and expressions for various human and social sciences.

Beyond abstraction and unifying conceptions

As demonstrated by Ricoeur's aporetics of time, the efforts of philosophers to produce in abstracto a unified theory of time have resulted in the formulation of unsolvable tensions, which eventually contributed to the acknowledgment of the irreducible plurality of the modes of temporality (Dubar, 2008). Such a plurality is by itself constitutive of the complexity of the philosophical study of time, and beyond, it sets the basis for establishing the heterogeneity of scientific temporalities (Fraser, 1966). At the same time, as discussed by Adam (1994) and Elias (1992) in regard to social theory, assumptions formulated by philosophers about time – especially the dualisms they express – are also shaping and limiting the way sciences conceive its meanings. As reminded by Adam (1994, p. 15) considering the development of sociological theories of time, we are not only facing an "incompatible array of definitions", but we are also confronted with "incommensurable ideas" informing our experience and understanding of the concept of time. Apprehending them according to a complexivist mind-set requires one to acknowledge the limitations of classical, logical demonstration whenever one has to interpret complex systems (Morin, 1977–2004/2008). The intelligibility of temporal phenomena requires thus the adoption of principles of thought that accommodate claims that may be complementary, contradictory and opposite at the same time (Morin, 1990/2008). Dialogical thinking may constitute the first epistemological principle to privilege.

Beyond dualistic approaches

Dealing with complexity requires one to think dialogically – rather than through binary oppositions – to establish and question links and relationships between notions and concepts and, by extension between and beyond disciplines (Alhadeff-Jones, 2010; Morin, 1977/1992, 1990/2008). As suggested by Adam (1994), in social sciences, most theorists find it necessary to confront the tradition of thinking in opposites (e.g., synchrony and diachrony, structure and change, individual and society, nature and nurture, quantity and quality, and objectivity and subjectivity) to seek ways to transcend it and to go beyond the boundaries of their own disciplines to do justice to their respective analyses. The adoption of such a position remains both unavoidable and challenging. In educational sciences, theoretical considerations about the definition and the meaning of time remain however scarce. As formulated by Slattery (1995, p. 613), most educational literature assumes that time is an external factor that constrains practices. At the margins of the discipline, authors such as Pineau (2000) and

Slattery (1995) have conducted reflection aiming at going beyond a reductionist understanding of time in education. However, their attempts demonstrate how difficult it is to avoid binary oppositions, such as a 'modern' conception of time (i.e., external and objective) and a 'postmodern' one that would privilege subjectivity, phenomenology and historicity (e.g., Slattery, 1995). It remains therefore crucial to explore theories that may allow us to go beyond the tendency to reduce temporal phenomena in education according to dualistic views.

The study of time in physics

Throughout the history of natural philosophy and science, each major shift in the understanding of the natural world has brought with it a reconceptualization of the nature of time and space (Adam, 1994; Lurçat, 1995). According to Adam (1994, p. 49), three clusters of approaches developed in physics appear to have a direct relevance for social and human sciences: the development of mechanics, quantum physics and thermodynamics. Their development reveals tensions between heterogeneous conceptions of time and, beyond, between principles of thought that establish specific relationships between order and disorder (Morin, 1977/1992).

From absolute to relative time in mechanics and quantum physics

In mechanics – the study of physical energy and its effect on objects – time is used as both a measure and a quantity to be measured. Until the formulation of Newton's laws, time was defined by the regular movements of celestial bodies (Lurçat, 1995). In his *Principia*, Newton (1687, as cited in Lurçat, 1995) redefines time by introducing a distinction between "absolute time" (i.e., true and mathematical) and "relative time" (i.e., apparent and common, measured with more or less accuracy, e.g., in hours, days, months or years). Newton's temporal order is expressed through the fact that time is conceived as a quantity: "invariant, infinitely divisible into space-like units, measurable in length and expressible as number" (Adam, 1994, p. 50). In addition, time is conceptualized as reversible: past and future are considered as identical. This reversible time is thought to operate in an absolute, unidirectional and irreversibly flowing time and to exist independent of any event, process or change. Privileging the symmetry of idealized motion, Newtonian time does not provide any means by which to tell the difference between earlier and later states (Adam, 1994, p. 66). Two centuries later, Newton's conception of an absolute temporal order was revised by Einstein's theories of relativity. With Einstein, time is no longer understood as an absolute; it is relative to observers and their frames of reference. The concept of *Eigenzeit* (local, proper or system-specific time) is introduced to elaborate that distinction and stresses the fact that time should be considered as an internal feature of the system of observation, dependent on observers and their measurements (Adam, 1994, p. 56). In addition, with Einstein's contribution, Newton's principles of an absolute and linear time, providing the rational connection between causes and their effects, appears limited to a specific range of phenomena, excluding those operating beyond the speed of light (Adam, 1994, p. 56).

Such phenomena are encountered in the subatomic world and constitute the core of quantum physics, which studies the properties of solids, atoms, nuclei, subnuclear particles and light. At this level, the form of causality that we experience as an integral part of our world is no longer relevant. The study of quantum phenomena requires the adoption of probabilistic assumptions rather than deterministic ones. At this level, reality cannot be considered as hard, material and permanent; particles' movement is unpredictable. Time and space lose their conventional meaning where actions seem to happen instantaneously across distance (Adam, 1994, p. 59). Furthermore, it is no longer possible to maintain objectivity: physicists need to take into consideration their own position to become intimately connected to the objects of their observation.

From reversible to irreversible time in thermodynamics

A third cluster of approaches informing the understanding of time emerged with the discovery of the laws of thermodynamics and the study of dissipative structures (e.g., a cyclone). The conception of time shifted from a model based on symmetry and reversibility to theories based on asymmetry, irreversibility and unidirectionality. Unlike Newtonian's principles, in thermodynamics energy can never be created or destroyed; it can only be transformed (first law). While the total energy of a system remains constant, useful energy is diminishing due to the dissipation into heat and thus rendered unavailable for work (second law). Accordingly, entropy represents the amount of energy no longer capable of being converted into work. It is interpreted as both a measure of disorder in a system and the degree of physical evolution. Thus, the measure of entropy allows an observer to distinguish processes on a 'before' and 'after' basis, introducing the idea that time has a directionality. Research conducted since the 1970s on dissipative structures (e.g., Prigogine & Stengers, 1984) demonstrated that such a direction differs depending on the phenomena considered. An irreversible process (e.g., dissipation of energy) can thus lead to increased disorder (e.g., molecular agitation) or play a constructive role and bring a system (e.g., atmospheric conditions) into a new state, characterized by a specific stability (e.g., a hurricane) (Alhadeff-Jones, 2008).

Beyond absolute universality and the disjunction between object and subject

The treatment of the idea of time in physics reveals additional limitations inherent to the development of Newtonian science and its influence over the simplifying conceptions of time spread throughout contemporary theories in human sciences. From a physical point of view, there is no such thing as an absolute and universal time. Without referring to philosophers' subjective experience of time or sociologists' social constructs, contemporary physics demonstrates the necessity to promote interpretations that take into consideration the relative position of the observers and the local and singular aspects of their temporal frames of reference. Furthermore, the principle of absolute disjunction between the object of study and the subject who perceives and conceives it becomes irrelevant from a temporal perspective. The understanding – as well as the measurement – of time requires the adoption of a principle of relationship between the observer's time and the temporalities involved in the phenomena studied. The act of observation changes indeed the outcome of the measurement process itself. Time and temporalities have therefore to be envisioned through the relationships and the processes they involve and not only through idealized absolute and universal features. As Slattery (1995, p. 623) reminds us, from a temporal perspective, the observation of change dynamics – in the physical world or in the group dynamics of a classroom – affects the way they unfold and therefore the rhythms they exhibit. The limitations inherent to the universalized and decontextualized temporal conceptions, traditionally adopted in educational theories and practices, should bring us to question the remaining prevalence of Newtonian temporal order and the neglect of alternative theoretical conceptions to conceive educational phenomena beyond an orderly and simplistic understanding of time (Slattery, 1995, p. 625).

Beyond reversibility, symmetry and linear causality

As conceived through the development of thermodynamics, complex systems cannot be understood as long as they are considered through temporal reversibility and symmetry. As a speech recorded on a tape loses its meaning when it is played in reverse direction, the evolution of a complex system cannot be simply 'rewound'; it involves directionality. In addition, like ink dropped into water constitutes an action that cannot be simply undone, there is a necessity to recognize and integrate the irreversibility of educational time and acknowledge the need to include events and history in any description or explanation (Morin, 1982, 1990/2008). Directionality and irreversibility may be obvious for historians, but as pointed out by Huebner (1975, as cited in Slattery, 1995, p. 613), they are far from being taken for granted in educational practice. The effort made by educators to establish clear and unambiguous goals in their pedagogical work appears thus as a result of the dominant 'clockwork mechanism' metaphor of time, resulting from classical physics (Slattery, 1995). It constitutes a problematic attempt to remove educators from the historicity of their practice, that is, the singular and irreversible movement through which students and teachers experience every instant as unique. In addition, the principle of linear causality – embedded in Newton's paradigm – providing the rational connection between causes and effects – appears limited too. As reminded by Slattery (1995, p. 618), it remains that most educators and researchers still envision reality as linear when they conceive time as an independent variable to be manipulated to improve educational outcomes (e.g., quantitative studies establishing educational effectiveness based on time measurement). Education, learning or development do not however constitute linear processes (e.g., Doll, Fleener, Trueit, & St-Julien, 2005). As exemplified by the 'butterfly effect', their influences are most often not proportional to the efforts they require. Complex phenomena, such as group dynamics or processes of sharing information, involve thus mutual causalities and feedback loops that defeat linear temporal representations and simple explanations.

The study of time in biology

The complexity characterizing the study of biological time is inherent to the diversity of temporalities and rhythms found among living organisms and the way they have been conceived throughout the history of life sciences. It refers, among others, to the study of phenomena involving intertwined time scales, multiple biological rhythms and complex (self-) organizational and evolutionary dynamics.

Metabolic, epigenetic and evolutionary time

Biologists traditionally identify three time scales that are of importance to human beings: metabolic, epigenetic, and evolutionary rates of change (Kalmus, 1966). The fastest changes in biological systems are called metabolic. They concern functions that are implied at the cellular level and are mostly determined by the temporality of chemical reactions. The functions of our organs, including our brains, are based on those cell activities and involve periods from a fraction of a second to a few minutes (Kalmus, 1966, p. 334). Epigenetic processes are implicated in the growth, development and aging not only of cells but of large organisms. They are slower than metabolic changes and depend on reactions (e.g., synthesis, transport and interaction) occurring at the molecular level. The life span of higher organisms (e.g., animals and plants) is measured in weeks, years and occasionally in centuries. Growth, development and aging occur only in conditions where the faster metabolic processes operate (Kalmus, 1966, p. 334). Epigenetic processes are the only ones accessible to our conscious experience. Evolutionary changes proceed at another – and usually much slower – rate. They presuppose the continuing and successful operation of metabolic and epigenetic processes as well. Harmonious functioning and the stability of the environment represent typically conservative influences that impose limitations and determine the possibilities of change. Evolutionary changes are carried by the molecules of DNA that can be influenced by mutation, recombination, selection and, at least in humans, historical processes (Kalmus, 1966, p. 334). Beyond the diversity of intertwined time scales, the recent history of biology and life sciences is also characterized by the reference to two distinct conceptions of time appearing as complementary, antagonistic and contradictory.

The classical time of chronobiology

Dominant perspectives in biology are deeply embedded in the epistemological assumptions framed by classical physics and Newtonian mechanics, privileging a conception of time used to measure and quantify duration and rate (Adam, 1994, p. 72). Such a temporal conception informs for instance the development of chronobiological research dedicated to the study of the temporal characteristics of biological phenomena. As an integrating discipline that has been ranked parallel with the more classical disciplines of development, genetics and evolution (Koukkari & Sothern, 2006), chronobiology defines a biological rhythm as a change driven from within the organism that is repeated with a similar pattern, probability and period. Its period, amplitude and phase can be expressed in numerical units, which provide a means to quantify the rhythm (Koukkari & Sothern, 2006, pp. 20–21). Because chronobiology refers to a time conceived as neutral, universal, invariant, measurable and expressible as a number, it privileges the measurement of cycles and periodicity, considered as repetition of the 'same phenomena', rather than the 'recurrence of something similar' (Adam, 1994, p. 81). Such a time appears as a powerful resource to establish regularities and constants ordering living phenomena. At the same time, it prevents one to conceive the variations that make the singularity and the renewal of evolving processes in spite of the fact that they are constitutive of the historicity of any living organism.

The irreversible time of evolution and the self-producing paces of life

In parallel with such a traditional temporal conception, biological temporalities are also constituted by phenomena that cannot be described and interpreted using the principles of classical physics. Thus, organic evolution can only be repeated and reversed very slightly and for a short way. On a larger scale, it appears therefore as irreversible and presupposes the idea of time as something unidirectional as it can be studied through stochastic models involving randomness and indeterminacy (Kalmus, 1966, p. 352). During the 1960s and the 1970s, new theories referring to notions such as self-organization, chaos or *autopoïesis* challenged the assumptions according to which the development and the evolution of living organisms are strictly organized according to predictable principles, regularity and order. From a temporal perspective, the renewed approaches of concepts such as adaptation, evolution, self, autonomy and emergence, privileged by innovative research in evolutionary biology, required the adoption of a theory of time characterized by fundamental asymmetry, irreversibility and unidirectionality of developmental and evolutionary dynamics (Alhadeff-Jones, 2008). Another significant temporal aspect characterizes the complexity of the study of time in biology. When considering living organisms, time does not only refer to the regularity of rhythmic changes that can be objectivized at different levels of organization. As formulated by Adam (1994, p. 87), temporalities are produced by the organism as a fundamental feature of living processes. Moreover, living beings not only produce their own time, but they have a sense of time, rhythmically organized, that endows them with memory, foresight and a capacity for synthesis (Adam, 1994, p. 87). Biological temporalities – as they appear through the study of biological rhythms – appear finally as fundamentally constitutive of any living phenomena.

Beyond reduction and disjunction

The specificities characterizing biological rhythms and the temporalities shaping the evolution and the development of living organisms reveal additional dimensions informing a complexivist interpretation of time. First, it challenges the principle of reduction according to which the understanding of a complex whole requires to be narrowed down to the knowledge of the basic elements that constitute it (Morin, 1982, 1990/2008). To understand metabolic, epigenetic and evolutionary temporalities, one has to take into consideration the relationships and mutual influences between phenomena occurring at different time scales within an organism. In addition, the observation of biological rhythms requires one to recognize the impossibility to isolate single elements and the necessity to link those temporal features to the knowledge of the wholes they belong to. Living temporalities appear thus as emergences generated by the complex interplay among internal factors (e.g., chemical and physiological processes) and external ones (e.g., circadian and seasonal changes or social interrelations).

Such observations remain however remote from traditional assumptions about the temporalities constitutive of educational phenomena. Educational studies of time traditionally rely on segmentation (Slattery, 1995). Isolated parts of complex organizations (e.g., schools, people and curriculum) are divided into coherent and cohesive segments (e.g., grade levels, control groups and disciplines) to be measured and evaluated. Quantified results may then be applied and generalized in other contexts to insure steady progress and sequential development; what results from this position is an overstated emphasis on manipulation of time (e.g., time management, timed tests and time on task) (Slattery, 1995, p. 612). Considering the recent history of physics and biology, it seems however preferable to adopt a principle of distinction rather than disjunction (Morin, 1982, 1990/2008) between the time associated with an object or a subject and the time of the environment that surrounds it. Thus, the time required to develop a critical capacity is embedded within a fabric of rhythms produced through classroom and school dynamics, psychological development and the life histories of the learners as well as through the development of the community they belong to. These temporalities cannot be isolated from each other. They are always inscribed in intertwined relationships.

From inherent order to self-organization and self-production

As exemplified by physical and biological phenomena, such as dissipative structures or biological evolution, explanations based on the absolute sovereignty of order and universal determinism are not sustainable. A complexivist understanding of time requires interpreting phenomena through the circular logic linking order, disorder, interactions and organization (Alhadeff-Jones, 2012; Morin, 1977/1992). As observed by Slattery (1995, p. 619) at a very practical level, educators and administrators experience every day the randomness and chaos that characterize their professional lives and how it impacts the decisions they take. Nevertheless, schools remain organized around a conception of time privileging predictability and stability, assuming that it can be controlled and managed. Educational temporalities should rather be conceived through both order and disorder. They require invariance and consistency as much as they display the critical influence of random interactions or fluctuations.

Another aspect inherent to self-organized living organisms is that they produce their own rhythms. The presence of the self-produced rhythmic and temporal patterns they exhibit provide us with a significant ground to conceive phenomena that emerge through the interplay between physical, biological and psychosocio-anthropological principles (Morin, 1977–2004/2008). In education, the assumption that the universe was created in time and space, and the neglect of the fact that living forms of organization produce their own temporalities, ground research efforts designed to manipulate time as an isolated, independent and quantifiable variable (Slattery, 1995, p. 612). It seems however preferable to assume that the rhythms of education emerge through their self-organization as a product of the order that constitutes them (e.g., repetition, periodicity and regularity) and the disorder that influences their evolution (e.g., accident, event and historicity).

The study of time in human sciences

Since the 19th century, psychology has had a long history of studying time. The studies conducted during the first half of the 20th century shifted from the earlier interest on ontology and consciousness of time to a narrower set of aspects focusing on experience, behavior and cognition (e.g., time perception, estimation of duration and intervals and time in regard of memory) (Adam, 1994, pp. 91–92). Contemporary research integrates the assumption that the study of human sense of time is no longer tied to an empty unit but rather differs according to the content of the experience itself. In addition, the human awareness of time appears as being critically related to language (Adam, 1994, pp. 91–92). What appears from this body of research is the implication of time in every aspect of our psyche (e.g., Adam, 1994, p. 93; Fraisse, 1957). However, the distinctiveness of human time remains problematic to establish as it seems predefined in the very aspects that are being studied and imposed on the studies;

those aspects appear thus as inseparable from social being (Adam, 1994, p. 94; Bergmann, 1992; Pronovost, 1996).

Time in social theory

From a sociological perspective, assuming that social phenomena are not reducible to individual consciousness, Durkheim (1912/1968) lays the first theoretical basis of a sociology of time. He postulates the existence of a "social time" whose constitution has to be seen as social and collective and whose expression reveals its sociocultural determination and variability. Through the contributions of Durkheim (1912/1968), Halbwachs (1952), Hubert (1929) or Mauss (1905/1966), the idea of time acquires a social dimension that results from the rhythms experienced by a society. Thus, social rhythms (i.e., experienced through festivals or rites and expressed through social time reckoning devices such as calendars) contribute to give coherence and meaning to the various durations, events and activities experienced individually and collectively (Bergmann, 1992; Pronovost, 1996).

For Mead (1969, p. 264, as cited in Bergmann, 1992, p. 83), "[h]uman acts are understood not as movements in an already existing time, but as emerging events that first constitute a present with a past and future horizon." If past events are irrevocable, their meaning and the way they are preserved, evoked and selected can be continuously recreated and reformulated, depending on their relationship with the present. Not only is the present constituted together with its time horizons, but the personal identity of the actor is constituted over time through social interactions that also lead to the construction of a common social time (Bergmann, 1992, p. 84).

For Sorokin (1943/1964) and Merton (Sorokin & Merton, 1937), the distinctiveness of social time relies on two aspects: first, it relates significantly to the activities (e.g., economical, religious, intellectual and artistic) that compose and give meaning to it; second, social time expresses the rhythm of social groups. Social activities therefore serve as references to distinguish the various categories of social time. Time appears thus as a relationship between activities (Pronovost, 1996, p. 21). In addition, Sorokin not only claims that time reckoning units such as weeks, months and years are social constructs and not natural units, but he goes further by assigning to each science its own form of time. Accordingly, social sciences are not served by a physical, mathematical, biological or psychological time, but they rather need an adequate conception of "sociocultural time" as one of their main references (Sorokin, 1943/1964). The main characteristics of the time of social sciences would be the use of purely sociocultural reference points, intercultural variability and unequal time flow, quality and effect in contrast to empty flow (Bergmann, 1992, p. 85). For Sorokin (1943/1964), sociocultural time refers to duration, synchronicity, rhythm and the intensity of change that affects other social phenomena. Its fundamental functions are their synchronization and coordination to serve as a referential to represent the duration and the continuity of events and to express the rhythm and the pulse of a social system.

Furthermore, Gurvitch's (1963) contribution stresses the multiplicity of social times, considered as always divergent and often contradictory. Their unification, which remains relative and linked to a hierarchy often precarious, constitutes an issue for any society (Gurvitch, 1963, p. 326). Through their diversity and plurality, social times remain heterogeneous. Through his distinction between "macro social times" and "micro social times," Gurvitch also identifies "depth stages" (*paliers en profondeur*) that particularizes sociological analysis. Society as a whole, institutions, social classes and individuals are characterized by specific times that must – according to Gurvitch – be considered through their dialectical relationships.

Toward a transdisciplinary conception of time

Social theories of time are all based on the assumption according to which time is fundamentally a social construction (Adam, 1994). This is a claim that plays a critical role to deconstruct the dominant conceptions of time that frame education as much as they are reproduced through it. At the same time, such a position implies that conventional analysis never goes beyond the strictly human nature of social life, assuming implicitly that "social time" is distinct from "natural time" (Adam, 1994, pp. 42–43). However, following the reflections of scholars such as Adam (1994), Bergmann (1992) or Elias (1992), it seems crucial to consider that it is not enough to define time – including educational temporalities – as social without referring to what is expressed by this notion. In other words, if time is conceived as a social construct, it remains critical to inquire what is symbolically represented and the multitude of phenomena it may encompass. Accordingly, the study of time in education should not be envisioned in isolation from research conducted in other disciplines. If the time of education is a social construct that has its own historicity, it remains bound to physiological or cosmological rhythms that are organized by chemical, biological and astronomical principles that cannot be reduced to the social meanings attached to them. It seems thus critical to challenge the assumption according to which the meaning of time in education could be ultimately reduced to some kind of foundational knowledge, whether philosophical, physical or sociological. The complexity of time requires one to move beyond monological or monodisciplinary discourses (Morin, 1977–2004/2008, 1990/2008) to embrace transdisciplinary perspectives (e.g., Nicolescu, 2002).

From philosophy, physics, biology and human sciences to educational theory

This chapter was built on the core assumption that to conceive time in educational theory, one has to question how this concept may be fragmented and reduced. Browsing significant contributions that emerged from philosophy, physics, biology and human sciences, we were able to get an insight about such complexity. More specifically, inspired by Morin's paradigm, we were able to identify a series of principles that need to be taken into consideration to conceive the idea of time and nurture the richness of the meanings associated with it. From there, at least two paths of research emerge. The first one raises the question of the specificity of educational temporalities. Assuming the fact that every scientific discipline and social praxis relates to specific forms of change that characterize their own temporalities, what does particularize educational temporalities? How may theorizing such specificities enrich our views on education, including emancipatory education? The second path raises additional conceptual issues. Assuming the necessity to embrace a complexivist interpretation of time in education, how can we theorize it according to such principles of thought? Based on which theories and concepts? How do we define time to accommodate the plurality of its expressions, and how do we conceive theoretically the relationships between heterogeneous temporalities?

Note

1 To envision the broad scope of research conducted around the study of time, see the collection of texts edited under the leadership of J.T. Fraser (1923–2010), founder of the International Society for the Study of Time.

References

Adam, B. (1994). *Time and social theory*. Cambridge: Polity Press.
Alhadeff-Jones, M. (2008). Three generations of complexity theories: Nuances and ambiguities. *Educational Philosophy and Theory, 40*(1), 66–82.
Alhadeff-Jones, M. (2010). Challenging the limits of critique in education through Morin's paradigm of complexity. *Studies in Philosophy and Education, 29*(5), 477–490.
Alhadeff-Jones, M. (2012). Learning disorders: From a tragic to an epic perspective on complexity. *Complicity: An International Journal of Complexity and Education, 9*(2), i–vi.
Ardoino, J. (2000). *Les avatars de l'éducation*. Paris: Presses Universitaires de France.
Bachelard, G. (2003). *Le nouvel esprit scientifique*. Paris: Presses Universitaires de France. (Original work published 1934)
Bergmann, W. (1992). The problem of time in sociology: An overview of the literature on the state of theory and research on the 'sociology of time', 1900–82. *Time & Society, 1*(1), 81–134.
Bergson, H. (1968). *Durée et simultanéité: A propos de la théorie d'Einstein*. Paris: Presses Universitaires de France. (Original work published 1922)
Chenet, F. (2000). *Le temps: Temps cosmique, temps vécu*. Paris: Armand Colin.
Doll, W.E., Jr., Fleener, M.J., Trueit, D., & St. Julien, J. (Eds.). (2005). *Chaos, complexity, curriculum, and culture: A conversation*. New York: Peter Lang.
Dubar, C. (2008). Temporalité, temporalités: Philosophie et sciences sociales. *Temporalités* [Electronic version]. *Revue de sciences sociales et humaines, 8*. Retrieved May 5, 2014, from http://temporalites.revues.org/137

Durkheim, E. (1968). *Les formes élémentaires de la vie religieuse.* Paris: Presses Universitaires de France. (Original work published 1912)
Elias, N. (1992). *Time: An essay.* Oxford: Blackwell Publishers.
Fraisse, P. (1957). *Psychologie du temps.* Paris: Presses Universitaires de France.
Fraser, J.T. (Ed.). (1966). *The voices of time.* New York: George Braziller.
Fraser, J.T. (1987). *Time: The familiar stranger.* Amherst, MA: University of Massachusetts Press.
Gonord, A. (2001). *Le temps.* Paris: Flammarion.
Gurvitch, G. (1963). *La vocation actuelle de la sociologie.* Paris: Presses Universitaires de France.
Halbwachs, M. (1952). *Les cadres sociaux de la mémoire.* Paris: Presses Universitaires de France.
Heidegger, M. (1964). *L'Etre et le temps.* Paris: Gallimard. (Original work published 1927)
Hubert, H. (1929). Etude sommaire de la representation du temps dans la religion et la magie. In H. Huber, & M. Mauss (Eds.), *Mélanges d'histoire des religions* (pp.180–229). Paris: Felix Alcan.
Husserl, E. (2007). *Leçons pour une phénoménologie de la conscience intime du temps.* Paris: Presses Universitaires de France. (Original work published 1916)
Kalmus, H. (1966). Organic evolution and time. In J.T. Fraser (Ed.), *The voices of time* (pp.330–352). New York: George Braziller.
Kant, E. (1963). *Critique de la raison pure.* Paris: Presses Universitaires de France. (Original work published 1783)
Koukkari, W.L., & Sothern, R.B. (2006). *Introducing biological rhythms.* New York: Springer.
Lurçat, F. (1995). Le temps de la physique. *L'enseignement philosophique, 46*(1), 7–33.
Mauss, M. (1966). *Sociologie et anthropologie.* Paris: Presses Universitaires de France. (Original work published 1905)
Morin, E. (1973). *Le Paradigme perdu: La nature humaine.* Paris: Seuil.
Morin, E. (1982). *Science avec conscience.* Paris: Fayard.
Morin, E. (1992). *Method: Towards a study of humankind (vol.1) the nature of nature* (J.L.R. Bélanger, Trans.). New York: Peter Lang. (Original work published 1977)
Morin, E. (2008). *La Méthode.* Paris: Seuil. (Original work published 1977–2004)
Morin, E. (2008). *On complexity* (S.M. Kelly, Trans.). Cresskill, NJ: Hampton Press. (Original work published 1990)
Morin, E. (2014). *Enseigner à vivre: Manifeste pour changer l'éducation.* Arles, France: Actes Sud.
Nicolescu, B. (2002). *Manifesto of transdisciplinarity* (K.-C. Voss, Trans.). Albany, NY: State University of New York Press.
Pineau, G. (2000). *Temporalités en formation: Vers de nouveaux synchroniseurs.* Paris: Anthropos.
Pomian, K. (1984). *L'ordre du temps.* Paris: Gallimard.
Prigogine, I., & Stengers, I. (1984). *Order out of chaos.* New York: Bantam Books.
Pronovost, G. (1996). *Sociologie du temps.* Bruxelles: De Boeck.
Ricoeur, P. (1985). *Temps et récit: Le temps raconté (vol.3).* Paris: Seuil.
Slattery, P. (1995). A postmodern vision of time and learning: A response to the National Education Commission Report 'Prisoners of time.' *Harvard Educational Review, 65*(4), 612–633.
Sorokin, P.A. (1964). *Sociocultural causality, space, time.* New York: Russell & Russell. (Original work published 1943)
Sorokin, P.A., & Merton, R.K. (1937). Social time: A methodological and functional analysis. *American Journal of Sociology, 42*, 615–639.

Chapter 2

Theorizing educational temporalities

The study of time in education

How is time conceived in educational research and praxis? Is there a specificity to consider time in education? How would it fit into existing debates about the contribution of educational theory and its relations with other disciplines? The aim of this chapter is to provide the reader with an exploratory framework to be able to position oneself in regard to such questions. To identify the core assumptions that frame the understanding of the idea of time in educational practices, theories and policies, the first section of this chapter introduces a distinction among four conceptions (chronometry, chronography, chronology and chronosophy) through which the idea of time may be visualized and translated. Embracing the diversity of temporal conceptions that shape education, the next section proposes a definition of time broad enough to be able to refer to multiple phenomena and specific enough to appear as a useful theoretical resource in educational research. Acknowledging the heterogeneity of educational temporalities further requires one to question how they can be studied and whether or not the attempt to theorize them carries any epistemological or institutional specificities. The third section identifies therefore two approaches (disciplinary vs. educational) that can be adopted to conceive the plurality of temporal phenomena in education. Because they refer to heterogeneous, hybrid and complex changes and transformations, their study necessitates a dedicated framework to describe and interpret how they relate to each other (temporal architecture and multireferential approaches). Recognizing the fact that the organization of multiple temporalities that shape education reveals complementarities, conflicts and contradictions as well, it is finally argued that the study of time in education requires one to consider both the epistemological questions that it raises and the cultural and political dimensions that are embedded in any attempt of theorizing social and historical phenomena.

Organizing heterogeneous conceptions of time in education

Considering both English- and French-speaking literature in education, only a very few resources appear to review systematically the existing references focusing on the idea of time in educational research. The study of time in education remains thus a fragmented and underdeveloped scientific territory. In English, the literature remains divided and – in spite of the quantitative abundance of publications – the majority of the contributions available are focusing on a limited number of topics (e.g., Ben-Peretz & Bromme, 1990). In comparison with the Anglo-Saxon literature, French-speaking publications remain quantitatively limited. Literature reviews available in French provide nevertheless alternate points of view (e.g., Cavet, 2011; Chopin, 2010; Delhaxhe, 1997; Lesourd, 2006); some contributions are more inclined to question the epistemological assumptions framing the treatment of the idea of time (e.g., Lesourd, 2006), to introduce it through a broader set of themes (e.g., Centre d'études et de recherche en sciences de l'éducation, 1993; St-Jarre & Dupuy-Walker, 2001) or to propose original and exploratory contributions that seem to have no direct counterpart in English (e.g., Pineau, 2000). Unfortunately, such references do not provide the reader with an exhaustive overview to articulate the existing literature focusing on temporal issues in education and discuss the underlying assumptions about the idea of time.

When considering the temporal dimensions of education, it seems at first relevant to establish a distinction between the implicit and the explicit treatment of time in educational research. Because education is about change, and the study of changes involves time, time appears as an unavoidable issue to consider in education. Most educational research assumes that time is an external factor that constrains learning and development or eventually provides researchers and practitioners with a framework to describe how educational processes evolve (Slattery, 1995). Such assumptions usually rely on a taken-for-granted view on time that does not constitute per se the topic of educational inquiry. Thus, most research in education considers time as a 'dimension' that does not require to be systematically questioned. When considering systematic reflections on time as a locus of inquiry in education, it is relevant to establish a further distinction between research on time considered as a "condition" for educational processes to unfold and time as an "object" of educational praxis (Lesourd, 2006, p. 10). Following Pomian's (1984) contribution as a historian, we can distinguish at least four ways (respectively identified as chronometry, chronography, chronology and chronosophy) the idea of time may be visualized and translated, whether time is taken for granted and considered explicitly as a condition for education or as an object of educational praxis.

Chronometrical approaches

Most educational research relies on a chronometrical approach to time. Time is represented through the indications associated with calendars (e.g., yearly, monthly or weekly school programs) or instruments of measure (e.g., clock or chronometer). According to Pomian (1984), chronometry suggests the presence of a time conceived as both cyclical and symmetric. It is grounded in the possible repetition of a cycle remaining invariant (e.g., 24 hours, weeks, months or seasons of the year). Time serves thus as an external structure that defines the points at which difference is being assessed to establish changes that occur (e.g., learning and teaching); to some extent, the phenomenon considered is no longer studied as 'becoming.' For instance, considering time as a condition for the educational process to unfold, research conducted on instructional time or academic learning time (cf. Chapter 6) relies on a specific metric scale as a means to redefine – and evaluate – most variables of the learning process and educational setting. The theories and methodologies that inform such conceptions come either from social sciences (e.g., time allocation) or psychology (e.g., time perception). Such a chronometrical conception of time is also found in studies conducted on the temporal aspects of school leadership and the organizational dimensions of teachers' work (cf. Chapter 6). Functional or dysfunctional patterns of activities constitutive of the educational organization are studied through the lens provided by predefined temporal structures (e.g., school schedules and calendars) considered either as a given or as a social construct. The contemporary literature on school rhythms (cf. Chapter 6) adds to chronometrical views provided by social sciences and psychology, those informed by chronobiology and chronopsychology; educational processes appear then to be determined by the learner's physiological and cognitive rhythms, considered as objective phenomena and studied through their periodic features. Considering time as an object of education, the chronometrical approach traditionally informs practices aiming at developing skills such as those related to "time management" providing learners with advices, prescriptions or strategies to avoid "time shortage" (e.g., Larsson & Sanne, 2005). A chronometrical view on time appears useful as it offers an 'objective' basis for measurement, synchronization and planning. It remains, however, limited to interpret human behaviors characterized by rhythmic repetition, including variations and irreversibility, continuities and discontinuities (cf. Chapter 7); it also excludes taking into consideration the intimate experience of time or the effects of the past, present and future (e.g., the accumulation of knowledge and experience, decay or aging). Such aspects appear at the core of the critiques formulated about classical conceptions of time found in mainstream educational theories (e.g., Ardoino, 2000; Ben-Peretz & Bromme, 1990; Hargreaves, 1994; Mayes, 2005; Papastephanou, 2013; Pineau, 2000; Slattery, 1995).

Chronographical approaches

A chronographical approach to time focuses on its qualitative attributes. It is found for instance through the successive notations characterizing chronicles based on the record of events established on a day-to-day basis. Chronicles typically mention events considered as abnormal, significant, surprising or extraordinary; repeated facts are usually neglected (Pomian, 1984, pp. iv–v). Chronicles focus on what happens in the present and conceive it as qualitative and discrete, assuming a simple relationship of anteriority between events (Pomian, 1984, pp. iv–v). In education, chronicles are produced through the practice of journaling, prescribed either to students (e.g., journal of learning) or to professionals. It can serve as a device to collect data to describe educational processes 'from within,' or as a learning artifact implemented to favor the development of self-critical reflection. Chronography is also found with the production of stories or tales. As such, it supposes a conception of time, perceived through both its continuity and its discontinuity, and may refer to the life of a person, a family, an institution or a group as interpreted in the present time (Pomian, 1984, pp. iv–v). Following a long tradition developed in social sciences and psychology, the production of stories or tales (oral or written) can be used as a methodology of research (e.g., narrative inquiry, biographical research and autoethnography) to interpret how educational processes and dynamics are experienced (cf. Chapter 7). In this perspective, the experience of time is conceived as a construct that can be interpreted through the theoretical lenses provided by phenomenology, psychology, sociology, history or linguistics. The use of narratives also characterizes approaches focusing on time as an object of educational praxis. Informed by humanistic and existentialistic psychologies (Mayes, 2005), it is found in curriculum theory such as Greene's (1975, as cited in Mayes, 2005), promoting students' narrative self-construction. It is also located at the core of life history and biographical approaches promoted in adult education as self-development and emancipatory practices (e.g., Dominicé, 2000; West, Alheit, Andersen, & Merrill, 2007).

Chronological approaches

A third approach to time found in educational sciences refers to chronology. According to Pomian (1984, pp. iv–v), in contrast with chronography and chronometry, chronological systems are oriented toward the past and bind quantitative and qualitative dimensions of time. Representing time through series of dates and names, successions of eras and their subdivisions, from an origin to the present time, such an approach is typically found in historical contributions (Pomian, 1984, pp. iv-v). It is used for instance to describe the evolution of a specific field or the development of educational practices themselves. Approaches referring to chronology constitute also a topic of education aiming at the development of a specific form of 'time awareness.' Mainly concentrated in history and language teaching, they are based on the transmission of a time-related vocabulary and the development of linguistic and historical skills grounding the capacity of sequencing (Hoodless, 2002). They may also be found each time the teaching of a discipline involves evolutionary aspects, as is the case in biology (e.g., Smith, 2010).

Chronosophies

A fourth way to represent time appears through the chronosophies that researchers, practitioners and policy makers either borrow or produce when they envision educational processes. Pomian (1984, pp. v–vii) defines a chronosophy as a questioning of the future, which claims to find answers to represent it, if not in details at least through its main characteristics. This generic term covers a large variety of practices and works, referring to different temporal horizons, goals and means to unfold the future. Chronosophies may focus on individuals, groups of people, and humanity as a whole or even the universe (Pomian, 1984, pp. v–vii). Because it transcends the present toward the future, any chronosophy aims to apprehend as a whole the trajectory of history, evolution or time. A chronosophy aims to replace an incomplete knowledge about evolution by a finite knowledge highlighting the meaning of everything that is supposed to happen (Pomian, 1984, pp. v–vii). Therefore, chronosophies are not limited to what is perceived or observed. They are legitimated by various techniques translating the future into an object of knowledge (e.g., clairvoyance, divination, astrology or the formulation of psychological, sociological or economic theories, based on their respective scientific apparatus)[1] (Pomian, 1984, pp. v–vii).

Considering scientific contributions and the policies they inform, every educational discourse is based – implicitly or explicitly – on one or more chronosophies determining the ways researchers, educators or policy makers interpret causal relationships between past, present and future learning or developmental opportunities. For instance, as shown by Leaton Gray (2004), locating educational projects in time serves as a rhetoric device invariably used by government policy documents to legitimate and advocate for educational changes. Such documents, as much as the practices they prescribe, are based on chronosophies referring either to children, adults or economic or social growth and development. They usually define themes related to "retardation" or "progression" (Leaton Gray, 2004) as they may be conceived in the educational literature based on psychology or social sciences. Educational research involves indeed assumptions about individual and collective development, suggesting for instance the specificity of ages of life or the existence of stages of development (e.g., Clark & Caffarella, 1999; Lerner, 2002; McDevitt & Ormrod, 2013). Considered as an object of educational practices, chronosophies are involved every time a representation of individual or collective future becomes a matter of learning. They are found for instance in research conducted on future time perspective and the role it plays in school achievement (e.g., McInerney, 2004). They also shape educational practices and theories whenever the ideas of anticipation, orientation, project, planning or scheduling are involved (e.g., Boutinet, 2008; Clegg, 2010).

Embracing the heterogeneity of time in education

The simultaneous presence or the distinction among heterogeneous temporalities (e.g., quantitative, qualitative, natural and social) legitimizes the assumption according to which there is a plurality of times, not only in appearances or through the symbolic expressions developed throughout the history of philosophy and sciences but also as a real and irreducible aspect of reality (Adam, 1994). Such an assumption provides the ground for a "pluralist chronosophy" (Pomian,

1984, p. 349) as a basis to avoid a reductionist approach to time, leaning toward the simplification of the plurality of times to a privileged – often hegemonic – expression. Formulating such a claim is critical for educational theory because it serves as a warrant against at least two pitfalls. The first one would be to reduce the complexity of educational temporalities to what can be measured according to the classical Newtonian's definition of physical time. The second one would be to reduce educational temporalities to a social construct operating only at the level of human mind. On the one hand, natural and social sciences have their own level-specific time concept. Biological time is insufficient for the description of the human social and historical world in the same way as physical time is inappropriate for the analysis of living nature and human psychology. On the other hand, considering that physical and biological times have no bearing on educational phenomena and only constitute social constructs remains problematic too. Natural conceptions of time are of central significance to educational theory and practice. They are significant because humans live in and interact with their physical environment as much as they also produce their own temporalities (e.g., biological rhythms). In addition, through their activity, humans design and create artifacts and technologies characterized by their own rhythms and temporalities.

Defining time in education

Embracing a pluralist chronosophy requires one to define more clearly the idea of time that underlies it. It appears particularly relevant to adopt Pomian's (1984) definition as it provides us with a terminology to envision the heterogeneity of temporalities involved in educational phenomena.

Time is about changes that may be related to each other

In agreement with a long philosophical tradition, the reality of time appears at first to be grounded in change; without change, there is no time. The multiple reality of change contributes thus to the diversity of time (Pomian, 1984, p. 350). Change is a necessary condition for defining time, but time cannot be reduced to it. A second aspect to take into consideration relates to the necessity to have multiple changes, occurring not too far from each other, so that they can be considered as related with each other (Pomian, 1984, p. 350). Such proximity remains however very relative: it depends on the types of phenomena considered (e.g., physical and social). To illustrate these two first points, we can consider the following: (a) the repeated changes of position characterizing the 24-hour rotation of the Earth around its axis (e.g., used to define the physical time expressed by traditional clocks); (b) the pace of the disintegration of a specific radioactive isotope (carbon 14) found in any living organism (e.g., used by archeologists or paleontologists to determine the age of prehistoric findings); (c) the successive transformations that characterize the evolution of a country or an institution (e.g., used as a basis to define their history); or (d) the series of changes that affect a living organism (e.g., used as a resource to determine the temporalities of its development or its evolution). From an educational perspective, such series or successions of changes may be considered for instance at the scale of a human being through embodied, discursive, cognitive, emotional, behavioral or social features.

Time is produced or observed by an entity that coordinates multiple changes

A third aspect (Pomian, 1984, p. 351) to consider is the fact that time emerges from a multiplicity of changes only if there is an entity (*instance*) (e.g., a physical phenomenon, a living organism, a person or a collectivity) that coordinates the changes included in this multiplicity. Such an entity may either produce or observe those changes themselves, or it can act on their representations, to integrate such changes into 'temporal relationships' (*rapports temporels*) (e.g., characterized by contemporaneity, anteriority-posteriority or simultaneity) (Pomian, 1984, p. 351) Thus, a person can experience a form of temporality by connecting in thought the qualitative or quantitative aspects of changes that are perceived as real because they are felt, perceived or reconstructed (Pomian, 1984, p. 351). Both a natural phenomenon (e.g., the rotation of the Earth) or a social institution (e.g., work) can produce a specific time through the rhythms that are constitutive of their own changes (e.g., alternance between day and night or succession of pauses and activities). In a similar way, through the production of a specific hormone, an organ can translate environmental variations (e.g., light–darkness) into biological processes that rhythm the organism (e.g., wake–sleep) (Pomian, 1984, p. 351). Any actors involved in the description or the process of an educational praxis may therefore experience, produce or observe such coordinated changes: observing one's own self-development, organizing activities to coordinate pupils' activity, comparing learners at different stages of their evolution and so on.

Time is produced or observed through the coordination of signals or signs expressing multiple changes

The coordination of a multiplicity of changes requires signals (e.g., beams of light, hormones, electric impulses and ink on a paper) produced by the entity to partially unify and modulate the multiplicity of changes and establish between them determined temporal relationships (Pomian, 1984, p. 352). Thus, physical time can be established through the alternance of states characterized by the presence or absence of light or by radiations emitted by specific radioactive isotopes. It can also be reconstructed by a human mind establishing correspondences between real or symbolized phenomena (e.g., the level of luminosity or the moves of the hands on the dial of a clock). Following a different logic, signs – rather than signals – can thus be used to determine temporal relationships

(Pomian, 1984, p. 352). The changes symbolized in a narrative or contained in documents can thus serve to establish – through their linguistic features – the evolution of a person or the historicity of a series of events. In education, signals may be observed through visual or auditory cues (e.g., movements and sounds), signs such as those expressed through language and communication, or symbolic features such as those associated with legal documents or physical spaces (e.g., buildings and classrooms).

The production or observation of time requires a 'program' that coordinates signals or signs

Finally, to produce signals that can be coordinated and serve as a basis to establish temporal relationships between changes – or their symbolic representations – Pomian (1984, p. 352) suggests that an entity requires a predefined program. The stability of such a program determines the accuracy through which identical temporal relationships can be reproduced (Pomian, 1984, p. 352). For instance, physical temporalities based on astronomical phenomena are determined by 'natural laws' (e.g., gravitation) that define the levels of variation and the spectrum of change that can be observed in specific phenomena. Biological rhythms are ruled by the 'instructions' coded in the genetic program of living organisms and the physical laws that determine chemical transformations. Social temporalities can be interpreted as the expression of norms and principles (e.g., social, historical and economical) defining the order ruling the succession of changes that affect human collectivities.

Conceiving educational temporalities

According to Pomian's (1984, p. 352) definition, time refers therefore to a class of quantitative or qualitative relationships. If one can perceive the entities, the changes they coordinate, the signals or signs they produce and the programs they execute, time itself cannot be observed. Such a definition is twofold. On the one hand, as shown through the examples provided, it is relevant to define the temporalities that characterize various levels of organization as they may be studied within various academic disciplines. On the other hand, it also provides us with a precise basis to envision the intertwined changes that shape educational temporalities. For instance, the temporal regularities and cyclic structures that characterize schools (cf. Chapter 4) and the periodic patterns that characterize dual education (cf. Chapter 7) both refer to rhythmic organizational changes that produce signs (e.g., information) and influence the learners and the educators' activity (e.g., knowledge and skills), according to programs defined by curriculum theories and educational policy. The example provided by research conducted in schools on didactic time (cf. Chapter 6) illustrates how a rhythmic succession of 'ignorances' provoked by the teaching setting and overcome by the learner may represent – when coordinated through a pedagogical set of instructions and the cognitive ability of the learner – the main determinant of the student's learning temporality. The use of educational biographies (cf. Chapter 7) illustrates how the writing of a narrative, characterized by the temporalities of one's own psychological and social life – when it is produced within the rhythm of an educational sequence of actions and shaped by the logics of linguistic rules – may transform the representations and the assumptions of the learner about one's own life.

Those examples demonstrate the validity of two core assumptions framing the temporal dimensions of education. First, educational phenomena are characterized by rhythms and temporalities that can be defined specifically, according to the components (i.e., changes, entities, signs or signals and programs) they involve. Second, the nature of the components constitutive of educational temporalities is hybrid; that is, they convoke simultaneously physical, biological, psychological, linguistic and social features. Educational temporalities cannot therefore be reduced to a specific subcategory of social time. They involve changes whose nature is not strictly social. For instance, the activity of learning (e.g., a language) involves neurological and cognitive modifications that are influenced by the educational process as much as they determine to some extent what can be learned and at which pace (e.g., the acquisition of a language will probably never be the result of an instantaneous or fast activity even in the best conditions). Ecological transformations that may be influenced by sustainable changes in consumption habits, promoted through education, are also inscribed in temporalities that exist beyond social time. Thus, physical, physiological or biological phenomena are ruled by 'principles' that are not 'constructed', even if the representations and the theories that describe them remain social constructs. Therefore, the specificity and the hybridity of educational temporalities require one to question how they can be studied and whether or not the attempt to theorize them carry any epistemological or institutional specificities.

Theorizing time in education

The 'theory question in education' and the 'education question in theory and theorizing'

According to Biesta, Allan, and Edwards (2014, p. 3), a common view in the English-speaking world is that the theoretical resources for educational research stem from a number of academic disciplines, such as psychology, sociology, philosophy and history. For these authors, looking at the role and the specificity of theory in education raises therefore two main questions. The first one – the theory question in education – interrogates how theories from a range of different disciplines pertain to the study of education. The second one – the education question in theory and theorizing – investigates what it means for particular theories to be used or applied within the context of educational research. Considering the issue of time, the questions formulated by Biesta, Allan and Edwards open up two distinct, but related, research paths. The first one (I will call it 'the time theory question in education') would suggest one to explore the temporal dimensions of education based on conceptions of time developed in various academic disciplines (e.g., physical time, biological time and social time). The study of time in education would thus be considered as a topic of research on which to apply assumptions and theories about time imported from other fields of study. The second part of this book will explore this path, locating some of the existing research conducted in educational sciences inspired by theories borrowed from philosophy, biology, psychology, linguistic and social sciences. The second path (I will call it 'the educational temporalities in theory and theorizing') would suggest one to consider the temporal aspects inherent to educational phenomena as a complex, whose understanding requires the adoption of a theoretical apparatus that goes beyond the fragmentation, and the reductionist conceptions of time inherent to disciplinary contributions. Referring to the notion of rhythm and to rhythm theories, the third part of this book is going to engage on this path, exploring the possibility to conceive education – and more specifically emancipatory education – through the rhythmic dimensions that produce and organize their temporalities. There is no reason to oppose these two approaches or believe that one is more heuristic than the other. However, there are good reasons to believe that both raise different questions and challenges from an epistemological and institutional point of view. They require therefore researchers to take a stance on the options they may privilege when choosing to study the temporal aspects of education. Because the 'time theory question in education' is implicit to the existing literature on time and education, even if it often remains at the margins of educational research, it seems important to focus at this point on the assumptions that may legitimate the relevance of the questions related to 'educational temporalities in theory and theorizing' as an emerging field of inquiry. To proceed, it seems necessary to identify what may constitute the epistemological specificity of research and theory developed under the umbrella of educational sciences.

The epistemological specificities of educational sciences

While the idea of education as an academic discipline in its own right and with its own forms of theory and theorizing may be rather alien to the English-speaking world, Biesta, Allan and Edwards (2014, p. 3) take the example of Germany to point out the fact that it is an important dimension of the way in which the academic study of education has developed in other settings. In France too, especially since the 1970s, many authors have explored what is at stake regarding the specificity of *sciences de l'éducation* both from an epistemological and institutional perspective (Association des Enseignants et Chercheurs en Sciences de l'Education, 2001; Charlot, 1995). Inspired in particular by Charlot's (1995) contribution, the position adopted in this book relies on the assumption that because of the nature of their object of study and their own historical development, the contribution and the value of educational sciences are embedded in the recognition of their epistemological specificities. Formulating such specificities appears as a crucial operation to locate the cores and the limitations of the knowledge produced within this field.

As conceived by Charlot (1995, p. 21), education can be defined as a body of practices and processes through which *l'humain* emerges within human beings. As such, education represents a movement of construction within which every human being is engaged. As an object of study, "[e]ducation can be analyzed as an *intentional action* exercised on others to bring them to become what they must be, to lead them (according to the etymology) where they must go" (Charlot, 1995, p. 24, stressed by the author, my translation). Its finalities can therefore be conceived through the doctrines that define the aims of education and shape its practices. It can also be defined as the practice implemented by parents whenever they have to make decisions regarding their children in reference to implicit and explicit principles of actions, more or less intuitively (Charlot, 1995, p. 24). From this perspective, studying education requires one to study such practices, their effects and the situations in which they occur. Finally, education can be conceived as the movement through which children, and later adults, built themselves up. Its study requires then to pay attention to the situations, encounters and influences embedded in the triviality of everyday actions and constitutive of the singularity of significant events as well (Charlot, 1995, p. 24).

For Charlot (1995, p. 27), studying education is challenging because of the ambiguity, uncertainty and hybridity that characterize it. It is difficult to apprehend it with rigor because it is at the same time, global and daily, referring to the presupposed educability of the subject and to the ideal principles according to which it must be evaluated. If other disciplines bypass such challenges by focusing on a particular perspective (e.g., anchored in psychology, sociology or philosophy), it remains that education is not an object like any other. Charlot (1995, p. 27) conceives it as a "bridge" allowing sciences to explore each other's fields of study. Such an object is at the same time specific enough for the ideas of "educational sciences" and "educational theory" to emerge and too broad, too multidimensional, for one single discipline to apprehend it fully (Charlot, 1995, p. 27). Research in educational sciences refers to notions and concepts borrowed from other disciplines, but at the same time they require one to elaborate specific objects of research to grasp the complexity of education (Charlot, 1995, p. 27). If disciplines considering education as a topic of inquiry (e.g., psychology, sociology or philosophy of education) are characterized by a specific entry point and find their legitimacy from their respective disciplinary background, according to Charlot (1995, p. 27), educational sciences and educational theory may claim a multidimensional approach that would appear similar to the one emerging in relatively new academic disciplines such as political sciences, management sciences and environmental or information sciences. Thus, for this author (Charlot, 1995, p. 36), the emergence and specificity of those new disciplines relate to their capacity to operate synthesis and articulate the production of conceptual knowledge and meaning, including within the course of action. However, educational sciences present the specificity of working on a transversal topic universally spread out among everyday practices (Charlot, 1995, p. 36).

Theorizing educational temporalities

Revisiting the temporal dimensions inherent to any educational phenomena constitutes a particularly relevant entry point to question the epistemological specificity of educational sciences and the role of educational theory. As a process of becoming, education is a matter of time. First, it is the time of personal history through which the individual becomes a singular person. It is also the time of collective history that produced the culture, which is appropriated through education. As a process of appropriation that carries meaning, education also refers to the time and history through which the individual develops affective and imaginary relationships with the others and with the world (Charlot, 1995, p. 22). Education is neither an absolute – it carries the mark of places and times through which it is built – nor can it be achieved; education refers to the movement through which the child becomes adult, but it also encompasses adulthood (Charlot, 1995, p. 22). Education also determines the way we learn to relate to time and the multiple rhythms of existence (Pineau, 2000). Education appears therefore as an ongoing movement made of intertwined temporalities. It is shaped by the complementary, antagonistic and contradictory temporalities that rhythm the activity and the life of learners, educators, institutions, society and knowledge itself. Educational temporalities constitute also a complex that produces the multiple threads that compose the physical, living, psychological and social fabric of human life.

When the temporal dimensions of education are defined based on time theories provided by other disciplines, time may either be considered as an abstract and universal idea or conceived through a multiplicity of unarticulated and potentially conflicting views. Indeed, phenomena such as learning, transformation or development can be 'observed' or 'measured' in reference to an external temporal framework. They can also be conceived as the expression of physical, biological, psychological or social determinants following their own specific temporal orders. Considering the temporalities involved in educational phenomena through disciplinary contributions carries therefore the risk of significantly reducing interpretations or explanations to a narrow set of dimensions that may remain fragmented. The consequence would be a truncated understanding of time conceived either as internal or external, as a quantity or as a quality, as natural or social and as a psychological experience or a social construct. What appears therefore as a significant theoretical issue is that even when the diversity of temporalities shaping education is acknowledged, the absence of organizing principles prevents scholars and practitioners to systematically establish and question their complementary, antagonistic and contradictory relationships. Indeed, physical changes that produce the alternance between days and nights, biological processes that shape the rhythm between rest and activity, psychological states that characterize the attribution of meaning to one's experience, or social dynamics that determine the synchronization of collective activity, all those phenomena rely on some forms of temporal organization that are fundamentally heterogeneous, even if they are closely intertwined with each other. The logic that rules their mutual influences cannot be grasped by a single theory or a single discipline. To understand how they are interrelated, it is therefore necessary to establish how they can be both organized and organizing. Because they represent such a hybrid field of study, educational sciences may provide an opportunity to envision such an organization.

Organizing complementary, conflicting and contradictory temporalities

Conceiving a temporal architecture

When envisioning the heterogeneity of theories of time, as a whole, the multiple sources, dimensions, aspects and levels of time all appear equally important. However, as pointed out by Adam (1994, p. 46), grouping existing perspectives on time (e.g., according to their different foci, emphases and philosophical traditions) is not enough to establish connections and meaningful relations between those diverse ideas. It does not provide explanations to interpret differences and incompatibilities between heterogeneous contributions. Acknowledging the fact that time is simultaneously implicated in all the cultural, living and physical dimensions of our being, but expressed differently in each of them (Adam, 1994, p. 49) is a core assumption of a pluralist chronosophy. To conceive the richness and variety of temporalities that shape educational phenomena, it is also required to conceive how they relate to each other. The approaches advocated by Adam (1994, p. 161) and Pomian (1984) point toward a conceptualization in terms of 'levels' as it necessitates an understanding of relations, interconnections and mutual implications among heterogeneous times. It prevents having to choose between perspectives on an either/or basis, and it encourages to see connections without neglecting the multiplicity of points of view.

Many recognize the relevance of discriminating the 'level-appropriate' meanings of time and to take account of them. For instance, Fraser (1981b, 1982, as cited in Adam, 1994, p. 162; Fraser, 1987) defines six "time-levels of existence" conceived as discontinuous (three for the physical universe, one for life forms and two for the human realm). However, as rightly pointed out by Elias (1992), such levels do not stand in isolation. They do not exist in parallel but in relation to each other, and it is in their relation that they have to be understood. For authors such as Adam (1994, p. 45) or Fraser (1987), adopting a pluralist perspective requires one to disregard disciplinary boundaries and dualisms as they are not suitable for the understanding of "multiple realities", "embeddedness" and "simultaneity" that characterize them. For Pomian (1984, p. 354), a plurality of temporalities always involves an "architecture" composed by hierarchical "stratums" – or levels of organization – that relate to each other through multiple feedback loops. Privileging the stratums of social life, the chapters of the second part of this book illustrate this aspect by showing how cultural, religious, economic, political and psychological temporalities have coevolved, influencing the ways time is experienced throughout the history of education.

There are however many difficulties associated with a level-based conceptualization of time. For Adam (1994, pp. 161–162), they relate to the tendency to reify such levels (as if they were existing per se) to conceptualize them hierarchically (as if some were more fundamental or simple than others) and to postulate clear cutoff points between them (as if they were structured). It is therefore critical to bear in mind the fact that we do not live 'in' those levels or that they stand in relation to each other (Adam, 1994, pp. 161–162). The idea of level remains a metaphor, and it is only one's understanding of time that requires to be connected and related, not time per se. In addition, as a hierarchical metaphor, such a description has to be considered as part of the framework of observation; it may have to be discarded or replaced if it prevents further conceptualization (Adam, 1994, pp. 161–162). It is crucial therefore not to consider such levels as stable and integrative but rather interpret them in terms of resonance and feedback loops (Lesourd, 2006, 2013). Modeling time through a level-based system of representation remains nevertheless the most appropriate strategy to emphasize the complexity of time (Adam, 1994, pp. 165–166) and establish some form of order to grasp the multiplicity of temporalities that influence educational phenomena according to complex causalities (Lesourd, 2013) and through different levels of experience (Roquet, Gonçalves, Roger, & Viana-Caetano, 2013). By establishing distinctions, it also provides us with a ground to conceive connections and relationships that are neither neutral nor symmetrical.

Privileging multireferentiality

From a theoretical and methodological perspective, what emerges from the previous considerations means that educational theory should provide researchers and practitioners with a vocabulary, a grammar and an architecture, that is, conceptual resources that enable one to organize and conceive the relationships among the various temporalities that are constitutive of educational phenomena. Embracing and studying the complexity of time in education requires the adoption of a position that conceives educational theory as "multireferential". According to Ardoino (1993), a multireferential approach proposes a "plural reading" of its objects, privileging different angles and involving different points of view and languages to enrich descriptions and interpretations. It also assumes that distinctive "systems of reference" are not reducible to each other (Ardoino, 1993, p. 15). The notion of multireferentiality, as it is defined and found in French educational theory since the late 1960s, stresses not only the complementarities among scientific disciplines but also their potential antagonisms. Multireferentiality postulates a fundamental (and probably irreducible) heterogeneity of perspectives mobilized. Conceived as others, and not only as different, they require to be actively articulated to contribute to the intelligibility of their objects (Ardoino, 1993, p. 15). Adopting a multireferential position in education suggests one to assume the beneficial and heuristic contribution inherent to the articulation of multiple theoretical and practical perspectives; it also requires doing the mourning of a homogeneous, ordered, overhanging and omnipotent point of view (Ardoino, 1993, p. 15). Multireferentiality is not about bringing an answer to the complexity of an issue; it is intimately related to such a complexity. Through the plurality of points of view and languages mobilized, it works as a reminder of the necessity to question epistemologies (Ardoino, 1993, p. 15), that is, the principles according to which one defines the legitimacy of the methods implemented to produce knowledge and their results. From this perspective, questioning the ways time is conceived in educational theory represents an initiative that cannot be conducted without interrogating simultaneously the legitimacy of the knowledge produced in other fields of study.

Recognizing conflicting views on educational temporalities

The previous sections stressed the epistemological issues associated with the articulation between heterogeneous temporalities, informed by scientific disciplines that also carry irreducible perspectives. Acknowledging such differences requires one to conceive simultaneously their complementarities as much as their antagonisms and contradictions. It requires questioning the ways their mutual influences are conceived. Such influences express indeed inequalities. Heterogeneous times do not relate with each other according to symmetrical ties. Dependencies exist between the multiple levels where time is observed or produced. For instance, physical temporalities (e.g., cycle of seasons) or biological rhythms (e.g., metabolic or epigenetic rates of change) determine aspects of our lives as human beings, including education, on which we have limited – if any – control. Reversely, human activity and education may also influence rhythms that characterize physical or natural phenomena (e.g., global warming and environmental sustainability). As individual and social beings, we are determined by social temporalities (e.g., through institutions such as work, family, education or religion) that we may recursively influence through the individual rhythms of our own activities (e.g., everyday habits, cognitive capacity and lifelong development).

The way we experience and conceive such mutual influences does not remain static. Such a temporal architecture is the product of history (Pomian, 1984): the ways time and temporalities are interpreted, defined and organized into hierarchical and interdependent levels have themselves evolved throughout the history of humanity following cultural and social influences. As for any other aspects of education, theorizing the relationships between heterogeneous temporalities relies on temporal conceptions and models, which are the products of a social and historical context. Selecting and privileging theories to conceive time in education translates therefore preferences, interests, ways of knowing or implications inherent to researchers' positionality. They remain fundamentally embedded in social, cultural and political dynamics that are the product of history. If the activity of theorizing time in educational sciences is not a neutral process, it requires to be assessed through the conflicting aspects – inherent to complementary and antagonistic views on time – it reveals. What emerges therefore from the adoption of a temporal architecture and the implementation of a multireferential approach is that theorizing educational temporalities requires one to conceive simultaneously the epistemological questions that are raised and the cultural and political dimensions that are embedded in it. The relationships among such epistemological, cultural and political dimensions are indeed at play whenever multiple temporalities need to be articulated and organized, either in theory or in praxis.

Toward a multireferential study of time in education

A lot has been written about time and education; however, the contribution of this literature remains relatively marginal and clearly disparate. To become an organized field of study that does not reduce the richness of views through which time may be conceived, additional work is needed. The idea of time must be reinvented to be enriched. There is so much more to study and to write about. The finality of further contributions should not be the development of a unifying theory. They should rather aim at fine-tuning the multireferential epistemology that is required to articulate various disciplinary contributions. They should also help us identify existing theories and concepts favoring the conjugation of heterogeneous perspectives as they relate to the diverse temporal aspects of life, including some that have been neglected so far, such as language, embodiment and the arts. Because education refers to changes that affect every level of existence, from the most material to the most spiritual one, and due to the diversity of the subdisciplines that constitute educational sciences, this field of study represents a privileged intellectual environment to theorize time according to non-reductionist points of view. Moreover, because educational sciences refer to a praxis that goes far beyond the production of knowledge, they also occupy a unique position to broaden one's understanding of time and confront the ways it is theorized with the social and cultural practices that inform every single aspect of everyday life. As it has been suggested, whenever multiple temporalities need to be articulated and organized, either in theory or in practice, there is a need to relate explicitly the epistemological, cultural and political dimensions involved. As it is going to appear in the next chapters, this is even truer when the aim of education is conceived through the lens of autonomy and emancipation.

Note

1 Pomian (1984, pp. vii–viii) distinguishes three types of – conflicting and complementary – chronosophy based on the pattern of evolution they represent: stationary (i.e., referring to the idea of eternity, represented through a horizontal line); cyclical (e.g., eternal recurrence, represented either through a circle or a sinusoidal line); or linear. Both cyclical and linear representations of time can be conceived either as ascending (e.g., the idea of progress, represented through an ascending line) or descending (e.g., the idea of decadence, represented through a descending line). Time can also be conceived without any determined direction or continuity; it refers then to a succession of divergent episodes that do not constitute any pattern.

References

Adam, B. (1994). *Time and social theory*. Cambridge: Polity Press.
Ardoino, J. (1993). L'approche multiréférentielle (plurielle) des situations éducatives et formatives. *Pratiques de Formation / Analyses, 25–26*, 15–34.
Ardoino, J. (2000). *Les avatars de l'éducation*. Paris: Presses Universitaires de France.
Association des Enseignants et Chercheurs en Sciences de l'Education. (2001). *Les sciences de l'éducation. Enjeux, finalités et défis*. Paris: INRP.
Ben-Peretz, M., & Bromme, R. (Eds.). (1990). *The nature of time in schools: Theoretical concepts, practitioner perceptions*. New York: Teachers College, Columbia University.
Biesta, G., Allan, J., & Edwards, R. (Eds.). (2014). *Making a difference in theory: The theory question in education and the education question in theory*. London: Routledge.
Boutinet, J.P. (2008). Penser l'anticipation dans sa (ses) crise(s). *Education Permanente, 176*, 8–22.
Cavet, A. (Ed.). (2011). Rythmes scolaires: Pour une dynamique nouvelle des temps éducatifs. *Dossier d'actualité de l'Institut National de Recherche Pédagogique, 60*.
Centre d'études et de recherche en sciences de l'éducation. (1993). *Temps, éducation et société: Actes du colloque de l'AFIRSE*. Caen, France: Université de Caen.
Charlot, B. (1995). *Les sciences de l'éducation: Un enjeu, un défi*. Paris: ESF.
Chopin, M.-P. (2010). Les usages du 'temps' dans les recherches sur l'enseignement. *Revue Française de Pédagogie, 170*, 87–110.
Clark, M.C., & Caffarella, R.S. (1999). Theorizing adult development. *New Directions for Adult and Continuing Education, 84*, 3–8.
Clegg, S. (2010). Time future: The dominant discourse of higher education. *Time & Society, 19*(3), 345–364.
Delhaxhe, A. (1997). Le temps comme unité d'analyse dans la recherche sur l'enseignement. *Revue Française de Pédagogie, 118*, 107–125.
Dominicé, P. (2000). *Learning from our lives: Using educational biographies with adults*. San Francisco: Jossey-Bass.
Elias, N. (1992). *Time: An essay*. Oxford: Blackwell Publishers.
Fraser, J.T. (1987). *Time: The familiar stranger*. Amherst, MA: University of Massachusetts Press.
Hargreaves, A. (1994). *Changing teachers, changing times: Teachers' work and culture in the postmodern age*. London: Cassell.
Hoodless, P.A. (2002). An investigation into children's developing awareness of time and chronology in story. *Journal of Curriculum Studies, 34*(2), 173–200.
Larsson, J., & Sanne, C. (2005). Self-help books on avoiding time shortage. *Time & Society, 14*(2/3), 213–230.

Leaton Gray, S. (2004). Defining the future: An interrogation of education and time. *British Journal of Sociology of Education, 25*(3), 323–340.

Lerner, R.M. (2002). *Concepts and theories of human development.* Mahwah, NJ: L. Erlbaum Associates.

Lesourd, F. (2006). Des temporalités éducatives: Note de synthèse. *Pratiques de Formation / Analyses, 51–52,* 9–7.

Lesourd, F. (2013). 'Boucles étranges' et complexité des temporalités éducatives. In P. Roquet, M.J. Gonçalves, L. Roger, & A.P. Viana-Caetano (Eds.), *Temps, temporalité et complexité dans les activités éducatives et formatives* (pp. 41–56). Paris: L'Harmattan.

Mayes, C. (2005). Teaching and time: Foundations of a temporal pedagogy. *Teacher Education Quarterly, 32*(2), 143–160.

McDevitt, T.M., & Ormrod, J.E. (2013). *Child development and education.* Boston: Pearson.

McInerney, D. (2004). A discussion of future time perspective. *Educational Psychology Review, 16*(2), 141–151.

Papastephanou, M. (2013). Philosophy, kairosophy and the lesson of time. *Educational Philosophy and Theory, 46*(7), 718–734.

Pineau, G. (2000). *Temporalités en formation: Vers de nouveaux synchroniseurs.* Paris: Anthropos.

Pomian, K. (1984). *L'ordre du temps.* Paris: Gallimard.

Roquet, P., Gonçalves, M.J., Roger, L., & Viana-Caetano, A.P. (2013). *Temps, temporalité et complexité dans les activités éducatives et formatives.* Paris: L'Harmattan.

Slattery, P. (1995). A postmodern vision of time and learning: A response to the National Education Commission Report 'Prisoners of time'. *Harvard Educational Review, 65*(4), 612–633.

Smith, M.U. (2010). Current status of research in teaching and learning evolution. *Science & Education, 19*(6–8), 523–571.

St-Jarre, C., & Dupuy-Walker, L. (Eds.). (2001). *Le temps en éducation: Regards multiples.* Sainte-Foy, QC, Canada: Presses Universitaires du Québec.

West, L., Alheit, P., Andersen, A.S., & Merrill, B. (2007). *Using biographical and life history approaches in the study of adult and lifelong learning: European perspectives.* Frankfurt am Main: Peter Lang.

Chapter 3

The functions and meanings of temporal constraints in education

Temporal influences and autonomy

Increasing one's autonomy requires the capacity to regulate the role played by 'external' influences and the impact of one's own actions over oneself and the environment. The term 'influence' refers therefore to a central notion, not only to theorize education but also to conceive the ideas of autonomy and emancipation. The assumption that frames this chapter is that to theorize what is at stake in a process of emancipation from a temporal and educational perspective, one must first describe and interpret the dynamics through which autonomy evolves and may be regulated. Such dynamics suggest the interplay between influences that occur through time and that determine how temporal experience itself is represented. Because we are considering changes and influences in regard to autonomy, it seems critical to explore in particular their constraining effects, that is, their capacity to limit or extend margins of freedom or agency. The aim of this chapter is therefore to circumscribe a theoretical framework to organize the way we are going to examine temporal constraints that shape human experiences and more specifically educational ones.

To proceed, this chapter is organized around five sections. The first one defines the notion of temporal constraint, which will serve not only as a generic expression referring to the heterogeneous forms of temporal influence that impact the development of individual and collective autonomy but also as a red line organizing the second part of this book. Because temporal constraints can be envisioned through their genealogy – from antiquity to the Early Modern period (cf. Chapter 4) and beyond (cf. Chapters 5, 6 and 7) – the next section briefly introduces the sociohistorical assumptions that frame such an evolution, considering especially the history of temporal norms, standards and their constraining effects as well as the mutual influences between dominant social times (e.g., religion and economy) and education. To conceive how temporal constraints can be interpreted from a sociological perspective, stressing both their functions and their meanings, the third section locates the core assumptions that define an institutionalist perspective. Accordingly, the institution of time is conceived based on its functional and symbolic dimensions. To illustrate their constraining influences in education, the fourth section explores how the normative aspects of time bind human activity in education. Finally, after having highlighted the importance of the symbolic dimension of the social imaginary of time, the last section of this chapter establishes the relevance of referring to the concept of rhythm as a privileged entry to describe, theorize and renew the way complex temporal phenomena may be represented, interpreted and analyzed in education.

Defining temporal constraints

Considering the emancipatory aim of education as the horizon of the reflection conducted in this book, it would be tempting to refer directly to the notions of power or control to conceive temporal influences and to use them to question the nature of the relationships among time, alienation and emancipation. There is after all a significant body of research around those notions in the sociology of time (Bergmann, 1992). Some of the contributions framing this literature are going to feed our reflection (cf. Chapter 8). However, to be congruent with the assumptions presented in the previous chapters, it does not seem appropriate to limit our reflection to such a sociological framework to conceive the dynamics of human autonomy. Because social and cultural life is embedded in physical and living environments, whether natural or artificial, it is permanently affected by changes whose temporalities escape the principles that rule human agency. Thus, phenomena such as climate change or ecological transformations, which have a direct impact on human activity (e.g., food reserves, geopolitical influences, migrations and employment) and represent a significant matter of concern in education cannot be reduced to an interplay of power dynamics. They may be understood as the results of human actions, constrained by political and economic interests, and represented through constructs that have been elaborated through history. They remain nevertheless ruled according to physical, chemical and biological principles whose causes and effects escape the realm of human agency; the constraints they involve cannot therefore be fully expressed through anthropological notions, such as control or power. The same is true for the artificial components that constitute and surround education. The changes that affect technologies, built environments or information evolve according to temporalities that are partially independent from human agency as they rely on material constraints. Even the symbolic dimensions inherent to cultural phenomena, such as language, body practices or the arts, are embedded in changes that are bound either by physiological or physical limitations (e.g., sensori-motricity and perception) that are partially autonomous from the social constructs that confer meanings to them. The temporalities that characterize those phenomena impact nevertheless social practices, including education, and eventually participate to some extent to the complexity of human autonomy.

Natural, artificial, technological or cultural aspects of our life influence and constrain human behaviors; they mediate power dynamics, but they do not manifest power or control per se. This is the reason why; it appears more appropriate to start the reflection around the emancipatory aim of education with the notion of constraint as an expression whose polysemy participates to a complex understanding of autonomy without narrowing it down to its strictly anthropological components. In its general understanding, this term evokes the exercise of force to determine or confine action; it appears as synonymous of coercion or compulsion. It also refers to some form of confinement, bound or fettered condition, that suggests a restriction of liberty or of free action (Oxford English Dictionary Online, 2015). The term is used in an anthropological as well as physical context; thus, it also expresses any special condition, such as a state of tension, into which a body is brought by the operation of some force and lasting during its operation (Oxford English Dictionary Online, 2015). If educational phenomena involve heterogeneous temporalities that can be conceived through their mutual interactions, then questioning the emancipatory aim of education may lead to conceive influences such as temporal constraints. Accordingly, temporal constraints refer to the effects of heterogeneous temporalities that confine, bound, restrict or put into tension the operations involved by educational phenomena, such as individual or collective learning, transformation or development.[1]

The position adopted in this book is that to theorize what is at stake in emancipatory dynamics, from a temporal perspective, one must describe first the phenomenology of temporal constraints and eventually depict how they have evolved through history. Focusing more specifically on educational praxis and theories, this represents the aim of the four chapters constitutive of the second part of this book. The analysis will suggest that the history of education is characterized by the emergence of successive, concomitant and intertwined strategies implemented to control existing temporal constraints (e.g., physiological, cognitive, discursive, environmental and social), and leads to the production of new forms of social constraints, expressed in education through the development of temporal discipline (cf. Chapter 4), temporal ideals such as the quest for temporal efficiency and rhythmic harmony (cf. Chapter 5), the internalized experience of temporal contradictions (cf. Chapter 6) and the necessity to cope with rhythmic discontinuities (cf. Chapter 7). To establish such a description, one must first determine how to frame and describe those temporal constraints and the ways they evolve. To proceed, we are going to adopt a sociohistorical lens and privilege an institutionalist perspective.

Framing the sociohistorical context that shapes educational temporalities

Referring to the history of temporal normativity

From a sociological and historical perspective, it is usual to consider time as a matter of social order and control. How a society defines and controls time is indeed at the core of the way power is exercised (Bergmann, 1992). Sociologists usually consider that the temporal order of social systems is expressed, on the one hand, in their time reckoning (i.e., the choice of temporal reference points) and the technology used to measure time (e.g., sundial, water clock, mechanical clock, wristwatch or atomic clock) and, on the other hand, through the temporal standardization of social behavior provided by their timetables. The normative content of time is therefore expressed in the establishment of social temporal norms whose ordering character comes from their effects on the structure and coordination of behavior (Bergmann, 1992, p. 99). Revisiting the history of human civilizations, authors such as Attali (1982), Le Goff (1980), Nowotny (1994), and Thompson (1967) have distinguished different periods characterized by specific relationships – intertwined, overlapping and succeeding to each other – among the experience of time, time measurement and the ruling system of power. Such an intertwined succession of temporal standards is going to provide our inquiry with a structure to consider the evolution of the relationship between temporal experiences and their constraining aspects.

Referring to the mutual influences between social times

For sociologists, time can be conceived as "a social construct which is the product of the diversity of social activities that it allows to coordinate, articulate and give rhythm to" (Sue, 1993, p. 62, my translation). Such a construct can however be envisioned according to different perspectives. Following Durkheim, one may conceive the specificity of social time as a unitary time – produced by each society – that fulfills a regulating, organizing and ordering function. Unlike this totalizing and abstract conception, another position may suggest that any social practice produces its own social time; accordingly, there would be a multiplicity of social times found at different levels of the social structure (e.g., institutions, social classes, groups and age cohorts) (Sue, 1993, p. 63). One may also focus more specifically on the times produced by social practices considered – legitimately or not – as the most significant ones among the representations carried by a society about itself (e.g., working time, leisure and education) (Sue, 1993, p. 63). In sociology of education, the perspective proposed by Sue suggests not only that social times are dynamic and that their organization evolves through history; it also supposes that their mutual influences are unequal and hierarchized. Regarding education as an institution, it stresses the fact that its formal organization appears directly related to the dominant social time, that is, the time considered as the most generative for the society, the one that defines its economy (Sue, 1993, p. 66). From this perspective, the institutionalization of vocational training (11th century), universities (13th century), religious schools (16th century) and the modern school (19th century), appear for instance as the product of complementary and antagonistic relationships among economical, religious and political spheres. Such a process of institutionalization also demonstrates the hegemony of working time as a key factor contributing to produce those forms of education and, recursively, reproduced by them. In the next chapters, such a perspective will bring us to pay specific attention not only to the evolution of the temporalities of educational praxis but also to the social context within which they unfold, especially considering the fluctuating role played by the temporal constraints imposed by other institutions, such as culture, religion or the economy.

The analysis of temporal constraints from a perspective centered on institutions

As discussed in the previous chapter, the adoption of a multireferential approach constitutes a relevant path to conceive the temporal architecture that sustains – as well as it may be supported by – the political dimensions of education. In *Education et Politique*, Ardoino (1977/1999) theorized a hermeneutical approach located at the core of French *Analyse Institutionnelle*, which interprets the political dimensions of education based on five distinctive and complementary perspectives, respectively centered on the persons (e.g., their psychological attributes), the interrelations and the groups (e.g., their psychosociological dimensions), the organizations and the institutions. According to the sociohistorical lens privileged at this stage of our inquiry, our reflection on temporal constraints is going to be framed by an institutionalist perspective focusing on both the functions and meanings associated with them. The following sections locate the core assumptions that define such an approach, privileging Castoriadis's contribution (1975/1997) to conceive both the dynamics through which time is instituted and their effects on education and society.

The functional and symbolic components of an institution

According to Dubet (2006), the notion of institution designates that most of social facts (e.g., customs, market rules or religions), as long as they are stable, impose themselves onto individuals and are transmitted from one generation to another. An institution may refer to all beliefs and all modes of behavior instituted by the collectivity. The term may also relate to facts, collective practices or cognitive and moral frameworks through which individual thoughts develop themselves: apparatus, laws, representations, activities that operate a transmutation from "nature" into "society" (Dubet, 2006, p. 634). For Castoriadis (1975/1997), such a conception explains the existence and the characteristics of an institution by the function that it fulfills in society, given the circumstances, and by its role in the overall economy of social life. However, an institution should not be reduced to its functions; it is also crucial to apprehend it through the symbolic dimension through which it gets to be known. Indeed, everything we experience in society is inextricably tied to a symbolic dimension that carries meanings (Castoriadis, 1975/1997, p. 117). For Castoriadis, the choice of symbols associated with an institution and its functions is neither freely chosen, imposed, neutral nor impenetrable (Castoriadis, 1975/1997,

p. 125). Symbolism refers to a capacity of invention, which is the mark of a social imaginary. According to this perspective, the institution can be defined as "a socially sanctioned, symbolic network in which a functional component and an imaginary component are combined in variable proportions and relations" (Castoriadis, 1975/1997, p. 132). Thus, conceiving time and education as institutions requires one to question both the functions fulfilled by the social, cultural and political use of these ideas and the meanings they carry symbolically in the social imaginary as well.

The identitary and imaginary dimensions of the time institutionalized in education

Castoriadis (1975/1997) distinguishes two forms of instituted time. The first one, inherited from philosophy, refers to a representation of time, conceived as a homogenous and neutral medium. This institution of time reduces its conception to a function of "bearings and marking" (*repérage*) (Castoriadis, 1975/1997, p. 209). Time can be apprehended through the repetition of identitary presents that are always identical and that can be counted. Instituted time as identitary relates to measurement, or the imposition of a measure on time, suggesting a segmentation into "identical" or ideally "congruent" parts (Castoriadis, 1975/1997, p. 209). This is the time of classical physics – a conception that grounds the scientific institution of time. This is also the calendar time, divided according to numbers, based on periodical natural phenomena (e.g., day, lunar month, seasons and year) (Castoriadis, 1975/1997, p. 209). For Castoriadis, this time is the product of the purification of a second form of instituted time: the time of "otherness-alteration". The later is the true sociohistorical time of a society (Castoriadis, 1975/1997, p. 200). It is a time of "bursting", "emerging", "creating" (Castoriadis, 1975/1997, p. 201). The time of otherness-alteration is the time of human experience constituted by the irreversibility of the succession of events and phenomena (Castoriadis, 1975/1997, p. 202). Loaded with significations, this "significant" time is conceived by Castoriadis as a time instituted as a "social imaginary" (Castoriadis, 1975/1997, p. 209). For him, there is a reciprocal relation of inherence or of circular implication between the two dimensions of time:

> Identitary time is 'time' only because it is referred to the imaginary time that gives it its signification of 'time'; and imaginary time would itself be undefinable, impossible to situate, ungraspable – it would be *nothing* without identitary time.
> (Castoriadis, 1975/1997, p. 210, stressed by the author)

Therefore, time must be instituted both as identitary and as imaginary to have a social existence (Castoriadis, 1975/1997, pp. 211–212). Identitary and imaginary time remain however inseparable from the time of social doing (Castoriadis, 1975/1997, pp. 211–212). The time of doing contains singularities that are not determinable in advance (e.g., irregularities, accidents, events and ruptures of repetition). Therefore, the time of doing is necessarily much closer to true temporality than the time of social representation is or can be (Castoriadis, 1975/1997, pp. 211–212). However, the social institution of imaginary time always tends to cover over, to conceal and to deny temporality as otherness-alteration:

> Thus, everything happens as if the time of social doing, which is basically irregular, uneven, changing, had always to be, in the imaginary, swallowed up by a denial of time through the eternal return of the same, its representation as wearing away and as corruption, its flattening out in the indifference of simply quantitative difference, its annulment in the face of Eternity.
> (Castoriadis, 1975/1997, p. 212)

The phenomenon described by Castoriadis is crucial to understand how temporal constraints operate at the symbolic level. Thus, the ways time is imagined and represented tend to take over the ways it is experienced in everyday life. Accordingly, the ordered representations of the time symbolized by clocks or calendars impose themselves to the flow of activity experienced spontaneously, including the discontinuities that randomly disrupt and pace human experience (Castoriadis, 1975/1997, p. 212). Such a phenomenon is for Castoriadis at the root of a specific form of temporal constraint where the social institution of imaginary time becomes a matter of alienation:

> Alienation . . . appears as a *modality* of the relation to the institution . . . [It] appears first of all as the alienation of a society to its institutions, as the *autonomization* of institutions in relation to society.
> (Castoriadis, 1975/1997, p. 115, stressed by the author)

In other words, whenever the representations of time (e.g., symbolic, metaphorical and discursive) gain autonomy in regard to the phenomena they are related to, they carry the potentiality to become not only constraining but also alienating. From an educational perspective, it means that it is particularly critical to establish how education participates to the institutionalization of specific representations of time and how it is shaped, and constrained, by such a social imaginary.

Interpreting the functional and symbolic aspects of time in education

According to the institutionalist position already defined to be described, the depth of the dynamics of temporal constraints requires the adoption of a 'binocular' approach, stressing both the organizational and symbolic aspects of time. A first lens magnifies the social functions the institution of time may fulfill; a second one filters how the institution of time may operate in the social imaginary.

In the following sections, we are going to explore how both aspects are intertwined. Considering examples related to school's temporal regularities, cyclic temporal structures, the temporal imagination conveyed by formal education, the functions of age norms, the structuration of the life-course, educational tracking, the representations of generation, and the perception of intergenerational inequalities, I will try to illustrate how both the functional and symbolic aspects of the institution of time are tight with specific temporal constraints.

The power of school's temporal regularities

Zerubavel (1981) explored four major forms of temporal regularity that refer to patterns of social events and activities: rigid sequential structures, fixed durations, standard temporal locations and uniform rates of occurrence. Students moving from grade to grade in a predetermined sequence – without having the freedom to choose their trajectory – illustrate well the first notion (Ben-Peretz, 1990, p. 69). Considering the symbolic nature of many "socially based irreversibilities" (Zerubavel, 1981, p. 4), Ben-Peretz (1990, p. 69) points out the fact that the sequential structure of curricula may be considered both as "natural" – if it was based on inherent characteristics of the subject matter – and as an imposed irreversibility understood as a symbol of the power structure of schools and subject matter experts. Another facet of temporal regularity is observed through the 'fixed duration' of many events as they express conventions that create certain temporal expectations in the participants (e.g., class or working-day duration). As noted by Ben-Peretz (1990, p. 69), exceptions to expected durations might be accompanied by normative-ethical overtones, such as leaving "too early" or staying "too late". Thus, the ways students, parents, educators or administrators negotiate the time devoted to specific pedagogical or administrative activities, or difficulties related to the implementation of innovative curriculum, could reveal tensions between organizational constraints and individual interests. In Western cultures, Zerubavel (1981) pointed out the fact that there is always an association among social activities, events and standard locations and time. In schools, planning, curriculum development and instruction tend indeed to impose norms of temporal location that may lead to the rejection of planned learning events if they are perceived as "unnatural" by students (Ben-Peretz, 1990, p. 70). The uniform rate of recurrence that characterizes formal organizations such as schools has also to be stressed. This "social rhythmicity" is "often quite independent of natural rhythmicity . . . sometimes even conflicts with it" (Zerubavel, 1981, p. 11). Temporal regularity has cognitive implications: "[It] adds a strong touch of predictability to the world around us, thus, enhancing our cognitive well-being" (Zerubavel, 1981, p. 12). This may explain why innovative curricula, or unusual teaching strategies, that lessen the predictability of an otherwise fairly regular temporal environment may lead to a sense of cognitive uneasiness in teachers and students (Ben-Peretz, 1990, p. 70). On another hand, one could consider such an experience of dissonance as a privileged opportunity to challenge the legitimacy of organizational temporalities.

The functions of school's cyclic temporal structures

For Connelly and Clandinin (1990), inspired by Zerubavel's contribution, the sociotemporal structure of schools is experienced as cyclic and rhythmic as it is ruled by the clock on a daily basis and by promotion on an annual basis: "Annual and daily cycles reflect in some complex way more general societal cycles, some of which are natural, such as the seasons, and some of which are conventional, such as the yearly calendar" (Connelly & Clandinin, 1990, p. 39). Those cycles can be interpreted in themselves and in relation to the sociotemporal order of other organizations (e.g., family and work). They also carry a personal meaning for those who experience it (e.g., students, parents, teachers and administrators), meanings that are negotiated throughout the organization of the everyday activities (Connelly& Clandinin, 1990, p. 39). Cycles, as described by Zerubavel, show a number of characteristics of importance to the study of schooling. One of those is that they have temporal boundaries that often exhibit exceptional rigidity and remain taken for granted: the beginning and ending of the school year, of the school day, of classes, and so on (Connelly & Clandinin, 1990, p. 40). Cycles are also structured; they have beginning, middle and end parts organized around clearly defined routines and rituals (e.g., class opening or end-of-the-day routines) (Connelly & Clandinin, 1990, p. 41). Another characteristic is that anyone participates in many contingent and overlapping cycles of activities that may be differentiated temporally (Connelly & Clandinin, 1990, p. 42). Based on their work in several Canadian schools, Connelly and Clandinin identified 10 school cycles according to their temporal duration: annual, holiday, monthly, weekly, six-day, duty, day, teacher, report and within-class cycles (Connelly & Clandinin, 1990, p. 42). Such cycles not only vary in duration, but they can also vary according to sequence, temporal location, and rate of occurrence. Thus, the same cycle (e.g., six-day cycle) orders in different ways the sociotemporal reality of different groups of participants (e.g., students, teachers, administrators and support staff) (Connelly & Clandinin, 1990, p. 45). Organizational rhythms may therefore be experienced in complementarity (e.g., students and teachers with the same daily schedule) or through antagonisms that require planning and scheduling to be balanced (e.g., the relationship between different school functions such as sports, library and special education and the regular class programs) (Connelly & Clandinin, 1990, p. 42). Another dimension of the cycles that define school order – mainly through schedules and calendars – is that they express a temporal regularity that structures social life by forcing activities into fairly rigid temporal patterns (e.g., routines, rituals and repetitive activity); such rigidity tends to prevent the emergence of spontaneous activities and the solving of unexpected problems (Connelly & Clandinin, 1990, p. 44). From a curricular perspective, the conventionality of school cycles and their reified objective status constitute therefore strategic points of entry – and resistance – to school reforms (Connelly & Clandinin, 1990, p. 57).

The bounded temporal imagination conveyed by formal education

School and family are the two main places where individuals are socialized to specific temporal notions and values (Pronovost, 1996, p. 135). At school, for instance, children learn to structure and organize their time, following a model analogous to working time. The measurement of achievement and the respect of the school order are defined according to temporal standards that are internalized very early in one's life. As noticed by Connelly and Clandinin (1990, p. 43), the primary definition of schooling is in terms of years, not in terms of what is to be known, even if the curriculum is experienced qualitatively through its various cycles. Adult and continuing education also perpetuates specific temporal conceptions, especially with the emergence through the 20th century of the "mythology" revolving around *éducation permanente* and lifelong learning (Pineau, 2000). For Ardoino (2000, p. 157), the language conveyed by educational institutions – especially in school – contributes to very insidious forms of alienation because it does not enable one to designate, describe or characterize the time of otherness and alteration. The order of instituted time refers thus to a chronology or a chronometry that even if it is associated with the ideas of movement and succession, refers nevertheless to a spatial order, frameworks and homogenous time units that remain interchangeable and reversible (Ardoino, 2000, p. 157). Ardoino suggests, for instance, that mathematical and geometrical forms and figures – such as circles, or a logarithmic spiral evoking the idea of reiteration or an arrow symbolizing the direction and irreversibility of time – limit one's representations (Ardoino, 2000, p. 157). Moreover, the language used by practitioners and researchers tends to make indistinct and takes for granted terms and expressions; even so they belong to heterogeneous temporal registers, such as the social time of the organization, the biological time of living organisms or the psychological time of the subjects (Ardoino, 2000, p.158). For Ardoino, temporality seems unthinkable without considering an explicit reference to the living and therefore to death: time "involves" us, it "affects" us, and "alters" us (Ardoino, 2000, pp. 159–160). Processes play indeed a crucial role. However, for institutional, legal, organizational, economical or administrative reasons, the existence of processes remains mostly ignored from the school logic; they are reduced to "procedures", "models", "policy" and "settings" (*dispositifs*) (Ardoino, 2000, pp. 159–160). To some extent, managers and policy makers are in control of the time of pedagogues. The time instituted by school is programmed and homogenized through the use of constraining time units; the meaning of duration becomes then pejorative ("it drags on") (Ardoino, 2000, pp. 159–160). In addition, such a setting dispossesses educators of their own notion of time due to the fact that their relationships with students remain intermittent and discontinuous; educators are therefore brought to imagine and abstract the lived time of their partners, which may prevent them to take into consideration differentiated biological and psychological rhythms (Ardoino, 2000, p. 161). For Ardoino, such phenomena are not conscious or deliberate; they rather belong to the order of (psychoanalytical) denial or Freudian slip (Ardoino, 2000, p. 162). They belong to the imaginary of instituted time.

The symbolic dimension of age norms and the institutionalization of the life course

Another way to approach the social imaginary of time and its constraining effects, as perpetuated by institutions such as education, is to consider the symbolic dimension of age norms (Settersten, 1999). Whether in family, in school or through continuing education, age always functions "as a convenient dimension with which to map social and cultural expectations about experiences and roles" (Settersten, 1999, p. 65). As an institution, education is organized (e.g., segmented or sequenced) around 'age structures' that reveal, formally or informally, social expectations and preferences. As pointed out by Settersten, because it is easily measured, objective, and universal, chronological age is particularly convenient and practical for administrative purposes and normative assessment, even though it contributes little to the understanding of human development (Settersten, 1999, p. 82). In education as for the rest of social life, the adoption of age norms constitutes a symbolic temporal constraint because it influences the ways one conceives life trajectories, including role transitions, rights, duties, resources, etc. Especially when they are taken for granted (e.g., internalized and naturalized), age norms influence representations regarding 'normal' or 'expectable life', perpetuating unchallenged conceptions of human life (Settersten, 1999, p. 93). Age norms are closely intertwined with the institutionalization of the individual life course (i.e., the organization of the sequence of successive life events and transitions that define familial, educational and professional trajectories) (Settersten, 1999, p. 19). As reminded by Settersten (1999, p. 23), historically, the state has come to play a greater role in structuring the life course, for instance by defining most of the "'ports of entry and exit' through which people move as their lives unfold". From an educational perspective, the institutionalization of the life course occurs for instance through pathways in secondary and higher education and in work organizations. Individual lives are therefore regulated and structured by social institutions and policies that create both constraints and new potentialities for individuals. They deeply influence the meaning perspectives through which individuals orient themselves and plan their actions (Settersten, 1999, p. 23) Whether the life course, as a whole, is more rigidly structured and experienced today, than it was before, remains up for debate (Settersten, 1999, p. 39). Considering the symbolic impact of education on individual life trajectories brings however one to question how much biographical choices remain 'chronologized' (i.e., bound to age), 'institutionalized' (i.e., structured by social institutions) and 'standardized' (i.e., exhibiting more regular patterns), or whether they display increased flexibility and idiosyncrasy (Settersten, 1999, p. 39).

Age constrains, educational tracking and generational representations

Age constrains and educational tracking constitute two expressions that illustrate well the concrete limitations associated with the symbolic value associated to age in education. In social theory, age constraints refer to inflexible formal requirements or restrictions, inherent to social roles or activities, that limit choices and opportunities, based on age differentiation or life stage (e.g., compulsory school is associated with childhood, and retirement benefits to old age). On the one hand, age-differentiated structures are convenient because they create "orderliness" in the entry to, and exit from, social roles and activities; on the other hand, they perpetuate 'ageism', as a form of discrimination that restricts opportunities depending on specific periods of life (Settersten, 1999, p. 42). In formal education, such issues appear for instance through 'educational tracking' implemented – either explicitly or tacitly – in primary and secondary schools. In such cases, the individual's performance, at critical points along the curriculum, determines the track onto which the student is placed; each educational track ultimately determines the range of future occupational positions to which one has access:

> Where educational tracks are explicit and strong, the individual has little or no opportunity to veer from that track once it has been assigned. In such a scenario, the likelihood of 'second chances,' whether to make up for past mistakes or to change earlier decisions seems slim.
>
> (Settersten, 1999, p. 49)

As reminded by Settersten (1999, p. 49), because "the practice of tracking goes against . . . ideals of equality and individualism, its existence . . . is often denied." In spite of remaining often 'hidden' from students and parents, such a phenomenon continues however to subsist.

If education, as an institution, shapes and determines age norms, life courses, and age constraints, its subjective meanings is also influenced by the experiences people have of learning and the way it is organized temporally. Biesta et al., (2011) have explored such dynamics by questioning the role of generations in understanding learning through the life course. According to these authors, the notion of generation refers, on the one hand, to family positions and relationships (e.g., child, parent, grandparent) and, on the other hand, to the notion of cohort which encapsulates a broader socio-economic outlook, as an age-based form of social identification, structured around people's shared experiences and the specific social and political events that have occurred throughout their life course (Biesta et al., 2011, p. 69). In both of these senses, the authors note that people's understandings of generational attachments lead them to adopt or recognize shared dispositions towards learning and education (e.g., generation is associated with specific skills, knowledge, and schooling experience) (Biesta et al., 2011, p. 73). Such conceptions may eventually influence the level of freedom perceived, in regard to the role taken by educational opportunities: for instance, older adults tend to see formal education as a guaranteed pathway to social mobility, while younger adults tend to view it as a necessary, but not a sufficient, condition for employment and a career (Biesta et al., 2011, p. 73). Conceived from a symbolic perspective, representations associated with generations constitute therefore another example of symbolic temporal constraints that may influence people choices and dispositions toward education.

Time-based discriminations and the representation of intergenerational inequalities

As noted by Schuller (1993, p. 345), whatever the rhetoric of public pronouncements in favor of lifelong learning, national policy and institutional practice still "encourage young people to stay on in education for as long as possible rather than to plan to re-enter later on." In formal education, time-based discriminations occur for instance through admission processes; they may express biases against older students (i.e., those who return to school or change occupations in their middle or later years) or older workers willing to follow training (Schuller, 1993; Settersten, 1999, p. 50). As pointed by Schuller (1993, p. 342), because shared representations around education are still so strongly associated with youth, discussions of equality in relation to education often ignore generational aspects, concentrating on other important dimensions such as class, gender or ethnicity. According to Temkin (1992, as cited in Schuller, 1993, p. 342), generational inequalities can however be identified through three different forms: first, by comparing the distribution of opportunities for life chances over the entire lifetimes of different groups of individuals; second, by choosing a historical or chronological period as the basic unit and then contrast people's experience within that unit regardless of their age or stage; and third, by choosing to compare people who are at the same stage of life or age, though this may be located at different historical times. According to each of those three perspectives, the study conducted in the United Kingdom by Schuller and Bostyn (1992, as cited in Schuller, 1993) presents evidences according to which intergenerational educational inequality has built up over decades. If the social effects of such discriminations are real and established, they remain determined by the importance given to the specific symbols of time (e.g., biological age, year of birth) mobilized in order to discriminate, assess and eventually quantify human experience.

Time and rhythm theory

Exploring after Castoriadis the influences and the constraints associated with the social imaginary of time should finally bring us to question the vocabulary used in order to depict and represent educational temporalities. So far, the terminology used mostly referred to time and temporalities, as defined in philosophy, physics, biology and human sciences. We have occasionally mentioned the term 'rhythm' without explicitly establishing how it relates to the idea of time. The last assumption formulated in this chapter is that this concept plays in fact a critical role in the understanding of the complexity of temporal phenomena, and that the evolution of its use reveals specific dimensions of the social imaginary of time.

Rhythms and temporal complexity

As documented by contemporary scholars (e.g., Henriques, Tiainen, & Väliaho, 2014; Michon, 2005, 2007; Sauvanet, 1999, 2000a, 2000b), the concept of rhythm is a nomadic one, which moved between disciplines (from philosophy, music, dance, poetry and literature, to physics, biology, psychology, sociology, economy, etc.), and which regularly appeared and disappeared from the history of human thought, including in the field of education. Considering the evolution of the use made of this concept, shifting the point of view adopted in this book from a temporal to a rhythmic perspective constitutes a strategic move for at least four reasons. First, the experience of rhythm constitutes a privileged way to access and describe the experience of time, providing us with a relatively accessible conceptual mediation to question and challenge fundamental existential, as well as more mundane or daily issues. Second, the adoption of a rhythmic approach appears particularly congruent with an epistemology valuing the complexity of human experience. As it will be developed in the following chapters, the concept of rhythm appears particularly appropriate in order to describe the temporal organization that characterizes complex living phenomena, involving aspects of one's existence that are both ordered and disordered (Alhadeff-Jones, in press). A third benefit associated with the use of this concept is that it brings one to conceive simultaneously the complementarities and antagonisms that characterize phenomena conceived through the lens of change and transformation. As argued by Spencer (1864, as cited in Henriques, Tiainen, & Väliaho, 2014, p. 6), rhythm can be considered as a fundamental property of the relationship between antagonistic forces. It fits therefore well any attempt to describe tensions inherent to temporal influences. Beyond natural phenomena, such as those observed in physics or in biology, it constitutes a privileged way to interpret constraining dynamics and even theorize the concept of power, as demonstrated in detail by Michon (2005, 2007). Finally, referring to rhythm theories significantly enlarges the spectrum of phenomena and fields of inquiry considered in order to analyze the effects of time. For instance, the preponderance of rhythmic references in the arts (e.g., dance, music, poetry, visual arts) appears as a privileged way in order to conceive their respective temporalities, and through them, the temporal constraints associated with sensible, esthetical, embodied and discursive practices. Even if rhythm theories have not reached yet the extent that characterizes the philosophical and scientific literature on time, such resources still require caution in order to be used appropriately. From the Greek origins of the term to its most recent applications, references to the concept of rhythm thus demonstrate the ambiguities and the ambivalences associated with the temporal descriptions associated with it (Michon, 2005, 2007; Sauvanet, 2000a, 2000b). Like the concept of time, the concept of rhythm can be interpreted according to an epistemology valorizing its quantitative (i.e., measurable), symmetric and repetitive dimensions, or – at the opposite – stressing its qualitative (i.e., sensible), free-flowing and irregular dimensions (cf. chapter 4). In addition, through the ubiquity of rhythms in one's life and their constant interactions, the use of this concept also raises critical questions about the relationships (including influences and causalities) between rhythms and the way they are conceived and theorized (Sauvanet, 2000a).

Rhythms: The fabric of time

There are as many ways to conceive rhythms than there are forms of temporalities. They can be categorized according to a similar typology. Sauvanet (2000a, p. 18) suggests for instance to distinguish cosmological rhythms (i.e., periodic cosmic rhythms, season cycle), biological rhythms (i.e., innate periodic processes of living organisms) and anthropological rhythms (i.e., periodic and rhythmic processes developed by and specific to human beings, such as historical, technical or artistic rhythms). If time and rhythm appear as two close parents, it remains nevertheless important to clarify how they are related to each other. As previously defined (cf. chapter 2), time refers to a class of quantitative or qualitative relationships; if one can perceive the entities, the changes they coordinate, the signals or signs they produce and the programs they execute, time itself cannot be observed (Pomian, 1984). It becomes perceptible through specific experiences; among those, one has to consider rhythmic ones. Thus, rhythms appear as what may characterize the relationships between changes. Rhythms refer to the specific way we perceive the signals (e.g., visual or auditory) and signs (e.g., language) characterizing the experience of time. As suggested by Sauvanet (2000a, p. 99), rhythms make humans be sensible to time; it is through rhythm that we can perceive it. For Sauvanet (2000a, p. 99), rhythm expresses the sense (in French: *sens*, as sensation, orientation and meaning) of time. First, rhythm makes time sensible, because it is what makes us be sensible to time; rhythm always appears as a differential of durations (e.g., alternance between strong and weak beat, high and low intensity of change). Second, rhythm gives time a direction, expressing both, repetition and irreversibility (e.g., difference): seasons reappear through the same cycle, but every year's weather features remain unique. Third, as a meaning, rhythm provides one with significations in order to interpret temporal phenomena. For instance, in poetry, the rhythm of a text is part of what gives meaning to the temporality of the text (Meschonnic, 1982, p. 214, as cited in Sauvanet, 2000a, p. 109). Rhythm does not provide us with an abstract measure of time (as a watch or a calendar); it gives it a concrete and oriented reality. For Wunenburger (1997, as cited in Sauvanet, 2000a, p. 103), as a multiple and differentiated phenomenon, rhythm could constitute the source, always concrete, active and actualized of the idea of time. In order to fully grasp the relationship between time and rhythm, one must also consider the interval itself (e.g., nothingness, blank, silence, emptiness), quantitatively as a near zero intensity, but qualitatively as a significant element of the temporal experience. According to Sauvanet (2000a, p. 113), such an interval is not only what allows one to perceive rhythm, but also to partially access time.

Studying the coevolution of education and time as institutions

Based on the assumptions developed in this chapter, the second part of this book is going to explore and contextualize how temporal constraints have evolved through the history of education, and what they may reveal about the relationships between time, rhythms and education. Three perspectives are going to be privileged. The first one is embedded into a sociohistorical approach that will serve as a backbone in order to contextualize the evolution of temporal norms and standards, to locate the successive hegemonic influences of specific social times (e.g., sacred, religious, trade, industrial, everyday life) and establish how they relate to educational praxis and theory. The second perspective will explore institutional and organizational dynamics that characterize specific aspects of formal and informal education throughout the ages. It will bring us to describe and interpret temporal constraints that shaped the history of education and its emancipatory aim. The third perspective will focus on the evolution of the social imaginary and the meanings associated with time, studying in particular how the rhythmic aspects of education have been conceived in theory and in practice.

Note

1 For a specific use of the notion of 'temporal constraint', see Mercier's (1992) research on the temporality of students' learning in mathematics education.

References

Ardoino, J. (1977/1999). *Education et politique*. Paris: Anthropos.
Ardoino, J. (2000). *Les avatars de l'éducation*. Paris: Presses Universitaires de France.
Attali, J. (1982). *Histoires du temps*. Paris: Fayard.

Ben-Peretz, M. (1990). Perspectives on time in education. In M. Ben-Peretz, & R. Bromme (Eds.), *The nature of time in schools: Theoretical concepts, practitioner perceptions* (pp.64–77). New York: Teachers College, Columbia University.

Bergmann, W. (1992). The problem of time in sociology: An overview of the literature on the state of theory and research on the 'sociology of time', 1900–1982. *Time & Society, 1*(1), 81–134.

Biesta, G.J.J., Field, J., Hodkinson, P., Macleod, F., & Goodson, I. (2011). *Improving learning through the lifecourse: Learning lives.* Florence, KY: Routledge.

Castoriadis, C. (1997). *The imaginary institution of society* (K. Blamey, Trans.). Malden, MA: Polity Press. (Original work published 1975)

Connelly, F.M., & Clandinin, D.J. (1990). The cyclic temporal structure of schooling. In M. Ben-Peretz, & R. Bromme (Eds.), *The nature of time in schools: Theoretical concepts, practitioner perceptions* (pp.36–63). New York: Teachers College, Columbia University.

Dubet, F. (2006). Institution. In S. Mesure, & P. Savidan (Eds.), *Le dictionnaire des sciences humaines* (pp.633–635). Paris: Presses Universitaires de France.

Henriques, J., Tiainen, M., & Väliaho, P. (2014). Rhythm returns: Movement and cultural theory. *Body & Society, 20*(3/4), 3–29.

Le Goff, J. (1980). *Time, work, and culture in the Middle Ages* (A. Goldhammer, Trans.). Chicago: The University of Chicago Press.

Mercier, A. (1992). *L'élève et les contraintes temporelles de l'enseignement, un cas en calcul algébrique.* Doctoral dissertation, Université de Bordeaux I, France.

Michon, P. (2005). *Rythmes, pouvoir, mondialisation.* Paris: Presses Universitaires de France.

Michon, P. (2007). *Les rythmes du politique.* Paris: Les Prairies Ordinaires.

Nowotny, H. (1994). *Time: The modern and postmodern experience.* Cambridge, MA: Blackwell.

Oxford English Dictionary Online. (2015). "constraint, n.". Retrieved September 5, 2015, from http://www.oed.com/view/Entry/39876

Pineau, G. (2000). *Temporalités en formation: Vers de nouveaux synchroniseurs.* Paris: Anthropos.

Pomian, K. (1984). *L'ordre du temps.* Paris: Gallimard.

Pronovost, G. (1996). *Sociologie du temps.* Bruxelles: De Boeck.

Sauvanet, P. (1999). *Le rythme grec d'Héraclite à Aristote.* Paris: Presses Universitaires de France.

Sauvanet, P. (2000a). *Le rythme et la raison (vol.1): Rythmologiques.* Paris: Kimé.

Sauvanet, P. (2000b). *Le rythme et la raison (vol.2): Rythmanalyses.* Paris: Kimé.

Schuller, T. (1993). A temporal approach to the relationship between education and generation. *Time & Society, 2*(3), 335–351.

Settersten, R.A., Jr. (1999). *Lives in time and place: The problems and promises of developmental science.* Amityville, NY: Baywood Publishing Co.

Sue, R. (1993). La sociologie des temps sociaux: Une voie de recherche en éducation. *Revue Française de Pédagogie, 104,* 61–72.

Thompson, E.P. (1967). Time, work-discipline, and industrial capitalism. *Past & Present, 38,* 56–97.

Zerubavel, E. (1981). *Hidden rhythms: Schedules and calendars in social life.* Berkeley, CA: University of California Press.

Part II

The evolution of temporal constraints and the rhythms of education

Chapter 4

The evolution of temporal discipline in education, from antiquity to the Early Modern period

Exploring the roots of the temporal orders of education

Following the considerations developed in the first part of this book, the aim of this chapter is to start exploring the nature and the evolution of the relationships between temporal constraints and education. Based on existing historical inquiry, considering successively antiquity, medieval times, Renaissance and Early Modern period, four examples have been selected to illustrate the increasing ordering and formalization of educational time through temporal and rhythmic discipline. The analysis conducted in this chapter does not focus on a single and coherent phenomenon studied systematically and longitudinally. It appeared indeed more relevant to adopt a strategy privileged by multireferential analysis: identifying and exploring heterogeneous phenomena that reveal multidimensional, complementary, antagonistic and conflicting issues characterizing educational praxis and theories more broadly. Therefore, the analysis is going to focus first on the temporalities characterizing early Jewish education as an example of traditional education aiming at preserving the social, cultural and political order of a community since archaic times. Next, we will explore the rhythmic dimensions that define 'musical education' during Spartan and Hellenic periods to demonstrate how, through specific rhythms, artistic and moral education were jointly conceived to perpetuate a specific form of social and political order. A third perspective is going to be introduced through the rhythmic analysis of monastic education, developed throughout medieval times, as it illustrates the coercive and transformational power of an educational system centered on the control of habits and routines. Finally, the evolution of school temporal organization, promoted through the introduction of new school regulations, is going to be described to reflect on both its role in the systematic spreading of economical rationality and its disciplinary effects.

Sacred time and the rhythms of archaic societies

As suggested by the work of anthropologists such as Evans-Pritchard (1940) or Mauss (1905/1966), taking into consideration the rhythmic dimensions inherent to the life of a community is crucial to describe the way a society functions and evolves. For Mauss, the order of social and individual lives is not the product of a linear, homogeneous and continuous process that would be determined by a set of stable attributes. It rather follows temporal alternances, more or less regular, that periodically influence the form of a society and the intensity of individual and collective experiences (Michon, 2005). Archaic societies – as later kingdoms and modern societies – were organized around the alternance of relatively long periods of weak sociality (characterized by daily routines during which individuals were more or less autonomous) and usually brief, intense periods (characterized by social concentrations, festivals, ceremonies, *potlatchs*, etc.) through which groups and persons were entering into a process of regeneration. For Michon (2005), Evans-Pritchard's descriptions complete well Mauss's analysis, suggesting that in such collectivities, the experience of time was also related to periods of conflict and alliance within society and on the outside. Attali (1982, pp. 15–17) suggests that the first measurement of time in archaic societies was linked to the necessity to anticipate the apparition of rain and sun to follow and control the renewal of food reserves and organize the continuity of the survival means for the community. As the source of environmental changes remained invisible, there was an incessant dialogue between magical thinking and the rational study of natural phenomena (Attali, 1982, pp. 15–17). Thus, the very first societies enclosed time in rigorous norms, fixed by myths and the requirements of agriculture and breeding. Each event had its own rhythm, its origin and its duration. Sacred tales gave meaning to the mutations of nature and the requirement of agriculture by providing narratives capable to explain and to anticipate natural phenomena. The possibility to announce a future as the renewal of the past was a condition of the group survival (Attali, 1982, p. 18). Gods were exerting their control and their power first through the service of the elders and then through specialized priests, astronomers and astrologists. Those determined the legitimacy of kings, who then protected them. With the emergence of large theocratic empires, the time of gods was still organizing social life, according to calendars and sacrifices; however, time became more and more structured according to the increased codification, rigor and repetition characterizing the evolution of routines and rituals (Attali, 1982, p. 19).

Sacred time and traditional education: The roots of Jewish education

The predominance of sacred time within traditional societies – organized around mythical beliefs, monarchic and religious authority – is congruent with a conception of "traditional education" (Gauthier & Tardif, 2005) organized around both the transmission of cultural models inherited from the past and the reproduction of the existing social and political order. From a temporal perspective, the master words describing traditional education could be 'reproduction' from an institutional perspective and 'repetition' from an organizational one.

Considering the history of the Western world, the nature and the specific functions played by the reproductive and repetitive aspects of educational praxis, as well as the forms they took, evolved throughout the ages and cultures. Such functions differed based on the position occupied within society, from farmers or craftspeople (who had to transmit their know-how) to aristocrats (who were inheriting advice and cultural references from their 'mentors'). In every case, reproduction and repetition were located at the core of both a 'technical' education, grounded in the initiation to a way of living, and 'ethical' education, referring to a system of values orienting one's actions and decisions. To identify the role played by the reproductive and repetitive functions of education in ancient times, the next sections explore the early history of Jewish education. Based on Drazin's (1940) and Morris's (1937) historical research, they illustrate the relationships between temporal constraints and the conservative dynamics through which this specific community has evolved.

Evolution of the preservative function of Jewish educational institutions

According to Morris (1937, p. 6), as for other traditional cultures, at the origin the practical training of the child, both religious and social, was embedded in the family activity itself. Teaching and learning as a continuous process disconnected from practice hardly existed in earlier times (Morris, 1937, p. 8). The emergence of what we would call today formal instruction, as a dedicated educational institution, came into being as a result of the political and spiritual crisis of the Babylonian captivity, following the destruction of the first temple in 586 BCE (Morris, 1937, p. 9). The synagogue (literally meaning 'assembly') appeared then as the first school for adults, an academy for higher learning (Drazin, 1940). People would come together once a week on Sabbath to discuss passages from the Scriptures. The teaching of children at that period, and for long afterwards, was still entirely in the hands of the parents (Morris, 1937, p. 10). Two centuries later Palestine came for the first time into actual contact with Hellenism. At that time, the first schools for boys of 16 and 17 were created. Their aim was based on the interpretation of the Scriptures, according to the tradition of the 'Oral Law'. The method implemented shared similarities with the Greek rhetorical school (Morris, 1937, p. 12). It is only after the destruction of the Jewish political institutions during the Roman wars (70 CE) that the development of popular education reached its final stage: the establishment of elementary school, publicly organized and controlled (Morris, 1937, p. 12). Because religious and national unity was threatened, education was thrown into a position of significant importance. To fill the void, "school became the focus of the vital energies of the community, invested as the main resource to preserve its existence" (Morris, 1937, p. 103). After that, elementary education spread very rapidly to be generalized to all boys (Morris, 1937, p. 12).

The rhythmic organization of traditional Jewish education

Within Jewish education, the religious motive used to represent the dominating factor (Drazin, 1940, p. 138). For the adults, the free teaching of the Oral Law was primarily intended to help the promotion of knowledge of the Torah (Morris, 1937, p. 43). As its observance was required in everyday practice, instruction was integrated with all the activities of life. The development of the intellectual faculty was only a "by-product" of that education (Drazin, 1940, p. 138). Especially after the fall of the second temple, learning was considered as an ultimate value because it was a matter of preservation of the people under adverse conditions (e.g., persecution and expulsion):

> Under such conditions a complex and elaborate school organization was neither possible nor even desirable. What was required was a school of a simple, mobile character, which closed one day and opened somewhere else the following day.
> (Morris, 1937, p. 47)

At that time, the rhythmicity of Jewish education's organization was therefore constrained by both the order of sacred traditions and the disorder of the political and social context in which it was rooted.

In practice, depending on individual differences, the age of three was considered as the starting point in family for both practical religious training as well as the beginning of a literary education (Morris, 1937, p. 60). As to formal education, or the entrance age to the elementary school, there was no strictly uniform practice. From the third century CE, the age of six became the norm (Morris, 1937, p. 60). During the Talmudic period (70 CE to 500 CE), school hours were long and without intermission, at least for the teacher engaged into individual teaching. The temporal organization of school was paced by the circadian rhythm: children began their lessons early, at sunrise or even before, and spent the whole day at school, returning home only in the evening (Morris, 1937, p. 63). The practice of studying during part of the night may also have been prescribed. On certain days (e.g., major festivals) lessons were probably not given. In comparison, approximately 90 festivals and other state holidays were regulating the pace of Greek education (Morris, 1937, p. 65).

Bible, liturgy and the Oral Law as determinants of the organizational rhythms

The origin of Jewish education revolved around the synagogue service. The Scriptural readings supplied both the content as well as the form of instruction, both in the academy and later in elementary education (Morris, 1937, p. 85). The temporality of the curriculum was therefore globally shaped by the time required to learn how to read the Pentateuch; it required originally seven years following the pace of a weekly reading and got gradually developed into a triennial and eventually an annual cycle in Babylonia (Morris, 1937, p. 85). With the shortening of the cycle of study, the curriculum was rearranged on a concentric plan, studying each year a little more of the weekly portion until the whole ground was covered (Morris, 1937, p. 88). Another aspect was the prominent place given to liturgy in the elementary school: the preparation of ceremonials and rituals associated with various festivals (e.g., Passover) were the opportunity for practical training and literary education for boys (Morris, 1937, p. 92). With the destruction of the Jewish political institutions, after the Roman wars, the content and the organization of Jewish education evolved to accommodate the new social and political functions attributed to education. The result was a system in which study and practice were distinct from each other even if conceived through the cooperation between school and families (Morris, 1937, p. 111).

Cultural memory and the role of repetition

As for other traditional communities, the main content of Jewish education was oriented toward the memories of the past, kept alive by a system of ritual and ceremony. In school, the literary education was therefore centered on the preservation and transmission of the sacred literature (i.e., the Hebrew Bible and Oral Law) (Morris, 1937, p. 117). Such an imperative had a significant consequence on the rhythmicity of learners' activity: elementary education was thus mostly based on memorization through repetition. The task was made particularly difficult due to two additional challenges. First, the educational system was fundamentally 'bookless'; it was literally the case in the academy with the study of Oral Law and mostly the case in elementary school due to the fact that scrolls were very scarce and expensive. Second, in the absence of a vowel system, the reading of Hebrew depended upon tradition; it had to be given by the teacher and memorized by the pupil verse by verse (Morris, 1937, pp. 117–120). The main instrument of literary education was thus 'rote repetition' (a characteristic also present in Greek education), supplemented with an elaborate system of practical training based on rituals (Morris, 1937, pp. 117–120). From a rhythmic perspective, the educational praxis was therefore determined by cultural and historical imperatives but also by linguistic and psychological factors. To secure speedy and reliable memorization, several "learning strategies" were developed (Morris, 1937, pp. 117–120). One of the numerous 'aids' to memorization was rooted in the old practice prevalent among the students of the Talmud of swaying to and fro during study. In addition, the organization of Biblical language, with its strongly marked rhythmic structure characterized by parallelisms, favored "musical speaking", if not formal 'singing', that constituted also a resource for memorization (Morris, 1937, p. 140).

Rhythms and musical education during Greek Antiquity

The history of Greek education covers a period of more than 15 centuries (from approximately 1000 BCE to 500 CE). Through its development, it evolved from a culture of "noble warriors" to a "culture of scribes" (Marrou, 1948/1981).

Through the inner conflicts and struggles that punctuated its history, different conceptions of education emerged (e.g., military and aristocratic at first and philosophical, mystic and sophistic later) (Marrou, 1948/1981). With the invention of Athenian democracy and the value attributed to rationality and argumentation, Greek thinkers were at the origin of the first systematic attempts to theorize education and reflect on the respective values of different educational approaches (Gauthier & Tardif, 2005, p. 25).

Due to the limitations imposed by the format of our reflection, the detail of the temporal aspects of Greek educational institutions and organizations will not be discussed here. Some of those aspects express indeed similarities with phenomena already introduced in the previous sections (e.g., role of traditional education, relationship between family and school and schedule of the day). Other aspects (such as the innovations developed through Athenian education), which have deeply influenced further educational forms, will be introduced in following chapters (e.g., the role played by the organization of the subject matter around separate subjects or branches of study and the separation between vocational learning and school education). Considering the purpose of this chapter, it appeared much more relevant to operate a selective interpretation of the Greek history of education, focusing on one of its most distinctive contributions: musical education. Musical education – and especially the role played by its rhythmic component – reveals indeed some of the critical tensions related to the contribution of Greek philosophy of education from a temporal perspective.

The artistic, conservative and disciplinary values of Spartan musical education

From the origin, poetry and singing played a critical role in Greek traditional education. 'Homeric education', which was at the roots of the history of Greek education since the eighth century BCE was characterized by the transmission of texts (e.g., *The Iliad* and *The Odyssey*) to an aristocracy inspired by chivalrous models (Marrou, 1948/1981). Learning by heart those epics was not unusual and – as for cantillation in Jewish education – singing such "lyric poetry" was a privileged medium for the transmission of values and poetry – the only archaic form of literature (Marrou, 1948/1981). In Sparta and for the early Athenians, the chief aim of education was to educate good citizens: "Individual excellence was stressed in its relation to public usefulness" (Drazin, 1940, p. 137). During the Spartan domination (eighth to sixth century BCE), Greek education was a military one and its aim was to produce "noble warriors" dedicated to their homeland (Marrou, 1948/1981). Their training was organized around physical and musical education: "gymnastic for bodies and music for the soul" (Plato, *Republic*, II, 376e, trans. A. Bloom). Music was a privileged medium because it was located at the core of the Greek culture: through dance, it was linked to gymnastic, and through singing, it served for the transmission of poetry (Marrou, 1948/1981). Music was not only a key component of Spartans' education;

it was also giving its pace to the city through the artistic aspects characterizing the multiple religious festivals organized by the state (Marrou, 1948/1981, pp. 43–44). If music education (both vocal and instrumental) was carrying spiritual, intellectual and artistic dimensions, its main function was however related to the military aim of Spartan instruction: reinforcing a sense of community and maintaining discipline and obedience. Music education was therefore conceived through its cohesive function (e.g., finding one's place in a chorus), its disciplinary value (e.g., following marching song) and the moral character they were both supposed to reinforce (Marrou, 1948/1981).

The notion of rhuthmos in Greek philosophy

To discuss further the role of music in Hellenic education, and to better understand the function attributed to its rhythmic component, it is necessary at this point to develop more in detail the meanings associated with the term 'rhythm' itself, as it evokes many significations. Etymologically, the term comes from the Ancient Greek *rhuthmos*, which was characterized by its own polysemy and the bundle of meanings that characterized its use throughout the history of Greek thinking. Following Benveniste's (1951/1966) landmark contribution, Sauvanet (1999) identifies several key aspects that emerge from the philosophical use of this term and help identify its current relevance.

At the origin, the term was used by Democritus (c.460–370 BCE) to designate the singular form taken by moving atoms (Sauvanet, 1999, p. 5). Originally, the term referred thus to a form or a figure in their relation to time, stressing two key aspects: order and movement. It evoked both, the ideas of 'form' (*skhema*) and 'flux' (*rheo*) and appeared as a marker of 'order' within the evolution of a thing. The Greek *rhuthmos* evoked a form as it is transformed through time (Sauvanet, 1999, p. 6) As a concept, *rhuthmos* referred to the idea of 'changing configuration' (e.g., aggregates of atoms). The term designated thus a 'fluid' or 'flowing form' that remains distinctive and characteristic rather than blurred. Throughout the successive conceptions referring to the term, the meaning of *rhuthmos* oscillated between two main interpretations: either it was conceived as "particular configurations of what is moving" or as "imposition of an order", revealing a preference for the metric rather than rhythmic (Sauvanet, 1999, p. 8).

It was only later, with Plato (c.428–348 BCE), Aristotle (c.384–322 BCE) and his disciple Aristoxenus (c.350 BCE), that *rhuthmos* became associated with music, dance or poetry describing human phenomena as they relate to nature (but not natural periodicity, such as cosmic time, as it is the case in contemporary use) (Sauvanet, 1999, p. 5, p. 125). Thus, Plato's conception associated *rhuthmos* to a succession of strong and weak beats, organized arithmetically, as they can be found in a dance or in music. Following Pythagorean's model, Plato's definition stressed the primacy of number and proportion. According to his view, to be rhythmic a phenomenon had not only to be repetitive, but such a repetition had to be ordered and measured through a number; rhythm referred therefore to a *metron* (i.e., a unit of measure) (Michon, 2012, p. 3.) Following Aristotle and Aristoxenus' systematic use, such a definition became widely adopted. Through the translation and the diffusion of the idea of rhythm, it remains often considered nowadays as the traditional definition of rhythmic phenomena, conceived first through their ordered, metric and measurable feature (Michon, 2012, p. 3).

Form, order, measure and reason were on one side with flux, disorder, movement and body on the other side: early reflections conducted around the concept of *rhuthmos* demonstrated however, through their twofold expressions, the inherent ambiguity this term carried on from the very beginning (Sauvanet, 1999). The term 'rhythm' is thus characterized by an irreducible duplicity that constitutes a significant feature associated with its use. As it will appear in the next chapter, it will nevertheless take centuries for Plato's and Aristotle's conception to be challenged and enriched to reintegrate its free-flowing and qualitative dimension (Michon, 2012).

The moral virtues of musical education according to Plato

Plato is probably the first thinker to have explicitly included the idea of rhythm in a theory of education. One of his contributions was to stress the importance of musical education – including lyric poetry but also speeches – which begins with the telling of tales in the earliest years of childhood. If the value of tales was to instill virtue and a certain theology, it also had to foster courage, moderation and justice (Dillon, 2004). The purpose of music for the mind was the making of a noble and beautiful character and to move one's life with the "harmony" and "rhythm" of moral perfection (Adamson, 1903, p. 125). Rhythm and harmony played a specific role in Plato's views:

> [They] insinuate themselves into the inmost part of the soul and most vigorously lay hold of it bringing grace with them; and they make a man graceful if he is correctly reared, if not, the opposite.
> (Plato, *Republic*, III, 401d)

As evoked in the chapter of *Republic* dedicated to "Melody and rhythm", every component of speech had to follow the disposition of a good soul: "good speech, good harmony, good grace, and good rhythm accompany good disposition" (Plato, *Republic*, III, 400e). As previously mentioned, for Plato rhythm appeared above all as a marker of order within the evolution of a human phenomenon as it was relating to its nature. It was assumed that there were natural rhythms of a well-regulated and manly life, and these were to be sought and adopted. Plato established therefore a strong connection between the order that characterized the symmetry of a rhythm (as found in poetry, music and other forms of artistic expressions) and the rightness of moral value that it may contribute to foster (Adamson, 1903, pp. 96–98). From an educational perspective, literature, melody and rhythm were not for Plato subjects to be apportioned to the hours of a school day: "they were rather formative influences always at work upon a highly intellectual and artistic people" (Adamson, 1903, p. 232). Through familiarity with poems, songs, rhythms, sculpture and paintings, Plato assumed that the learner unconsciously grew to be like them, reflecting in habits and character elements of their material and social environment (Adamson, 1903, pp. 231–233). Furthermore, rhythms were located at the core of an ethical conception of education.

Following Plato, Aristotle and his successors perpetuated this approach. A whole body of doctrines related to the expressive and moral attributes associated with musical modes (e.g., Dorian, Phrygian and Lydian) was later developed according to theories establishing their respective moral virtues (Marrou, 1948/1981, p. 211). However, as noted by Marrou (1948/1981, p. 211), Plato and his successors did not take into consideration the technical evolution of music throughout the Hellenic period. Influenced by an abstract conception of music, privileging measurement and metric, Plato's musical education was therefore no longer connected with the expressivity of the music of his time. In addition, in spite of its deep insight about the role played by rhythms in the development of the person, his conception was perpetuating naive ideas about the moral 'efficiency' of music as a means for enhancing personal and social discipline (Marrou, 1948/1981, p. 210). For Marrou, both the conservative and abstract views of Plato's conception of musical education, and its divide from the artistic expressivity of music itself, may explain the progressive decline of musical education until the second century BCE, when music was no longer conceived at the same level as literature or gymnastics in the curricula.

Rhythm and religious education during medieval times

The medieval period started with the surge of barbarian invasions between 376 and 406 CE in Europe, invasions that provoked the fall of the Roman empire in 476 CE. One of the consequences of those political changes was the rise of the educational role played by the Christian Church during the fourth century. Contesting and criticizing the pagan culture inherited from the Greeks, the activity of Christian scholars and monks progressively took over as the main source of formal instruction in Europe, exercising a monopoly on culture and teaching (Jeanmart, 2003, para. 23). During the peak of barbarian invasions and until the fifth century, monasteries were the only places where religious education and study were provided. After the sixth century, the monastic school served as a model for the institutionalization of presbyteral and episcopal schools (Jeanmart, 2003, para. 27). As analyzed in detail by Jeanmart (2003, 2007), such a system promoted the ideal of an education based on docility and obedience. It deeply influenced the further developments of educational institutions throughout the Renaissance, the Early Modern period and the Industrial Revolution until today.

Against idiorhythmy

To understand how monastic education was able to impose obedience and docility, it is needed at first to refer to the rhythms of individual and collective life. Monastic education was indeed based on the development of a method constituted against 'idiorhythmy', that is, all the phenomena through which people aim at finding and following a particular (*idios*) rhythm and those experiences where individual freedom is understood as the conquest of one's own rhythm (Jeanmart, 2007). The "fight" against idiorhythmy appeared as a locus of power dynamics that translated through very coercive and at the same time very subtle means ruling the individual and collective life (Jeanmart, 2007, p. 139). The idea of idiorhythmy relates to the original meaning of the Greek term *rhuthmos*. It refers to the individual way of moving as it may be inscribed in the interstices of the natural and social order (Jeanmart, 2007, p. 139). It evokes subtle forms of experience such as moods, unstable configurations and depressive or exalted episodes – the opposite of the traditional understanding of the term 'rhythm' as a form of regular order (Jeanmart, 2007, p. 141). Originally, specific forms of Eastern monastic experiences, such as those of the anchorites (living by groups of two or three) or the hermits (living alone), were based on the capacity to remain isolated from the rhythms of the social world; they perpetuated therefore some kind of idiorhythmy that involved a form of autonomy from external power (Jeanmart, 2007, p. 141). Through the rupture with the outside world, anchorites and hermits were following their own rhythms of life, refusing external authority. As suggested by Jeanmart, they were also escaping the monastic structure and the obedience to a higher form of authority, such as the abbot's. Monastic experiences that emerged in the Western part of Europe (e.g., cenobitism) were constituted against those practices because they were condemning the principle of such autarky, especially the freedom it provided to follow one's own desires (Jeanmart, 2007, p. 144).

The temporal order of monastic education

One of the main characteristics of the monastic schools was their aim: to fully transform those who were entering monasteries, breaking down and deconstructing their secular culture and habits (Jeanmart, 2003, para. 30). To guarantee a rupture between the monks and the outside world, monastic education required the development of a specific pedagogical method, based on the institutionalization of asceticism, through the adoption of a body of practices (the monastic rule) formalizing individual and collective life to rule collective practices and prevent the individual excesses brought by a solitary life (Jeanmart, 2003, para. 30). As described by Jeanmart, the exclusive reading of the Bible was thus conceived as an ascetic practice requiring silence to purify the soul. Psalms had to be memorized. Through the practice of *ruminatio scripturis*, the monks had to ruminate day and night the holy words. The aim was not just memorization;

the repetitive reading was conceived as a tool against external temptations, aiming at gathering all the attention of the soul to avoid any distraction (Jeanmart, 2003, para. 33). Such an educational conception required dispositions of the mind that belonged to the register of obedience: simplicity, humility, discretion, conformity to the will of God, self-denial, abnegation, docility and so on (Jeanmart, 2003, para. 34). Another aspect of those practices was based on the imitation of Christ's way of living (*sequela Christi*). The stress was particularly put on a selection of everyday gestures and behaviors. It required for instance a permanent effort to control 'bad thoughts'. Such an education was therefore exclusively focusing on habits (Jeanmart, 2003, para. 43–45). The importance of clocks, the rhythm and the succession of daily activities became central to this organization. The key aspect of monastic education was to prevent monks to follow their own rhythms by imposing a single, dominant pace (Jeanmart, 2007). The collective life was therefore constrained by the adoption of a shared rhythm of life defined with great accuracy by the times devoted to prayers. Devoted to a time conceived as sacred, individuals' own temporality was radically subjugated (Jeanmart, 2007).

From religious time to the time of the merchants

After the fall of the Roman empire, there was no general political structure in Europe anymore. As summarized by Attali (1982, p. 63), no calendar and no temple were controlling the proliferating violence. Until the eighth century, Europe was almost empty, and cities remained very small. Economy and money did not exist. From the seventh to the 10th century, the Christian order emerged, contributing to redefine and spread a new calendar. In this environment, the first Christian convents represented islands of order, following the rhythm of prayer and clerical time. The emergence of monasteries, autonomous and powerful, able to resist to attacks or revolts, progressively instituted the Christian order. In two centuries, they succeeded at imposing a new pace, a new calendar and a new way of counting hours and days (Attali, 1982, p. 63). In the middle of a world dominated by agricultural rhythms, Benedictine monasteries were following a different time based on discipline and predictability and dedicated to God. Their bells rang the pace of canonical hours (Attali, 1982, p. 65). During the eighth and the ninth centuries, this way of living started spreading out and got adopted throughout the empire. Because it was helping estimating time, the influence of bells over urban and rural rhythms became significant (Attali, 1982, p. 71). With the new millennium and the increased power of cities, the control of time was taken over by civil authorities, which used the belfry's bells to pace activities (Attali, 1982, p. 77). With the technical advances, the first clocks appeared during the 12th century, using weight and water (Attali, 1982, p. 90). During the 14th century, all the European cities started displaying clocks at the top of their towers. Dials were introduced during the 15th century, when the need to read time more accurately emerged. The display of minutes was introduced toward the end of the 17th century. Upper classes started using those artifacts first. As suggested by Attali, punctuality became urban ideal, and owning a clock became a sign of success for merchants. The rhythm of trade increased (Attali, 1982, p. 99). As described by Le Goff (1980), the end of the Middle Ages is thus marked by a transition from "God's time" to "merchants" time. Time became secular. If the Catholic Church was still defining the beginning of the era and the beginning of the year, the normalization was in fact the result of the merchants' pressure: the organization of fairs required unity of time and synchronism of time measurement throughout the year (Attali, 1982, p. 126). To the variable hours of Roma and the canonical hours of the Church, mechanical clocks imposed the substitution of equal hours dividing the day in 24 similar sections. Because in town, work was more complex than in the fields, it could no longer be measured by the task realized; thus, working time determined the income and became a core issue of social order. The length of the working day became crucial for the safety of the cities. It was delimiting unemployment, regulating the poor in the city and therefore controlling violence (Attali, 1982, p. 129). On one hand, with the organization of European cities, the periodical circulation of tradesmen and merchants – who followed agricultural and maritime rhythms – paced the social body. On the other hand, it remained regularly regenerated by carnival as a main opportunity for the bodies to experience collectively raw violence in a permissive context (Attali, 1982, p. 144).

The organization of instruction and the institutionalization of school's time during the Early Modern period

Throughout the Early Modern period (16th to 18th century), the institutionalization of school and vocational education was embedded in organizational modalities that were rooted in medieval practices, such as those implemented respectively in monasteries (e.g., reciting, singing and read aloud, reflecting and copying in silence with assiduity, punctuality, exactitude and speed) or through the guilds' mentorship (e.g., observation and imitation of the master's gestures) (St-Jarre, 2001, p. 18). During medieval times, the lack of attention, idleness, absence, lateness, error and slowness were already apprehended by the collectivity as sources of temporal disorder that had to be kept under control to preserve the social order (St-Jarre, 2001, p. 18). With the invention of the first mechanical clocks during the 14th century and the economical surge, which emerged at the end of the medieval period, the temporal organization of educational practices became more refined and structured. The time of the everyday activities could then be measured, planned and therefore rationalized and individualized thanks to the measurements provided by hourglasses, clocks and specific schedules (St-Jarre, 2001, pp. 20–21). In this context, the increased rationalization of the temporal organization of education contributed to the ongoing transformations of the rhythms characterizing the period of *Ancien Régime*. The increased control over movement and discourses – promoted by the new regulations and the formalization of schedules implemented at that period – reveals the rhythmic dynamics through which power and authority were progressively shifting from religious principles to an economical logic practically imposed and internalized through educational praxis.

The temporal economy of instruction throughout the Early Modern period

Throughout the Renaissance, with the increase of knowledge and especially the reception of Greek classics, the old structure of study previously developed in schools and universities started to become obsolete. The multiplication of books to study introduced a new form of tension. Since the end of the 14th century, "temporal pressure" became indeed an ongoing matter of concern among humanistic thinkers who were prescribing advice to improve temporal organization, method and planning (Dohrn-van Rossum, 1997, p. 262). Hourglasses appeared in this context to help people determine deadlines and control the pace of study. Until then, the study of classical authors was typically organized around the structure of the text's content; texts were therefore providing learners with the pace of study. Such a temporal organization remained prevalent in many universities at that time; the complexity of their structure was preventing the introduction of time measurement and 'hours of study'. The curricula of the different faculties were therefore structured by *ordines legendi* (literally, 'the order of reading'), a sequence of books divided into chapters and sections. The time measurement of classes was following 'points' whose progression could be controlled. Overrunning the schedule was eventually punished by deductions from the professors' salary (Dohrn-van Rossum, 1997, p. 268). With the use of the hourglass, an abstract measurement of time was introduced in school organization. Limited 'studies and teaching units' started to be used to structure the time of study according to a delimited timeframe, independent from the contents transmitted. Such a timeframe was going to become an additional tool to control teaching practices. In Europe, school schedules were introduced around 1550 in the regulations of municipal schools to limit teaching time and determine teachers' workloads; however, it is only after the Reformation that they became a common practice (Dohrn-van Rossum, 1997).

Since the end of the 16th century, one of the main challenges inherent to school organization was to provide teaching to a large group of students simultaneously. The numbers of students, their heterogeneity and the diversity of contents to transmit were, as many sources of disorder, susceptible to hinder instruction (St-Jarre, 2001, p. 21). Inspired by monastic education, Jesuits started organizing instructional time around several principles. Attention was conceived as a key principle. Teaching time and learning time were conceived through the hierarchy of sacred texts and the grouping of students based on age and level of knowledge (Chartier, Julia & Compère, 1976, as cited in St-Jarre,

2001, p. 21). Differences of levels were converted into temporal differences: the more a discipline was important, more time was allocated to its study (Dohrn-van Rossum, 1997, p. 267). During the 17th century, Comenius (1592–1670) – a Czech Protestant monk – developed an encyclopedic curriculum to rationalize instructional time. The program was distributed through seven levels, 30 hours a week; disciplinary contents were grouped by level in a single handbook used by monitors teaching simultaneously. Time and contents were organized based on a predetermined order that allowed instructors to conceive a progression and a sequence by year, by month, by day and by hour (Chevallard & Mercier, 1987, as cited in St-Jarre, 2001, p. 21). In France, the efforts led by the Catholic scholars La Salle (1651–1719), Démia (1637–1689) and Batencour (c.1650), to provide instruction to the largest group of young people possible, brought them to standardize the learning context through the categorization and the compartmentalization of the various elements involved (i.e., pupils, knowledge and classes). Academic subjects were divided according to temporal sequences linked to each other following a logic going from the simplest to the more complex issues. Contents were ordered and introduced through a predetermined number of steps. Considering the time allocated to them – on a daily, weekly or yearly basis – such a temporal organization was translating the importance given to the subjects taught (St-Jarre, 2001, p. 22). More fundamentally, it was also revealing the increased importance given to an economical rationality, characterized by a logic of efficiency, over the traditional principles inherent to a strictly religious authority.

The disciplinary nature of school temporal organization

The study of school schedules – ruling the whole school life since the end of the 17th century – reveals further the tight connections existing among temporal constraints, discipline, the exercise of power and the temporal organization of human activity. As noticed by Foucault (1975/1995, p. 150),

> In the elementary schools, the division of time became increasingly minute; activities were governed in detail by orders that had to be obeyed immediately: 'At the last stroke of the hour, a pupil will ring the bell, and at the first sound of the bell all the pupils will kneel, with their arms crossed and their eyes lowered. When the prayer has been said, the teacher will strike the signal once to indicate that the pupils should get up, a second time as a sign that they should salute Christ, and a third that they should sit down' (La Salle, *Conduite des écoles chrétiennes*, 1783, pp. 27–28). In the early nineteenth century, the following time-table was suggested for the *Ecoles mutuelles*, or 'mutual improvement schools': 8.45 entrance of the monitor, 8.52 the monitor's summons, 8.56 entrance of the children and prayer, 9.00 the children go to their benches, 9.04 first slate, 9.08 end of dictation, 9.12 second slate, etc.
> (Tronchot, p. 221)

What emerges from Foucault's account is not only the 'machinery' that enables power to be exercised and obedience to be maintained. The elaboration and the implementation of school schedules expressed the fundamental rhythmic aspects that are constitutive of power dynamics and the way they are embodied and codified (Michon, 2007). Comparing military and school discipline, Foucault (1975/1995, p. 151) illustrated how disciplinary control imposed not only a series of particular gestures but more fundamentally a logic of efficiency and speed grounded in the "correct use of the body". Throughout the Early Modern period, in schools, the succession of gestures was imposed by a sequence of signals, whistles, drum rolls and commands that had at the same time to accelerate the learning process and teach rapidity (Foucault, 1975/1995, pp. 180–181). In parallel with the introduction of techniques that gave a pace to the learning of reading and writing, and surveillance tasks devolved to pupils, the school organization was also based on a system of penalties and rewards following a hierarchical and graded basis. Behaviors were ruled by a "micro-penalty of time" implemented to punish lateness, absence, interruption and inattention as well as inappropriate expressions, such as "incorrect" attitudes or irregular gestures (Foucault, 1975/1995, p. 178).

Considering the evolution of the role played by the rhythmic organization of educational praxis, from traditional to monastic education, what emerged through the Early Modern period appears therefore as threefold. First, it demonstrates the extreme minutia through which gestures and language could be controlled and prescribed through educational regulations. Second, it illustrates the rhythmic dimensions inherent to the exercise of power, involving corporeal and discursive techniques required to impose the specific discipline characterizing an order determined by an 'economical' logic. And third, it exemplifies how the 'theorization' of such disciplinary principles contributed to develop and perpetuate a specific imaginary of time based, among others, on principles such as abstraction, measurement, efficiency and obedience.

The temporal and rhythmic dimensions of power in education

Within traditional societies, the predominance of sacred time was related to the role played by an educational system especially aimed at preserving the social and political order of a community. Such a function appears clearly through the temporalities characterizing traditional Jewish education and the ways it was shaped by its origins, its purposes, its content and its activity as well. Jewish education's cultural and social determinants, psychological requirements and linguistic and religious features, conceived all together, help in understanding the complexity of the rhythms that characterized this form of traditional education. In addition to the periodicity inherent to its repetitive and reproductive functions, the early history of Jewish education also exemplifies the role played by discontinuities and the movement of history. The evolution of Jewish traditional education appeared thus as the result of the conjunction between the slow development of the community and the acceleration provoked by external political events, a movement that stimulated its transformations and eventually its stabilization.

The early history of Greek education provides us with another perspective on the relationship between external and internal temporal constraints in education. Both Spartan and Hellenic models of instruction find their roots in a lyric tradition characterized by a specific rhythmic organization and conceived as a privileged way to transmit traditional moral values. During the Spartan hegemony, the rhythms transmitted through musical education were fulfilling esthetic, social and political functions as well, contributing to both the early cultural influence of Sparta and the consolidation of the stability of its totalitarian regime. Supporting a more humanistic conception of education, the use of the idea of rhythm in Plato's educational theory reinforced the already presumed relation established between esthetic experience and morality. It located at the center of the educational process the internalization of external rhythms as a key principle for the transmission of moral attributes. Doing so, it also perpetuated a conception of rhythm stressing its abstract, ordered and measured nature rather than its free-flowing aspect.

The development of monastic education through the medieval period illustrates well both at the micro and macro levels the power of an educational system centered on the control of individual and collective rhythms. At the level of the persons, the behavioral rules implemented through monastic education proved the efficiency of a system organized to prevent the development of individual autonomy and reinforce submission and obedience. It also demonstrated the transformative effects associated with techniques and methods focusing on the strict regulation of mental and embodied routines and habits. At the societal level, the rhythmic stability that characterized those communities appears retrospectively as a key aspect of the progressive hegemony of the Christian Church in Europe and the imposition of its own temporal norms.

Finally, the successive organization of the school's temporal features, since the Renaissance throughout the Early Modern period, illustrates well the progressive transformations that affected the principles ruling the collective experience of time. Supported by technological advances, the transformations of schools' organization reflect a deeper cultural, social and political shift from the predominance of a strictly religious order to the increasing weight given to the prescription imposed by an economical rationality. In schools and in universities, both the necessity to accommodate a larger number of heterogeneous students and the increase of knowledge got translated in the temporal economy of pedagogical practices. The organization of the classroom activities integrated therefore principles and techniques inspired by monastic education revised through the lens of efficiency. It determined contents and pedagogical methods as well. From this perspective, the proficiency of new school regulations appearing during that period reveals further the constraining and disciplinary nature associated with the rhythmic organization of education.

References

Adamson, J. (1903). *The theory of education in Plato's 'Republic'*. London: Swan Sonnenschein & Co.
Attali, J. (1982). *Histoires du temps*. Paris: Fayard.
Benveniste, E. (1966). *Problèmes de linguistique générale (vol. 1)*. Paris: Gallimard. (Original work published 1951)
Bloom, A. (1991). *The Republic of Plato* (A. Bloom, Trans.). New York: BasicBooks.
Dillon, A. (2004, May). *Education in Plato's Republic*. Paper presented at the Santa Clara University Student Ethics Research Conference (May 26, 2004). Retrieved August 10, 2014, from https://www.scu.edu/character/resources/education-in-platos-republic
Dohrn-van Rossum, G. (1997). *L'histoire de l'heure: L'horlogerie et l'organisation moderne du temps*. Paris: Maison des Sciences de l'Homme.
Drazin, N. (1940). *History of Jewish education from 515 BCE to 220 CE*. Baltimore: The Johns Hopkins Press.
Evans-Pritchard, E.E. (1940). *The Nuer: Description of the modes of livelihood and political institutions of a Nilotic people*. Oxford: The Clarendon Press.
Foucault, M. (1995). *Discipline and punish: The birth of the prison* (A. Sheridan, Trans.). New York: Vintage Book. (Original work published 1975)
Gauthier, C., & Tardif, M. (Eds.). (2005). *La pédagogie: Théories et pratiques de l'Antiquité à nos jours*. Montréal: Gaëtan Morin.
Jeanmart, G. (2003). Le rôle de l'obéissance dans l'éducation antique et médiévale [Electronic version]. *Philosophique, 6*, 61–98. Retrieved August 7, 2015, from http://philosophique.revues.org/186
Jeanmart, G. (2007). *Généalogie de la docilité dans l'Antiquité et le Haut Moyen Âge*. Paris: Vrin.
Le Goff, J. (1980). *Time, work, and culture in the Middle Ages* (A. Goldhammer, Trans.). Chicago: The University of Chicago Press.
Marrou, H. (1981). *Histoire de l'éducation dans l'Antiquité. Le monde grec (vol. 1)*. Paris: Seuil. (Original work published 1948)
Mauss, M. (1966). *Sociologie et anthropologie*. Paris: Presses Universitaires de France. (Original work published 1905)
Michon, P. (2005). *Rythmes, pouvoir, mondialisation*. Paris: Presses Universitaires de France.
Michon, P. (2007). *Les rythmes du politique*. Paris: Les Prairies Ordinaires.
Michon, P. (2012). *Notes éparses sur le rythme comme enjeu artistique, scientifique et philosophique depuis la fin du XVIIIème siècle*. Retrieved December 12, 2013, from http://www.rhuthmos.eu/spip.php?article540
Morris, N. (1937). *The Jewish school*. London: Eyre & Spottiswoode.
Sauvanet, P. (1999). *Le rythme grec d'Héraclite à Aristote*. Paris: Presses Universitaires de France.
St-Jarre, C. (2001). L'organisation du temps en éducation: les cadres de référence. In C. St-Jarre, & L. Dupuy-Walker (Eds.), *Le temps en éducation: Regards multiples* (pp. 15–41). Sainte-Foy, QC, Canada: Presses Universitaires du Québec.

Chapter 5

Temporal efficiency and rhythmic harmony, two competing educational ideals at the turn of the 20th century

The invention of instructional time and the rise of rhythmic education

This chapter provides an overview of the development of two trends that have marked the development of educational theory since the beginning of the 20th century. The first part of this chapter aims at explaining why and how the first attempts to rationalize scientifically educational temporalities emerged at the end of the 19th century. To proceed, the temporal environment that characterized the modern period – from the Industrial Revolution to the Second World War – will be briefly described. Such a contextualization will set the stage to interpret both the main features characterizing the institutionalization and organization of modern school's time and the early research conducted to study the implementation of 'instructional time', understood as an attempt to rationalize educational temporalities. The second part of the chapter introduces a body of educational theories focusing on the concept of rhythm, which approximately at the same period fulfilled a specific critical, social and political function. To locate such contributions, the cultural impact of the Industrial Revolution and the evolution of the concept of rhythm between the 18th and the early 20th centuries will be briefly discussed. Such a social and intellectual contextualization will serve the purpose of explaining the rise and the hope invested at the turn of the century in contributions such as Jaques-Dalcroze's eurhythmics, Bode's rhythmic gymnastics and Steiner's anthroposophy.

The Industrial Revolution and the emergence of productive time

From the 17th to the 19th century, as it became more accurate, the advance in watch technology created a new time, divided and constant, that enabled the methodical measurement of working time. Such a mutation participated to the transformation of the organization of economic exchanges (Attali, 1982). With the advance of the Industrial Revolution and the development of mass production, the flow and the repetition of time were no longer organized around environmental constraint or trade; they were divided according to production periods, interrupted by breaks required to restore machine's forces. Power was transferred to those who could impose a work schedule and pay accordingly (Attali, 1982, p. 187). With the transition to industrial capitalism, where task-oriented time division gave way to work according to the clock, time reinforced its disciplinary character, and the optimization of time use became compulsive (Bergmann, 1992). Following the diffusion of capitalist values, valorizing speed and efficiency, idleness was perceived as both useful and dangerous, so it had to be contained and controlled. What was at stake was the codification and monitoring of daily and weekly breaks, long enough to recover from work but not too long to avoid idleness, leading to revolt (Attali, 1982, p. 192). At the beginning of the 19th century, labor code emerged as a new social calendar that determined work and rest schedules. With the introduction of the time clock, workers were paid by the hour and not by day anymore. Saving time became a social obsession and a requirement experienced by everyone (Attali, 1982, p. 210). Individual freedom was constrained by the norms and moral considerations that shaped the structuring of time and the division of activities (Bergmann, 1992). Criticizing the way production was organized until then – grounded in the subjective time requirements determined by the workers – Taylor started advocating around 1860 for the introduction of a "scientific and systematic study of time" set by the management, using chronometers to discipline and model the workers' activity (Attali, 1982, p. 212). Taylor's doctrine, and later Ford's organization of assembly lines, contributed to generalize the reification of working time.

The institutionalization and organization of modern school's time

As detailed by Compère (2001), the generalization of schooling emerged in Europe between the 16th and 18th century. At the end of the 17th century, the basis of the rational organization of school time – as we know it today – was already set. The first laws regulating school activity appeared during the 19th century. After the First World War, they led to the legislation of compulsory education. Such laws were revealing a mind-set valuing an economical conception of instructional time, instilled by the spirit of the Industrial Revolution. The will of the states was to systematically intervene into the organization of school time and regulate the daily, weekly and yearly rhythms. The principles of time management were located at the core of schools' rules, stressing for instance punctuality and regularity. Such interventions contributed to rationalize primary teaching and brought more practical, economical and efficient solutions to the education of lower classes (Compère, 2001). In the United States, in the 1840s, inspired by the model of the Prussian school system and the principle of the division of labor, a "graded school" system (divided according to ages and attainments) was introduced as a way to maintain the uniformity among an increasing heterogeneous population of migrants and prepare them for the workforce (Gutek, 1986).

As noted by Michon (2007, p. 162), added to agricultural, industrial and religious disciplines, school was the last vector that enabled from the 17th to the 20th century the dismantlement of the rhythmic habits of the populations, inherited from the *Ancien Régime*, to prepare them for new economical tasks imposed by the rising dominating classes. Through a succession of ruptures, from the abolition of night work for children to the legislation increasing the minimal age required to work, the universal dimension of compulsory education was progressively introduced. Through this movement, it was also – more symbolically – the assimilation of childhood to schooling that was instituted (Pronovost, 2001). Through those transformations, what was at stake was the education of workers to be able to follow the pace of an activity with a sustained attention. The aim was to increase schoolwork efficiency by fading individual differences and equalizing the time of activities to be realized. Indicators of productivity and efficiency were defined based on the measurement of time required to accomplish specific tasks, the conduct of pupils, teachers' practices and learning evaluation (Anderson, 1984; Berliner, 1990).

In between the two world wars, curricula became more specialized in Western countries, and the school day – which was organized until then according to the importance given to each academic discipline – became segmented in same-length periods of approximately 50 minutes. Teachers' work itself became more systematically divided according to their different activities (e.g., teaching, preparation and surveillance) (St-Jarre, 2001). With the tools provided by the Industrial Revolution (e.g., chronometers), the school organization was adapted to new work standards: productivity and maximal efficiency, specialization, standardization, hierarchical organization and timing of the tasks, management of the productivity and evaluation based on predefined temporal measurement.

Theorizing instructional time

The social and cultural transformations occurring in the school organization were accompanied by theoretical innovations. Instructional time, as a dimension constitutive of the activity of teaching and learning, was a matter of research since the end of the 19th century. Its status varied depending on the dominant scientific paradigm (Delhaxhe, 1997). In the United States in particular, its study became a significant tradition of research (e.g., Anderson, 1984; Berliner, 1990; Borg, 1980; Chopin, 2010; Delhaxhe, 1997). Since the first studies were conducted, two axes of research emerged that were going to characterize the future treatment in the United States of time issues related to learning and teaching. The first one related to the study of the impact that the quantity of teaching time had on students' learning. The second one was focusing on the specificity of the quality of time dedicated to teaching, associated with a more detailed theorization of the concept of time (Berliner, 1990; Chopin, 2010; Delhaxhe, 1997). For Berliner (1990), instructional time may currently be conceived as a "superordinate concept" referring to a family of more or less elaborated notions such as allocated time, engaged time, time on task, academic learning time, transition time, waiting time, aptitude, perseverance or pace.

Allocated time, engaged time and time on task

In the current literature, the notion of 'allocated time' is usually defined as "the time that the state, district, school, or teacher provides the student for instruction. . . . Sometimes this is called *scheduled time* to distinguish it from the time actually allocated by teachers" (Berliner, 1990, p. 4, stressed by the author). When time provided for instruction emerged as an object of research in education, it benefited from the newly developed survey method adopted to gather information about allocated time for instruction (Berliner, 1990). Authors such as Holmes (1915), Mann (1926) and Payne (1904) (as cited in Borg, 1980) started collecting descriptive data showing the gap existing between the reality of time allocated to instruction and the official recommendations. At that time, researchers started questioning the existence of a relationship between the quantity of time allocated to teaching and its efficiency. The first inquiries conducted were based on the assumption that 'efficient' teachers were characterized, among others, by their capacity to manage optimally the time available (Delhaxhe, 1997, p. 109). A second core assumption, which remained very pregnant during the following decades, was that exposure to teaching had to remain strongly and linearly correlated to students' learning (Husén, 1972, as cited in Chopin, 2010). Considered by many people around the world to be an important indicator of instructional productivity, the study of allocated time remained throughout the 20th century a topic monitored by the research community in many countries (e.g., Amadio, 2004; Berliner, 1990; Cavet, 2011).

According to Berliner (1990, pp. 4–5) "engaged time" is usually defined as "time that students appear to be paying attention to materials or presentations that have instructional goals. . . . [It] is always a subset of allocated time. A synonym for engaged time is 'attention'." "Time on task" is usually defined as "engaged time on particular learning tasks" (Berliner, 1990, pp. 4–5). It is used in conjunction with the specific curriculum or instructional activities prescribed to measure students' specific engagement. Historically, a key concern related to the temporality of learning activity refers to the students' level of engagement, a preoccupation that goes back to Currie (1884), James (1904), Rice (1897) and Thorndike's (1913) studies (as cited in Berliner, 1990, p.8) around active learning processes and attention. In 1926, Morrison designed and described scales for studying attention among high school students that are still used today. His work stimulated a number of studies of attention and achievement, but this line of research was eventually dropped (Berliner, 1990).

Toward the commodification of educational time

Considering the evolution of educational theory and the role devoted to its temporal dimensions in the United States, notions associated with the concept of instructional time translated the new rational and economical mind-set directly inherited from the Industrial Revolution (e.g., the role of mechanical repetition), the rise of capitalism (e.g., the importance of efficiency), the development of empirical science (e.g., the prevalence of quantification and abstraction) and the 'taylorization' of learning and teaching activity (e.g., the importance of division and systematic organization). Considering the contemporary interest for the literature on instructional time, the contributions made by the research initiated at the turn of the century around this notion fulfilled to some extent the perceived need to reinforce school efficiency. From a critical point of view, however, one of the main effects of those contributions has been the reinforcement of the legitimacy of a language that eventually saturated the temporal imagination conveyed by formal education, reinforcing an economical conception of time, conceived as an abstract and quantified commodity, whose measurement and manipulation appeared as crucial to regulate learning and teaching activity. The normativity legitimized by those early scientific works thus contributed to reduce the understanding of the temporal aspects of educational experience to the segmentation, the repetition and the counting of a succession of "identical presents", serving a function of "bearings and marking" (Castoriadis, 1975/1997) located at the core of the temporal norms sustained by formal instruction.

The cultural impact of the Industrial Revolution: The emergence of proper time

Besides the direct impact of the Industrial Revolution on working conditions and workers' everyday routines, the turn of the 19th century was also marked by another phenomenon located at the core of the way people were experiencing time. During the 18th century, the horizon of the future became dynamic. Throughout the next century, the idea of progress entered the history of the human race and "temporalized" it (Nowotny, 1994, p. 16). The period between 1880 and 1918 laid the foundations for drastic changes people experienced in the sense of space and time (Kern, 1983, as cited in Nowotny, 1994, p. 19). The invention and technological improvements of the telegraph, the radio and the telephone were erasing spatial distances. The electrification of cities negated for the first time the difference between day and night. New ways of seeing and capturing movements were created with the cinematograph (Nowotny, 1994, p. 19). With those significant cultural changes, a new sense of subjective time emerged, raising new preoccupations. People were trying to determine how "real" was their own experience of time and how to clarify the relationship between the "public time" of the calendar and the "private time" of their feelings and their bodies (Nowotny, 1994, p. 22). As they started perceiving the increase of speed in the different areas of their lives and discovering the illusion of the worldwide simultaneity, people were also becoming more aware of how little the temporal control of bureaucracies and institutions was changing. The struggle for the social recognition of "proper time" – as self-time from the perspective of the individual – and its representation in the global, standardized system of world time became a political fact (Nowotny, 1994, p. 41). At the social level, the codification of time became ubiquitous through working-time regulations, lifetime regulations and retirement age regulations (Nowotny, 1994, p. 31). With the temporalization of proper times, social inequalities did not disappear. They were translated into "temporal inequalities", depending on individuals' capacity to control and negotiate the tensions existing between one's own history and social temporalities (Nowotny, 1994, p. 32). In Europe, during the first decades of the 20th century, alternative educational approaches started to emerge in reaction to the social and cultural transformations that were unfolding and especially to their temporal features. Observing the consequences associated with industrialization, the rise of capitalism and their effects on education (e.g., compartmentalization, specialization, intellectualism and neglect of the embodied aspects of education), several educational theories were formulated and invested by many scholars as a hope for political and cultural renewal (Hanse, 2007). One of the main characteristics of those theories was their explicit focus on the rhythmic aspects of individual and collective life.

The evolution of the concept of rhythm between the 18th and the early 20th centuries

To grasp the meaning and the extent to which the concept of rhythm got invested by educators, and the social impact of their theories and practices at the turn of the 20th century, it is particularly relevant to first locate how the term 'rhythm' reemerged two centuries earlier. The role it played in German Enlightenment and Romanticism reveals indeed meanings that contributed to reinforce new connections between the rhythmicity of human experience and the way it was going to be organized and expressed, especially through the arts. The interest raised by the notion of rhythm in scientific and philosophical studies, at the end of the 19th century, also constitutes one of the grounds that explains the significant rise of interest for rhythmic theories in education during the following decades.

The contribution of the German Enlightenment and Romanticism

According to Couturier-Heinrich (2004), the concept of rhythm reemerged as a key theme in Germany between 1760 and 1830. During that period, it appeared in research conducted in many disciplines, such as anthropology, history, philology, poetics, philosophy, medicine and natural sciences. At that time, the dominant conception was to refer rhythms to Plato and Aristotle's views (e.g., cycles, numbers and proportions), stressing their formal aspects (Michon, 2012a). However, during a relatively short period, from 1785 and 1805, the idea of rhythm got associated with new meanings and new values, especially in philology and poetics. Authors such as Moritz (1756–1793), Goethe (1749–1832), Schiller (1759–1805), Schlegel (1772–1829) and Hölderlin (1770–1843) started challenging Plato and Aristotle's rhythmic conception. For instance, with Moritz, rhythm was no longer a formal and linear succession of contrasted stresses; the alternance of slow and fast movements constituted what provided a poem or a dance with its own value and beauty (Couturier-Heinrich, 2004). Schlegel was the first one to apply the idea of rhythm (*rhythmus*) beyond verses to a whole literary work. Rhythm was no longer used in reference to a metric; it was rather used to qualify a literary genre. Following the same direction, Hölderlin showed that rhythm was determined by techniques, rules and the specific way of processing that characterized the writing process. Such theoretical innovations contributed to the formulation of new types of assumptions about the role played by rhythms and the temporalities of language and the arts (Couturier-Heinrich, 2004). For Plato and Aristotle, rhythms used to refer to the principle organizing the succession of elementary and complex units composing poetry, music and dance, an approach congruent with a quantifying conception of time. Beyond such formal and ordered attributes, the concept of rhythm appeared after Moritz, Goethe, Schiller, Schlegel and Hölderlin more closely related to what gives its autonomy to a text and – beyond the narrative – to the subjects that produce or experience an art form (Meschonnic, 1982; Michon, 2012a). Such innovations eventually contributed to reintroduce the qualitative aspects of rhythm already present in the original meaning of the word *rhuthmos*.

The renewal of interest for the scientific and philosophical study of rhythms at the end of the 19th century

Following this first wave of German contributions, Wagner (1813–1883) and especially Nietzsche (1844–1900) reinitiated a discussion around rhythm during the second half of the 19th century. Denouncing the disappearance of rhythm in the arts of their times, such a phenomenon was then interpreted as a sign of the dysfunctions associated with the mutations of society (Hanse, 2007, p. 33). 'Arrhythmia' – the lack of rhythm – was no longer conceived as an individual issue; it became clearly associated with social changes related to the cultural and economic shifts characterizing modernity. From the 1880s to the 1940s several trends of research emerged studying the rhythmicity of psychological and social life (Michon, 2005, 2012b). In social sciences, through his research on labor and rhythmic forms of works among "primitive people", Bücher (1896) studied the archaic connections existing between economy and rhythmicity. He formulated the thesis according to which rhythm represented an 'economic evolutionary principle' serving as both a means to lessen the burden of labor and a source of esthetic pleasure. According to Bücher's thesis, dance and poetry originated in labor rhythms. In France, Durkheim (1912/1968) theorized how the rhythms of large gatherings of people contributed to regenerate the feeling of belonging and transform or reinforce institutions; doing so he grounded a first conception of social time. Mauss (1925/2012) developed this idea further, considering social rhythms, as well as the rhythms of the body and language, at the core of the process of individual and collective individuation. Observing the transformations affecting Europe since the second half of the 19th century, Simmel (1900/2004) and Tarde (1901/1989) were questioning how the social flow of interactions was evolving under the influence of capitalism, especially with the emergence of large cities, the increased use of currency in social interactions and the development of new media (e.g., the press, telegraph and phone) (Michon, 2005). In philosophy, the approach developed by Bergson (1888/1970) appeared as a critique of mainstream scientific conceptions that were "spatializing" time, that is, reducing continuity and the irregularly moving aspect of duration to a succession of equally numbered intervals. If Bergson only referred metaphorically to the notion of rhythm, his contribution introduced nevertheless a new way to conceive rhythms that characterize movement, mutation, and transformation no longer understood according to some form of "order" but rather considered through their "organization" (Michon, 2012b, p. 7). A few years later, Bachelard (1931, 1936) formulated the first grounds of his "rhythmanalysis", arguing that interruptions and discontinuities were at the core of the intuition of duration. In the United Kingdom, at the same period, Whitehead's (1929, 1938) contribution also stressed the role played by events, instability, unpredictability and movement within organized phenomena unfolding through time (cf. Chapter 7).

The rise of rhythmic education at the turn of the 20th century

In Germany, at the turn of the 20th century, the interest for the notion of rhythm started expanding from the artistic, scientific and philosophical fields to the social and political ones. In between those spheres, education played a critical role in the spreading of this notion (Hanse, 2007). Discourses around "arrhythmia" and its projection on the "social body" became more popular as people were witnessing the growing impact of capitalist values celebrating productivity and competition (Hanse, 2007, p. 222) and perceiving their negative effects on communities and individuals' balance. The interest for rhythm was exacerbated among those who were educated but felt they were losing their influence, threatened – on the right – by the increasing power of businessmen and – on the left – by proletarians envisioning to replace social order through a revolution (Hanse, 2007, p. 222). In this context, scholars from different horizons (reformist and conservative as well) started conceiving the role played by a new form of 'rhythmic education' as a resource to fight against the materialistic mind-set grounding the rise of capitalism and the intellectualism that was characterizing the educational system. Instruction was perceived more and more as compartmentalized and specialized and less and less taking into consideration the balance among "body, soul and mind" (Hanse, 2007, p. 224). If the ethical virtues of rhythm in education were praised since antiquity, during the first 30 years of the 20th century, especially in Germany, many people considered rhythmic education as a real hope for cultural and political renewal (Hanse, 2007).

At the core of the educational trends that were emerging at that time, one may find, according to Hanse (2007), the impulsion of Schiller (1795/1943) and his views on education. For him, the conquest of freedom did not require revolt against the oppressor; it rather required the harmonization of human capacities through art and esthetic education. Disheartened by the violence exerted throughout the French revolution, Schiller assumed that the reconciliation of humans with themselves constituted the premise of political liberation. Art was not conceived therefore as an escape to reality; it constituted rather the best way to create a new kind of people able to transform the state without violence and without contradiction between ends and means (Hanse, 2007, p. 26). Such a vision was particularly valued among members of the cultivated classes, who were more inclined to elaborate indirect strategies of social action privileging art and body education as a way to bring individuals to change rather than exerting more radical social pressures (Hanse, 2007, p. 40). Hence, a large movement emerged during the first decades of the century, privileging the idea that rhythmic education was valuable – beyond its esthetic interest – to help individuals find balance, increase their well-being and eventually change their ways of living collectively (Hanse, 2007; Toepfer, 1997); similar concerns were thus found in music (e.g., Jaques-Dalcroze, 1921), dance (e.g., Laban, 1921/2014, 1948), gymnastics (e.g., Bode, 1920/2014) and spiritual education (e.g., Steiner, 1920/1995) as well.

Emile Jaques-Dalcroze's eurhythmics

Inspired by his own pedagogical experience, the Swiss composer and pedagogue Jaques-Dalcroze (1865–1950) formulated a project to reform musical education through the development of a dedicated training focusing on the body (e.g., Jaques-Dalcroze, 1921; Pennington, 1925). He founded his first school in Hellerau (Germany) in 1910 and then created his own institute in Geneva (Switzerland) in 1914; later, other schools were created in London, Paris, Berlin, Vienna, Stockholm and New York.

Criticizing methods that reduced musical skills to the technical ability developed when learning to play an instrument, Jaques-Dalcroze conceived musical education at the core of a process of development that embraced the person as a whole, considering one's sensibility, sense of order and creativity. Music had to help one to create one's own style in accordance with one's temper and respect a frame that enables collective work. At the junction between music and body movement, rhythm appeared as an element that enabled the awakening of an individual's lively forces and at the same time canalized and structured them (Hanse, 2007). For Jaques-Dalcroze, developing a child's or an adult's rhythmic sense required one to organize the relationships among one's faculties, to introduce more flexibility and reinforce one's 'nervous system', to identify blocks and problems within internal coordination to eliminate them, to shape instincts without repressing them and to solve inner conflicts without violence. Such a work had to result in a "purification" of the body that freed the mind, the sensibility and creativity, promoting self-mastery and spiritual and ethical elevation as well (Hanse, 2007). Like Laban's dance education, such an approach was conceived as the first step toward a larger project of societal renewal, aiming at the constitution of a better-coordinated and more brotherly community (Hanse, 2007, p. 253).

From a pedagogical perspective, Jaques-Dalcroze's ideas were close to Rousseau's (1712–1778) and Pestalozzi's (1746–1827) views on education. His method was based on a conception of the individual as a whole and learning as an internal process. The educator's role was seen as a supportive one, remaining at the side of the learners, trying to awaken their faculties without any imposition. Trying to respect children's nature, their curiosity, their need to play, to move, and to manipulate, as well as their own rhythm of learning, Jaques-Dalcroze prescribed an intuitive approach starting from concrete actions (e.g., experiencing rhythms and internalizing them) and moving progressively toward the recognition of abstract principles through intuitive reasoning (e.g., recognizing and reproducing specific rhythms). Only when a well-established consciousness of rhythms, sounds and a good mastery of one's body were reached could the study of an instrument begin. In addition, the method was based on a personal relationship with the learners throughout their path toward autonomy and self-mastery (Hanse, 2007, p. 225). The originality of the approach also relied on the fact that it was taking into consideration individuals' own characteristics (e.g., age, constitution, aptitudes, defaults and ethnical and geographical origins) (Hanse, 2007, p. 235).

Jaques-Dalcroze's musical pedagogy, like Plato's, was not primarily aiming at the mastery of an instrument. Its purpose was much more holistic. In comparison with the early intuitions grounded in the Platonician conception of musical education, Jaques-Dalcroze's eurhythmics represented however a significant advance. It provided educators with a detailed method to conceive a pedagogy articulating movement, artistic practice and personal development, based on an extended body of empirical evidence and a more systematic process of inquiry. If its current legitimacy and contemporary evolution appear fundamentally grounded in those qualities (Mathieu, 2014), like Plato's pedagogical views, Jaques-Dalcroze's contribution remains however limited when comes the time to accurately determine the nature of the relationships that connect embodied skills and psychological, spiritual and social development.

Ossip Mandelstam's ideal of popular rhythmic education

In 1918, working as an employee for the People's Commissariat of Education, the Russian poet Mandelstam (1891–1938) seems to have organized a Rhythm Institute, whose precise objectives remain unknown but which appeared directly related to his own practice of eurhythmics (Michon, 2005, p. 192). His personal interest for Jaques-Dalcroze's method and his political commitment inspired a short essay he wrote in 1920, titled "Government and Rhythm", (Mandelstam, 1920/1979) in which he attempted to analyze the contemporary social context and the role that rhythmic education could play in the constitution of the emerging state. As noticed by Michon (2005, p. 192), in spite of the shortness of this text, this may have been the first theoretical attempt to use the idea of rhythm as both a descriptive tool and a political utopia.

For Mandelstam (1920/1979, p. 108), rhythm had to be seen as "an instrument for social education". Accordingly, eurhythmics had nothing to do with "estheticism", which appeared as "an accidental veneer" resulting from a fashion among the European and American bourgeoisie; it was even more incorrect to regard it merely as "hygiene" or "gymnastics" (Mandelstam, 1920/1979, pp. 109–110). As noted by Michon (2005, p. 193), what was at stake for Mandelstam was to go beyond traditional dualisms (e.g., spirit–body or work–play) through an individualizing synthesis that had to serve as political justification for the introduction of rhythmic education in the school system. For Mandelstam, 'rhythm' had to be differentiated from 'cadence' as it was found at work, in gymnastics or in sports. While cadence was homogenizing, rhythm appeared as a means to promote subjectivity and diversification among individuals and groups. From this perspective, rhythmic education had to be controlled by the government (Mandelstam, 1920/1979, p. 108) as it had to participate in the production of individuals who would form a "true democratic collectivity" rather than "undifferentiated masses" constituted of "amorphous persons" and "unorganized individuals" (Mandelstam, 1920/1979, p. 108). Rhythmic education was therefore conceived as a prerequisite to help individuals being more 'adjusted' and therefore abler to participate to the social ideal promoted by the People's Commissariat of Education.

For Michon (2005), one of the main contributions of Mandelstam's essay was that it constituted the blueprint of a theory of individual and collective emancipation in which the qualities of rhythm played a crucial role. Mandelstam's educational contribution may thus rely on the fact that he was able to foresee the political dimension inherent to rhythmic education; retrospectively, however, it seems that he failed to anticipate how collective rhythms could be instrumentalized according to totalitarian views that were antithetic to his own beliefs. As for Jaques-Dalcroze, at the core of his contribution remained the distinction made between the mechanical and alienating aspects of embodied rhythms – promoted by industrial production – and the free-flowing and bonding dimensions of human rhythms. In congruence with his views, similar reflections were emerging simultaneously in the field of gymnastic education. Jacobs (1922, as cited in Toepfer, 1997, p. 126), for instance, formulated at the same period the idea that the formation of a "redemptive proletarian culture" depended on "renewal through rhythm", a thesis embedded in the conventional Marxist argument according to which workers' alienation was directly linked to the stultifying and meaningless working conditions characterized by the mechanical repetition of assembly lines (cf. Chapter 8). To explore further the relationships between rhythmic constraints and embodied education, as they emerged at that time in educational theory, it is appropriate to introduce further the theoretical reflections conducted in the field of gymnastics education.

Rudolf Bode's rhythmic gymnastics

Bode (1881–1971) was a renowned exponent of the German body-culture (*Koerperkultur*), a heterogeneous movement conceived as a way to reform life and society in general and give birth to a "higher *Mensch*" whose "duty" was "to consider the body as a sacred temple" (Wedemeyer-Kolwe, 2004, p. 13, trans. Crespi, 2014, p. 33). Unlike Jaques-Dalcroze and Laban's progressive visions, Bode's contribution to rhythmic gymnastics was grounded in a much more conservative conception, assuming that social progress was actually threatening to destroy the beauty of 'natural rhythms'. For him, the body was seen as the foundation of the resistance to industrialization itself (Toepfer, 1997, p. 384). After having studied eurhythmics, Bode established in 1913 his own school in Munich; by 1925, his courses of gymnastics were taught in 130 different cities in Germany (Wedemeyer-Kolwe, 2004, p. 28, as cited in Crespi, 2014, p. 34).

Strongly opposed to Jaques-Dalcroze's methods, he embarked on a pedagogy that developed bodily rhythms independently of music or artwork. For Bode, eurhythmics was based on confusion between "rhythm" (*rhythmus*) and "measure" (*Takt* in German, from the Latin *tangere*, to beat), perpetuating a narrow and mathematical understanding of rhythm (Toepfer, 1997, p. 125). He contested the idea that such a technique could bring an organism to develop a specific rhythmicity. Privileging a vitalist perspective, he assumed that "lively forces" were the only ones to be really productive and that the right rhythms already existed within the organism (Hanse, 2007, p. 312). One of Bode's major influences was Klages's writings on rhythm, which asserted that excessive rationality or intellectual analysis was a source of "arhythm" or unnatural, strained, discordant, stifled movement (Toepfer, 1997, p. 127). In *Rhythm and Its Importance for Education*, Bode (1920/2014) introduced a "total" concept of rhythm similar to other contemporary views on movement education, such as those expressed by Klatt and Jacobs (1922, cited in Toepfer, 1997, p. 125). Bode's rhythmic gymnastics was privileging 'qualitative' objectives (rather than 'quantitative' ones, such as sportive achievements). His aim was to develop bodily movements derived from "rhythms in nature" – which he never clearly defined – with the view of making the body expressive in the performance of everyday actions

(Toepfer, 1997, p. 128) and preserving the individual's lively forces to sustain a resistance to the "attacks" of the will. Will and rationality were conceived as hegemonic sources serving utilitarian ends that ultimately were weakening the natural forces constitutive of human nature. Beyond the standards of a gymnastic method introduced as a defense of imagination and creativity, against mercantile values and the emerging hegemony of quantification, Bode's method was building up a critique against capitalism and democratic rules themselves. Values such as freedom and equality were perceived as counter-natural and dangerous (Hanse, 2007, p. 355) as they were introducing "splitting" and "destructuring" forces within a social body already perceived as "degenerated". Privileging "synchronicity" – as a supreme sign of unity with nature with other bodies and with movements external to the body – linking it to a "German concept of rhythm" appealing to national propaganda (exemplified by the massive gatherings organized in totalitarian countries, such as those organized in Germany a few years later), Bode's anti-intellectualism finally made him susceptible to follow national socialism's ideology (Toepfer, 1997, p. 128).

Bode's theoretical and political antagonisms with Jaques-Dalcroze's eurhythmics, and the very characteristics of his approach, raise interesting issues regarding the use of the notion of rhythm in education. They interrogate the extent to which rhythmic education has to be conceived as a mean to enrich, or rather to resist, the hegemonic pace characterizing a given society. They also require taking position regarding the 'threats' that justify the definition of a new set of pedagogical principles to experience time differently (e.g., lack of coordination and imposition of social pace over natural rhythms). By asserting the independence of movement over music, and stressing the inner origin of people's body rhythms, Bode's tribute also questions whether it may be desirable to foster some form of 'authentic' rhythms and how to conceive their origin and their locus (e.g., internal versus external). Through his contestation of a Platonician and Aristotlician conception of rhythm, and through his anti-rationalist theses, Bode's contribution also interrogates the qualities of the pedagogy required to promote and sustain the learners' sense of balance. Considering the anti-democratic and anti-intellectual grounds that came as significant by-products of Bode's rhythmic gymnastics, this approach finally demonstrates the ambivalence of an emancipatory project that aims at fostering more autonomy from social and economic pressures at the expense of people's very own humanity.

Rudolf Steiner's anthroposophy and eurhythmy

Steiner (1861–1925) was an Austrian philosopher and esotericist thinker who led the anthroposophic society, a spiritual movement finding its roots in German idealist philosophy and theosophy. Positioning himself as antiliberal and anti-Marxist, his vision was inspired by contributions produced at that time within heterogeneous disciplines, such as architecture, medicine, agronomy or pedagogy. With the installation of its headquarters in Dornbach (Switzerland), the movement progressively extended its cultural and religious program aiming at leading a pacific social reform (Hanse, 2007, pp. 50–52). In 1919, Steiner opened his first school (Waldorf School) in Stuttgart to serve the children of the employees of the Waldorf-Astoria cigarette factory. Throughout the century, the movement grew, leading to the creation of thousands of schools worldwide.

Like Jaques-Dalcroze, Steiner valued the role of physical well-being. However, his educational theory (e.g., Steiner, 1920/1995) privileged the spiritual dimension of human development rather than its embodied aspects. Believing that humans are spiritual beings who had to accommodate to their life on earth, Steiner conceived human development as a process of ongoing reincarnation through which humans have learned to use their senses to better perceive the surrounding physical world. For him, the main issue associated with human evolution was that the progressive conquest of the world led to the decline of spiritual consciousness. Considering Greek and Roman antiquity as the golden age of physical existence, Steiner recognized the benefits of rhythm as a core educational principle and fundamental component of the art (Hanse, 2007, p. 77). In the speculative system he elaborated, humans were considered as rhythmic beings as they were constantly connected to the 'pulse' of the cosmos. The irregularities experienced because of the increasing influence of their working environment brought people to move away from the "correspondences" between "astral movements" and their natural inner rhythms (Hanse, 2007). For Steiner, the human capacity to detach oneself from the rhythms of the natural environment was at the same time a condition for freedom and a source of perturbation for the "human species", which appeared as struggling with modern life's lack of balance. For him, the only way out was for humans, through their inner evolution, to find a rhythm that they could one day transmit to the world (Hanse, 2007, p. 183).

Rhythm is therefore a prevalent component of Steiner's educational contribution, expressed through multiples subthemes (Mathisen, 2016). The Waldorf education is embedded within a rhythmic conception that focuses on the dynamic interactions and correspondences between various aspects of human psychology. Thus, learning and development relies on teachers and pupils' capacity to articulate "feeling", "thinking" and "willing" (Mathisen, 2016, p. 54). Phenomena such as sympathy and antipathy, memory and imagination, and humor and seriousness are conceived as polarities interacting rhythmically. Steiner's contribution also relies on a developmental theory, organized around seven-year periods, that informs educational tasks and possibilities that may be assigned to pupils (Mathisen, 2016).

The role played by rhythms in Steiner's pedagogy is present in the repertoire of activities prescribed in Waldorf schools, including movements, singing, storytelling, the use of imagination, rhythmical counting in mathematics and so on (Mathisen, 2016, p. 55). It is also constitutive of the relationships between pupils and teachers and the way they talk and listen to each other (Mathisen, 2016, p. 58). In addition, the Waldorf school schedule is also organized around a regular daily routine intended to emphasize rhythms inherent to daily, weekly, monthly and seasonal cycles (Taplin, 2010), including periods of outdoor recess (Ullrich, 2008) and "school festivals" as markers of the ending of the educational program and the celebration of children's inner renewal through the reconnection with their deep nature and a "reconstituted community" (Hanse, 2007, p. 271). Waldorf school organization also takes into consideration the rhythmicity between sleep and wakefulness, assuming that the experience of sleeping has cognitive effects on memory, as much as they participate in the spiritual elaboration of events (Mathisen, 2016, p. 57).

Steiner's contribution also appears through its reference to "eurhythmy", a movement art usually accompanying spoken texts or music, which includes elements of role play and dance, designed to provide individuals and classes with a "sense of integration and harmony" (McDermott et al., 1996). Steiner's eurhythmy was distinct from Jaques-Dalcroze's method. It was not based on musical rhythm but rather on an esoteric conception of language understood not as a code but as a "universal mean of expression of the human soul" (Hanse, 2007, p. 272, my translation). For Jaques-Dalcroze, music and rhythm had to enable the creation of a sustainable connection between the body and the spiritual to reestablish balance and coordination; the movement's order and unity was based on a rational principle, shaping the body rhythms, and susceptible to counter the over-intellectualization of traditional education. For Steiner, the "spiritualization" of the body was rather based on "inner necessity" grounded in "natural laws" that automatically expressed themselves when subjectivity and rationality were eliminated from body expression (Hanse, 2007, p. 274).

Steiner's legacy to educational theory remains controversial. On the one hand, the practical principles he introduced to organize the school activity around specific rhythms constitutes an example of the significance of his pedagogical contribution, whose value is regularly asserted through empirical studies (Mathisen, 2016). On the other hand, his approach to 'spiritual science' and the underlying esoteric theory that grounds the principles of his 'eurhythmy' do not fit within the contemporary scientific standards of educational sciences. From an epistemological point of view, Steiner's theory of rhythms illustrates the limitations of a rhythmic theory according to which "everything is rhythm" and "rhythm is everything" (Sauvanet, 2000, p. 54). Steiner's conception, like Bode's, remains thus problematic because it positions on the same level rhythms that are fundamentally heterogeneous (e.g., astronomical, physical, musical or linguistic), and it establishes correspondences between them (e.g., influences) according to principles that cannot be always rationally demonstrated.

Rhythmic theories in education and their epistemological pitfalls

From a temporal and rhythmic perspective, the Industrial Revolution and the cultural transformations that occurred at the turn of the 20th century fed a twofold movement in the evolution of educational research and theory. On one side, they contributed to refine and rationalize even further the temporal discipline already introduced in school organization during the previous centuries. On the other side, they participated in the emergence of a countermovement favoring the development of a more holistic conception of education, carrying away Plato's earlier intuitions regarding the moral and psychological effects of esthetic rhythms and systematizing approaches privileging the role played by rhythmic experiences – especially artistic and embodied ones – in the development of more well-balanced individuals and collectivities.

The reinforcement of those two trends remains nevertheless problematic. On the one hand, the main issue associated with the study of instructional time is that – in congruence with the positivist principles grounding empirical sciences – it emphasizes a reductionist interpretation of time in education, neglecting the qualitative richness of temporal experience and ignoring its political and existential implications. On the other hand, inquiries promoted by rhythmical theories of musical, gymnastic or spiritual education lacked the epistemological rigor required to define with accuracy rhythmic phenomena and the nature of their (mutual) influences. Such developments demonstrate the fact that theorizing rhythmic educational phenomena, considering all together their empirical, political and epistemological dimensions, requires therefore one to frame more systematically the meanings associated with the use of the concept of rhythm itself (cf. Chapter 9).

As it will appear in the next chapters, throughout the following decades, the attempts to theorize the temporal dimensions inherent to education will become broader and 'thicker'. On one side, early studies on instructional time are going to lead to the development of a whole body of empirical study. On the other side, rhythmic theories, such as eurhythmics, rhythmic gymnastics or anthroposophy will continue to expand their influence, but their contribution will remain at the fringe of the development of mainstream educational sciences. The critical function they may have fulfilled in between the two world wars, and the hope they were carrying, will partly reappear through references made to a new set of notions rooted in the development of biology.

References

Amadio, M. (2004). Instructional time: Introduction to the open file. *Prospects, XXXIV*(3), 267–270.
Anderson, L.W. (1984). *Time and school learning: Theory, research and practice.* New York: St-Martin's Press.
Attali, J. (1982). *Histoires du temps.* Paris: Fayard.
Bachelard, G. (1931). *L'intuition de l'instant.* Paris: Stock.
Bachelard, G. (1936). *La dialectique de la durée.* Paris: Presses Universitaires de France.
Bergmann, W. (1992). The problem of time in sociology: An overview of the literature on the state of theory and research on the 'sociology of time', 1900–82. *Time & Society, 1*(1), 81–134.
Bergson, H. (1970). *Essai sur les données immédiates de la conscience.* Paris: Presses Universitaires de France. (Original work published 1888)

Berliner, D.C. (1990). What's all the fuss about instructional time. In M. Ben-Peretz, & R. Bromme (Eds.), *The nature of school time: Theoretical concepts, practitioner perceptions* (pp. 3–35). New York: Teachers College Press.

Bode, R. (2014). Rhythm and its importance for education (P. Crespi, Trans.). *Body & Society*, *20*(3/4), 51–74. (Original work published 1920)

Borg, W.R. (1980). Time and school learning. In C. Denham, & A. Lieberman (Eds.), *Time to learn* (pp. 33–51). Washington, DC: US Department of Education.

Bücher, K. (1896). *Arbeit und Rhythmus*. Leipzig, Germany: Hirzel.

Castoriadis, C. (1997). *The imaginary institution of society* (K. Blamey, Trans.). Malden, MA: Polity Press. (Original work published 1975)

Cavet, A. (Ed.). (2011). Rythmes scolaires: Pour une dynamique nouvelle des temps éducatifs. *Dossier d'actualité de l'Institut National de Recherche Pédagogique, 60*.

Chopin, M.-P. (2010). Les usages du 'temps' dans les recherches sur l'enseignement. *Revue Française de Pédagogie*, *170*, 87–110.

Compère, M.-M. (2001). L'histoire du temps scolaire en Europe. In C. St-Jarre, & L. Dupuy-Walker (Eds.), *Le temps en éducation: Regards multiples* (pp. 93–115). Sainte-Foy, QC, Canada: Presses Universitaires du Québec.

Couturier-Heinrich, C. (2004). *Aux origines de la poésie allemande: Les théories du rythme des Lumières au Romantisme*. Paris: Centre National de la Recherche Scientifique.

Crespi, P. (2014). Rhythmanalysis in gymnastics and dance: Rudolf Bode and Rudolf Laban. *Body & Society*, *20*(3/4), 30–50.

Delhaxhe, A. (1997). Le temps comme unité d'analyse dans la recherche sur l'enseignement. *Revue Française de Pédagogie*, *118*, 107–125.

Durkheim, E. (1968). *Les formes élémentaires de la vie religieuse*. Paris: Presses Universitaires de France. (Original work published 1912)

Gutek, G.L. (1986). *Education in the United States: An historical perspective*. Englewood Cliffs, NJ: Prentice-Hall.

Hanse, O. (2007). *Rythme et civilisation dans la pensée allemande autour de 1900* [Electronic version]. Doctoral dissertation, Université Rennes 2, France. Retrieved January 15, 2014, from https://tel.archives-ouvertes.fr/tel-00204429

Jaques-Dalcroze, E. (1921). *Rhythm, music and education* (H.F. Rubinstein, Trans.). London: Putnam's Sons.

Laban, R. (1948). *Modern educational dance*. London: MacDonald & Evans.

Laban, R. (2014). Eurhythmy and kakorhythmy in art and education (P. Crespi, Trans.). *Body & Society*, *20*(3/4), 75–78. (Original work published 1921)

Mandelstam, O. (1979). Government and rhythm. In J.G. Harris (Ed.), *Mandelstam: The complete critical prose and letters* (J.G. Harris & C. Link, Trans.) (pp. 108–111). Ann Arbor, MI: Ardis. (Original work published 1920)

Mathieu, L. (2014). *Un regard actuel sur la rythmique Jaques-Dalcroze*. Retrieved February 5, 2016, from http://rhuthmos.eu/spip.php?article1186

Mathisen, A. (2016). Rhythms as a pedagogy of becoming: Lefebvre, Whitehead and Steiner on the art of bringing rhythmical transformations into teaching and learning – Part II. *Research on Steiner Education*, *6*(2), 52–67.

Mauss, M. (1925/2012). *Essai sur le don: Forme et raison de l'échange dans les sociétés archaïques*. Paris: Presses Universitaires de France.

McDermott, R., Henry, M.E., Dillard, C., Byers, P., Easton, F., Oberman, I., & Uhrmacher, B. (1996). Waldorf education in an inner-city public school. *The Urban Review*, *28*(2), 119.

Meschonnic, H. (1982). *Critique du rythme: Anthropologie historique du langage*. Lagrasse, France: Verdier.

Michon, P. (2005). *Rythmes, pouvoir, mondialisation*. Paris: Presses Universitaires de France.
Michon, P. (2007). *Les rythmes du politique*. Paris: Les Prairies Ordinaires.
Michon, P. (2012a). *Aux origines des théories du rythme: L'apport de la pensée allemande des lumières au romantisme*. Retrieved December 12, 2013, from http://rhuthmos.eu/spip.php?article632
Michon, P. (2012b). *Notes éparses sur le rythme comme enjeu artistique, scientifique et philosophique depuis la fin du XVIIIème siècle*. Retrieved December 12, 2013, from http://rhuthmos.eu/spip.php?article54
Nowotny, H. (1994). *Time: The modern and postmodern experience*. Cambridge, MA: Blackwell.
Pennington, J. (1925). *The importance of being rhythmic*. New York: G.P. Putnam's Sons.
Pronovost, G. (2001). Temps sociaux et temps scolaire en Occident: Le brouillage des frontières. In C. St-Jarre, & L. Dupuy-Walker (Eds.), *Le temps en education: Regards multiples* (pp. 43–58). Sainte-Foy, QC, Canada: Presses Universitaires du Québec.
Sauvanet, P. (2000). *Le rythme et la raison (vol. 1): Rythmologiques*. Paris: Kimé.
Schiller, F. (1795/1943). *Lettres sur l'éducation esthétique de l'homme*. Paris: Aubier.
Simmel, G. (2004). *The philosophy of money* (T. Bottomore & S. Frisby, Trans.). London: Routledge. (Original work published 1900)
Steiner, R. (1995). *The spirit of the Waldorf school*. Hudson, NY: Anthroposophic Press. (Original work published 1920)
St-Jarre, C. (2001). L'organisation du temps en éducation: Les cadres de référence. In C. St-Jarre, & L. Dupuy-Walker (Eds.), *Le temps en education: Regards multiples* (pp. 15–41). Sainte-Foy, QC, Canada: Presses Universitaires du Québec.
Taplin, J.T. (2010). Steiner Waldorf early childhood education: Offering a curriculum for the 21st century. In L. Miller, & L. Pound (Eds.), *Theories and approaches to learning in the early years* (p. 92). London: Sage.
Tarde, J.G. (1989). *L'opinion et la foule*. Paris: Presses Universitaires de France. (Original work published 1901)
Toepfer, K. (1997). *The empire of ecstasy*. Berkeley, CA: University of California Press.
Ullrich, H. (2008). *Rudolf Steiner*. London: Continuum International Publ. Group.
Whitehead, A.N. (1929). *Process and reality*. New York: The Free Press.
Whitehead, A.N. (1938). *Modes of thought*. New York: Macmillan.

Chapter 6

The rise of temporal double binds in formal education throughout the second half of the 20th century

Internalizing the conflicting nature of temporal constraints

Educational temporalities are composed by heterogeneous rhythms and regulated by various temporal norms. They appear as hybrid. As shown in the previous chapters, they relate to discursive, corporeal and social activities characterized by rhythms and constraints of different natures. If such a hybridity is inherent to educational phenomena (cf. Chapter 2), it seems that it is only during the second half of the 20th century that it grew as a matter of concerns and reflection for those experiencing and studying them. Based on this hypothesis, the aim of this chapter is twofold. On the one hand, its first purpose is to depict the intellectual evolution that influenced, since the 1950s, how time and the experience of time have been conceived in schools. On the other hand, this chapter also aims at describing the movement through which people involved in formal education have internalized not only the hybrid dimensions of educational temporalities but also their conflicting nature. To proceed, this chapter discusses the effects associated with the implementation of strategies that renewed the perception of the idea of autonomy in formal education, especially in regard to students' and educators' time. Three lines of inquiry will be discussed: at the classroom level, the development of studies related to instructional and didactic time; at the school level, the implementation of nongraded curricula or learning cycles; and at the level of school policy, the contribution of chronobiological and chronopsychological research. At those three levels, what emerged is that the internalization of the hybrid and conflicting aspects inherent to educational temporalities constitutes the key feature of a new form of temporal constraint, characterized by tacit contradictions (double binds) that may lead to increased defensiveness, confusion and helplessness among the people involved in schoolwork.

From the homogeneity of school time to the heterogeneity of learning rhythms

Between the 1920s and the 1960s, the temporal organization of school evolved in Western countries following two main influences: on the one side, the extension of parents' daily working time – especially the increase in women's professional activity – and on the other side, the emergence of leisure time and the role assigned to school in the democratization of this new culture (Sue & Caccia, 2005, p. 19). At the beginning of the 1960s, the adjustment of school temporal organization was conditioned above all by economic factors (Sue & Caccia, 2005, p. 19). In the United States, an effort was particularly made to systematize conceptions of learning time to formulate scientific models that could support the temporal reorganization of schools. The research on instructional time, initiated at the beginning of the 20th century, reappeared in the late 1950s, stimulated by landmark references, such as Bloom's (1953, as cited in Berliner, 1990) study of students' thoughts during college classes, Carroll's (1963) model of school learning, or Jackson's (1968) *Life in Classroom*. Studies conducted during the following years found positive correlations between time on task and achievement, but the magnitude of the relationship remained open to dispute (Berliner, 1990, p. 10). The results of the studies conducted during that period progressively shifted the perspective adopted by educational researchers, moving their focus from schooling to learning. With such a change, research in educational psychology became central (Chopin, 2010).

The revival of instructional time

For Berliner (1990), the value of research on instructional time came from the interpretive framework it provided as well as its contribution for prediction and control. At the core of the literature on time and instruction remained several models considered as significant contributions (e.g., Bloom, 1968; Carroll, 1963), later revised to establish the "academic learning time" model (Delhaxhe, 1997). Carroll's (1963) model of instructional time did not describe the learning process per se; as noticed by Delhaxhe (1997), it should rather be conceived as a description of the "economy" of the school process. For Berliner (1990, p. 13), Carroll's model provided a theoretical resource that could generate "testable" and "quantifiable" hypotheses about school learning. For the first time in educational research, it gave concepts such as "aptitude", "perseverance", and "opportunity to learn" a common unit (i.e., time) that could serve to describe the functional relationships between those "variables" and a "measure" of school learning (Berliner, 1990). Carroll's model defined the 'degree of learning' in some particular content areas as a function of the time spent on learning in that area divided by the time needed to learn. Accordingly, time spent on learning is affected by (a) the time allocated for learning (opportunity to learn) and (b) the percentage of time actually spent engaged in learning (perseverance). Time needed to learn is affected by (c) the time actually needed to learn (individual's aptitude), (d) the quality of instruction and (e) the learner's ability to understand instruction (Berliner, 1990; Carroll, 1963; Delhaxhe, 1997). For Bloom (1974b, as cited in Delhaxhe, 1997), Carroll's model provoked a significant shift in research on learning and teaching, first, because it defined most variables of the learning process in terms of time, a unit of analysis that could be used at different levels (e.g., years, months, hours or minutes). In addition, references to time opened up the possibility to use a strict metric scale, facilitating the process of comparison.

Through his theorization, Carroll believed he found a way to "uncouple" notions of aptitude, sometimes thought of as "intelligence" or "ability", from notions about genetic endowment and social class effects on the ability to learn (Berliner, 1990, p. 13). Rather than being characterized as "smart or dumb", "bright or dull", "gifted or disabled", students could be classified only as "fast or slow", a variable that schools could eventually accommodate to (Berliner, 1990, p. 13). In itself such ideas were not new,[1] but for the first time, they were empirically grounded based on quantifiable evidence. Another aspect of Carroll's contribution was that the model relied on several variables controlled by the teacher (e.g., the quality of instruction and the time allocated for learning), which suggested more responsibility for time management (Chopin, 2010, para. 14). While not denying the importance of some general factor of intelligence, Carroll's definition of aptitude contributed to the promotion of a more differentiated view of learning and pedagogy, based for instance on multiage classroom groupings, ungraded schools or the ability to place a student at any level in any subject area, favoring children's own way of proceeding in different disciplines (Berliner, 1990, p. 14). For the supporters of the approach, defining perseverance as the time a student was willing to be engaged in instruction and conceiving engagement, attention or time on task as behavioral and quantifiable instructional time measures contributed to demystify concepts such as motivation (Berliner, 1990, p. 15). With Bloom's (1968) "mastery learning" model, Carroll's notion of aptitude was later used to predict time required by an individual to reach a determined level of competency and manipulate teaching variables so that most students could reach it.

Academic learning time

In the United States, the concept of academic learning time found its roots in Carroll and Bloom's models. It was developed in the early 1980s through the realization of the large-scale *Beginning Teacher Evaluation Study* (Denham & Lieberman, 1980). According to Berliner (1990, p. 5), academic learning time (ALT) is usually defined as a part of allocated time in a subject matter area (e.g., physical education or mathematics) in which a student is engaged successfully through activities or materials related to educational outcomes that are valued. Academic learning time is traditionally conceived in relation with other concepts, such as allocated time, time on task, success rate, transition time, waiting time, perseverance or pace (cf. Berliner, 1990, p. 5, for definitions). The development of this concept appears closely related to research conducted on class management (e.g., flow activity), linking student levels of engagement to the strategies implemented by teachers to sustain their continuous involvement (Delhaxhe, 1997). According to Delhaxhe (1997), most of the research conducted on time variables after the publication of the *Beginning Teacher Evaluation*

Study either focused on the application of the ALT model to improve students' performance or explore variables that influence academic learning time (e.g., teacher's enthusiasm, student's level of anxiety, diversity of ages in the classroom or number of interactions within the classroom).

Prisoners of time

Between 1980 and 1990, studies conducted on academic learning time dominated American research on time in education, representing more than half of the studies referenced by the ERIC database (Chopin, 2010, para. 18). Their impact went beyond the scientific field and reached the political sphere. In 1991, the US government established the National Educational Commission on Time and Learning (NECTL) charged with "exploring the relationship between time and learning and making recommendations for how the nation's schools should restructure the use of time to enhance student learning" (Aronson, 1995, p. 6, as cited in Chopin, 2010, para. 18). As the role played by allocated time came back at the center of attention in the United States, research on time and learning was no longer focusing exclusively on the relationships between the quantity of instruction and student achievement. Such studies also started questioning the limitations of teachers' activity within the school temporal framework (Chopin, 2010, para. 19).[2] Thus, the report of the NECTL (1994), titled *Prisoners of Time*, challenged educators to fix the design flaw in the ways schools were organized as well as the way time was allocated for academic purposes (Slattery, 1995, p. 615). The assumption framing this document was that if standards were established in "core academic areas", then time could become a "flexible resource"; curriculum and time were therefore conceived both as "quantifiable objects capable of external manipulation" (Slattery, 1995).

The emergence of didactic time

As pointed by Chopin (2010, para. 35), the use of Carroll's model raised the risk of perpetuating a reified and misleading conception of learning time, as if each student was characterized by a specific one, independent of any pedagogical dimension and preexisting to the teaching setting. For this author (Chopin, 2010, para. 44), the interest raised by the research conducted on academic learning time expresses the evolution of the understanding of time in the process of teaching and learning. Until then, time was considered as an "input" of the system; through research conducted on academic learning time, it became a time "produced" by some actions engaging teacher and students (Chopin, 2010, para. 18). At this level of analysis, a new dimension of time emerged, qualified by Chopin as "processual" to stress the fact that time progressively became a "construction" rather than just a "natural" variable (Chopin, 2010, para. 18). If Carroll and Bloom's contributions both assumed the existence of a specific learning time characterizing each student and determining the conditions of one's learning, research conducted during the 1980s and 1990s was rather drawing attention on the relationship between student's own time and the didactic time that characterized the instructional setting (Chopin, 2010, para. 18).

In French-speaking countries, research on didactic time usually referred to the specificity of the temporality involved in the construction of knowledge. The emergence of this concept (e.g., Chevallard, 1991; Chevallard & Mercier, 1987) aimed at introducing an epistemological shift in the way time was conceived. As stressed by Chopin (2010, para. 44, my translation), it refers to "the time *of* the construction of knowledge and not simply the time *through which* knowledge is constructed." For instance, in France, Mercier (1995) developed the notion of students' "didactic biography" to describe how the succession of "ignorances", provoked by the teaching setting and overcome by learners, were representing the main determinant of students learning temporality. Assuming the processual dimension of time suggested one to stress the interdependency and the consubstantiality of the student's learning temporality and the teacher's teaching temporality (Chopin, 2010). From a methodological perspective, it questions and focuses on the decisions made by the teacher regarding the articulation between teaching and learning to elaborate models that could describe their activity (Chopin, 2010). Thus, for Chopin, if the legal time defining the school setting and the didactic time characterizing the learning process are interdependent, it does not necessarily mean that the former completely determines the latter: didactic time has its own autonomy, and its "efficiency" relies on the conditions provided for teachers to control the creation and the diversification of the teaching process (Chopin, 2011).

Internalizing hybrid and ambiguous temporal constraints

When considering the development of research on instructional time, academic learning time or didactic time, from the perspective of temporal constraints, ambiguities remain. Considering students' and teachers' autonomy, the impact of those studies are twofold. By revealing the increased importance given to the temporality of learning, the theorization of instructional time participated in the autonomization of learning's time itself. Until then, teaching was at the center of the attention as an activity whose temporality had to be externally defined, organized and controlled (e.g., through school policy). Through this development, the locus of control shifted, focusing on the learners and the way they interact with their teachers. Because the locus of temporal influence changed, the temporal constraints that determined students' achievement are no longer appearing as exclusively external to classroom organization. They became variables that could be controlled and managed by teachers, who internalize them as fundamental components of the learning setting – components they not only have control over but also the responsibility to manage. With the relative increase of their autonomy and responsibility regarding the management of their time, students' and educators' activities no longer appear as exclusively constrained by external (e.g., institutional) requirements; they are rather interpreted through internalized, self-imposed temporal pressures.

From an epistemic and symbolic perspective, research conducted on instructional, academic learning and didactic time are also marked by ambivalence. At the core, such literature purposefully prevents one to consider how the very subjective and even existential meaning associated with temporal experience determines the learning outcome. It remains confined to the pace of observable behaviors and a temporal scope limited to the study of the formal setting (e.g., school or classroom) rather than integrating the student's or teacher's life temporalities as a whole. Despite the fact that such efforts were initially aimed at empowering educators and learners, they restrain how people may perceive themselves and envision the meaning of their education, limited by a conception of time still defined as natural, external, abstract, quantifiable and measurable. However, with the further development of alternative conceptions of the temporalities involved (e.g., didactic time), such research also provided an opportunity for scholars and practitioners to renew their conceptions of educational temporalities, stressing their processual dimension. From that perspective, with studies focusing on the rhythms of learning activity, time is no longer exclusively conceived as a variable that constrains the learning outcome; it rather has to be envisioned as a product of the educational activity, defined through the evaluation of the succession of qualitative changes (e.g., discursive, corporeal and social) affecting the learning situation. Educational time appears thus as a bundle of heterogeneous rhythms emerging from the learning situation itself. Through the evolution of the study of instructional time and its effects on educational practices, what emerged therefore is a renewed conception of temporal constraints more ambiguous, more hybrid and more internalized than before.

The impact of differentiated learning on teacher autonomy

For P. Perrenoud (2001, p. 289), the structuration of school curricula in years or cycles, the yearly and weekly organization of school and the implementation of schedules defining the time dedicated to each discipline all constitute aspects that allow the belief that school temporalities are constraining or prefiguring work organization. Perrenoud considers however the fact that in reality, broad margins of interpretations remain and that the fine-tuning of time management often depends on strategies adopted individually and collectively by teachers, based on their sphere of autonomy; recursively, such practices determine the way organizational temporalities are structured in the long term (Perrenoud, 2001, p. 289). Through the modern history of education, one finds multiple trends characterized by the experimentation of alternative modalities of school temporal organization. In the following section, two approaches (nongraded schools and the implementation of learning cycles) are briefly introduced to discuss how the temporal organization of differentiated curricula relates to professionals' heterogeneous and potentially antagonistic experiences of time and autonomy.

From the development of nongraded schools to the implementation of learning cycles

As summarized by Anderson (1992), nongraded elementary schools emerged at the end of the 19th century from uncoordinated efforts to question graded practices and be more sensitive to differences in children's learning styles. In the United States, several programs, such as Dewey's Laboratory School or Stoddard's Dual Progress Plan, were based on a differentiation of students' activity and privileging more flexible curricular and school organization patterns (Anderson, 1992, pp. 2–3). In Europe, many scholars (e.g., Petersen, Montessori, Freinet and Ferrer) were emphasizing, in one way or another, children's freedom to develop their own potential at their own pace, promoting practices based on multigraded or multiage pupil grouping, individualized instruction, differentiated staffing (i.e., teacher aides), cooperative teaching, emphasis on learning outcomes rather than coverage of content, holistic assessment practices and so on (Anderson, 1992, pp. 4–5). In the United States, after the Second World War, the idea of nongradedness started gaining favor, benefiting during the following decades from the increasing impact of practices such as multiage grouping and team teaching, which started getting traction in the late 1950s (Anderson, 1992, p. 7). More recently, such principles were found in the development of initiatives based on the concept of 'learning cycle' (*cycle d'apprentissage*). In French-speaking countries (e.g., France, Switzerland and Canada) for instance, after periods of experimentation initiated during the 1970s, public school policies have been revised to promote new forms of school organization during the 1990s. As summarized by O. Perrenoud (2005, p. 47), the key principles of pedagogical action based on learning cycle can be organized around three axes: first, the individualization of the educational trajectory (*parcours de formation*) (e.g., managing differentiated paths within a cycle and the sequence of learning situations); second, the redefinition of learning situations favoring engagement (e.g., project-based learning, problem solving, research-oriented activities, group work and team teaching); and third, the promotion of pedagogical differentiation (e.g., adjustment of the content according to students' capacities, skills and knowledge and adjustment of teaching and learning methodologies to embrace the diversity of learning styles).

Pedagogical tensions inherent to the implementation of differentiated school time

Considering the temporal organization of schoolwork, P. Perrenoud (2001) suggests that organizational issues are located in tension between two polarities: on one side, the fear of losing time, and on the other, an attitude favoring students' own rhythm and the values defended by progressive pedagogies. Thus, when programs overestimate the pace of the "average" student, they generate massive failure; when they are based on the weaker students' rhythms, they raise protests against the "leveling down" of public school (Perrenoud, 2001, p. 292). In addition, curricula that accommodate the students' rhythms carry a double risk: for the fastest students (e.g., gifted ones), accelerating the pace of their instruction at the expense of their socialization, their balance and their belonging to an age-based cohort can create another form of suffering; for the slowest ones, the risk of exclusion only shows later, when they leave a class or a school that "protected" them (Perrenoud, 2001, p. 293). As formulated by Perrenoud (2001, p. 293), such tensions raise at least two main questions: how to induce and sustain an optimal tension for each student and how to avoid gaps between slow and fast students becoming too deep, up to the point where they become irreversible. For this author, the pedagogical issues are located at three levels. First, it is a matter of "optimizing learning processes" (Perrenoud, 2001, p. 296) (i.e., finding the "right timing"): educators must be able to design curricula that are in line with the developmental capabilities of the learners, and they should be able to choose when students may enter into specific learning activities (Ben-Peretz, 1990, p. 69). At a second level, they must be able to provide 'slow' students with more time, either by adjusting curricula with different lengths (with the risk of creating important disparities in age) or by fixing learning goals that have to be reached at the end of pluriannual cycles; it may also require educators to privilege other axes of differentiation than the time of study (e.g., stressing the development of skills or core concepts rather than specific contents). Finally, the organization of schoolwork itself should be revised. One must question the ways its efficiency and modalities are conceived to promote a culture, rules, division of labor, models of cooperation, communication and decision making that enable collective work around each student (Perrenoud, 2001, pp. 306–310).

Organizational tensions and inner conflicts inherent to professionals' subjective experience of time

The development of learning cycles – among other strategies aiming at promoting differentiated pedagogy within schools – suggests one to conceive the temporal organization of learning activities in close relationship with the temporal organization of curriculum design and implementation. Beyond teachers' individual responsibilities, such an achievement is conditioned by the negotiation, the implementation, the regulation and the management of the standards and expectations that constrain the organization of learners' and teachers' activities. It reveals therefore organizational tensions. Observing the evolution of non-graded schools in America, Anderson (1992, p. 8) points out for instance the critical role played by the rapid turnover of school principals, superintendents and teachers in the dilution of such innovative practices over time. Moreover, the relationships between the ways curriculum designers, administrators and teachers perceive time constitutes another critical issue to consider (Connelly & Clandinin, 1990; Hargreaves, 1994; Lafleur, 2001; Reviol, 2001).

Based on his empirical study of collective bargaining agreements, Hargreaves (1994) established a distinction between different ways educators and managers perceive and experience time in their work at school. His research suggests that the way curricula are prepared and implemented is lived differently depending on one's position in the organization and one's specific way of experiencing time. On the one hand, administrators tend to privilege a technical-rational conception of time, understood as a "finite" resource or "means" which can be "managed", "manipulated", or "reorganized" to accommodate selected educational purposes (Hargreaves, 1994, p. 96). On the other hand, teachers' temporal experience fits into what Hall (1989) interprets as a "polychronic" conception of time, including disorder, unpredictability, the daily effervescence of the classroom and the multiple rhythms of the students (Hargreaves, 1994, p. 101). According to Hargreaves, such differences may perpetuate vicious circles at the organizational level due to ongoing incompatibilities inherent to the positions occupied. Taking into consideration such tensions constitutes also a relevant way for this author to analyze the differences of status (also rooted in gender differences) between administrators and teachers and the power dynamics they perpetuate. Accordingly, the "micropolitics" of time within the school organization can be interpreted through notions such as "separation" (that explains how the distance from the classroom is proportional to the experience of a "slower" experience of time) and "colonization" (that describes how administrators instrumentalize teachers' time for their own ends) (Hargreaves, 1994, p. 101).

As illustrated by Hargreaves, teachers are affected by heterogeneous temporalities, including those imposed by school schedules and those related to teaching, evaluation, school report writing, parents' meetings, professional development or extracurricular activities (Hargreaves, 1994, p. 101). In her research on temporal tensions experienced by primary teachers, Reviol (2001) developed a categorization to interpret such antagonisms. According to her study, potential conflicts occur for instance between the teacher's personal aspirations and the institutional expectations; work planning and unexpected events; the richness and the quality of the teaching activity; the multiple expectations toward teachers and their limited availability; urgencies and priorities; and temporal continuity and interruptions. Temporal conflicts also emerge from the different rhythms of the classroom's actors (e.g., students and teachers) or from the lack of coherence and constancy between the temporalities characterizing the beginning and the end of the school year. They also involve tensions between "wasted" and "well-invested" time or professional and extra-professional time (Reviol, 2001). It finally appears that the way teachers deal with such tensions is not homogeneous; additional conflicts may therefore emerge among teachers themselves.

Struggling with normative hybridity and heterogeneous temporal positions

The development of nongraded schools and the implementation of learning cycles reveal two additional expressions of temporal constraints experienced in formal education. First, they illustrate the deep tensions inherent to the conflicting values that shape contemporary educational practices. As discussed previously (cf. Chapter 5), the evolution of the temporal ideals shaping formal education follow indeed two antagonistic principles: on one side, the logic of efficiency dictated by economical rationality, and on the other side, the value of equity responding to a democratic and humanistic ideal. The implementation of differentiated learning exposes how such values get blended. Thus, for practitioners, everyday pedagogical acts are shaped by the dual moral imperative to be at the same time 'efficient' and 'fair'. To some extent, every choice made by educators in their classrooms translates temporal dilemmas that express the tensions between a 'rational' use of the 'temporal resources' available and the respect of the learners' singular rhythms to provide them with 'equal' chances to succeed. Educators seem therefore to have internalized such a normative hybridity, as a mix of conflicting values they are required to respect and nurture. The second expression of temporal constraint emerges with the diverging perspectives that characterize professionals involved in formal education. Thus, educators are not only required to find strategies to solve the temporal dilemmas they internalized; they are also forced to deal with colleagues who experience similar tensions differently, according to their own preferences and the positions they occupy in the institution. Diverging temporal positions constitute therefore an additional form of systemic constraint that shapes everyday activity.

The renewed interest for the rhythmic dimensions of education

After the end of the Second World War, probably due to the emergence of new paradigms (e.g., structuralism and system theory) that were incompatible with the "fluidity" it suggested, the concept of rhythm lost its traction and progressively disappeared from the scientific and philosophical landscape (Michon, 2012). At the origins of its reappearance during the 1980s and the 1990s in the vocabulary used by educators and policy makers, one finds the development of two emerging fields of study: chronobiology and chronopsychology.

Chronobiology and education

The term 'chronobiology' emerged in the mid-1960s to unify the study of temporal characteristics of biological phenomena (cf. Chapter 1). Biological rhythms are typically categorized into three major groups: ultradian (< 20 h) (e.g., heartbeat, breathing and brain waves); circadian (20–28 h) (e.g., alternance wake–sleep and body temperature); and infradian (> 28h) (e.g., menstrual cycle) (Koukkari & Sothern, 2006). Research on the relationships between internal biorhythms and external rhythms (e.g., cosmic and social) brought chronobiologists to study the rhythmic variations of factors found in the environment that exercise an influence on biological rhythms and are able to modify their parameters. Such environmental factors have been designated as "time giver" (*Zeitgeber*), "entraining-agent" or "synchronizer" (Reinberg, 1979, p. 48). Chronobiologists have categorized time givers in classes: for instance, ecological time givers (e.g., day–night alternance) or societal ones (e.g., work organization, education and meal times) (Sansot et al., 1981, as cited in Pineau, 2000). For Reinberg (1979), the most significant synchronizer for human beings is of socio-ecological nature: it is the alternance between activity in the light and rest in the darkness linked to the conditions of our social life. From an educational perspective, biological rhythms are determined by, as well as they influence, various aspects of the everyday life: wake-up time, sleep time, meal time, work schedule, life conditions, time organization, presence or absence of parents; seasonal schedule changes are also important synchronizers that affect sleep and are particularly felt by the youngest children. The research on children's biological rhythms has contributed to develop knowledge on the relationships between physiological rhythms and behaviors and the way they fluctuate throughout the day and the week (Testu, 2008).

Chronopsychology and learning

Going beyond the strictly biological aspects of living rhythms, chronopsychology takes into consideration the temporal dimension in the study of human behaviors per se. More specifically, it studies human behaviors focusing on the way they change, considering their own periodic variations. As a scientific field, chronopsychology emerged with the development of the psychology of time (e.g., Fraisse, 1957). Most chronopsychological research was initially dedicated to the study of active adults, their physical and intellectual performance variations at work, and the fluctuation of their levels of vigilance, attention and cognitive processes over 24-hour, weekly or yearly periods (Testu, 2008). In the field of education, pioneer work was conducted at the turn of the 20th century (Sue & Rondel, 2001; Testu, 2008). Those studies were among the first ones to measure the periodic variations of students' behaviors and performances in school, taking into consideration variables such as age, the nature of the task, the type of memory, the day of the week or the hour of the day. More accurate work emerged during the past 50 years, exploring in depth the temporal variations of student performance (Testu, 2008). During the past decades, even if it remained a marginal field of inquiry, chronopsychological research applied to school environment contributed to a better understanding of the fluctuations of cognitive activity and behaviors (e.g., attention, tiredness, hyperactivity and bullying) among students, taking into consideration the moment of the day or the week, age, personality traits, type of task and contextual dimensions (e.g., geographical) but also to the family's temporal pattern and parents' work patterns (Testu, 2008).

Taking into consideration biological and psychological rhythms within school organization

In France, studies conducted in the fields of chronobiology and chronopsychology contributed during the 1980s to the emergence of debates around 'school rhythms' *(rythmes scolaires)*,[3] channelizing the reflections and discussions among policy makers, school leaders, parents and researchers in education, in psychology and in medicine (Sue & Caccia, 2005). For French chronobiologists and chronopsychologists, school and societal rhythms were not adapted to the reality of children's rhythms. The lack of synchronization between children's biological clocks and their environment was considered as a major source of tiredness, lack of attention and learning difficulties but also exhaustion, anxiety and demotivation, especially for vulnerable children (Cavet, 2011). Such studies contributed to several reforms oriented toward the reorganization of school schedules. Such debates around school rhythms familiarized the public to issues associated with educational temporalities. Reports ordered by the French government during that period prescribed changes affecting students' workloads, the number of class days or the modulation of teaching sequence based on age, topics or pedagogical method chosen; they also insisted on the necessity to harmonize the different times experienced by the children within and outside school (Sue & Caccia, 2005, p. 22) (cf. Chapter 7). Various initiatives experimented new forms of temporal organization in primary schools to open them to their social environment, to increase their connections with nonprofit organizations and to provide opportunities to make learning be more concrete. The traditional daily and weekly organization of time was challenged (Fotinos & Testu, 1996; Husti, 1999; Sue & Rondel, 2001). The advance of the research developed in chronobiology and chronopsychology stressed the importance of considering the biological and psychological rhythms of the child and more specifically their impact on the quality of learning (Sue & Rondel, 2001). What was at stake was the design of the temporal organization of the school system to take into consideration both the heterogeneity of students (including their biological and psychological rhythms) and the decompartmentalization of the structures through which they were taken in charge (Fotinos & Testu, 1996; Husti, 1999; Sue & Rondel, 2001).

The quantification of biological rhythms and its dual effects on the social imaginary of educational time

From a theoretical perspective, the contribution of chronobiology and chronopsychology to educational sciences is twofold. First, research conducted in those fields of study provides scholars, practitioners and policy makers with knowledge that enriches the understanding of the hybridity of educational temporalities. One of the contributions made by chronobiology to educational sciences comes indeed from the multiplication of the explanatory principles required to interpret educational situations. Learning rhythms can no longer be reduced, neither to an expression of social time (even if their meanings remain socially constructed), nor to a strictly physiological approach. The rhythms determined by biological principles (e.g., time required by the nervous system under specific circumstances to learn or participate in learning activities) as well as social temporalities that shape the learning setting (e.g., rhythms that characterize verbal and nonverbal interactions and the evolution between learners, educators and the collectivities they belong to) are both constitutive of the hybrid time studied by educational theory.

A second aspect inherent to chronobiological and chronopsychological approaches is that they perpetuate a numbered notion of time that limits the representations through which the human body may be depicted and envisioned. As for Plato's rhythmic conception, the epistemology framing research on biological rhythms remains bounded by the assumption that it may (and therefore should) be quantified. Those rhythms are conceived mainly through the measurement of their periodicity. From that perspective, chronobiological and chronopsychological research represent the latest and the most internalized expressions of a metric conception of rhythm that echoes the hegemonic views around quantified time previously discussed.

The case of biological rhythms is exemplary of the difficulties inherent to the dual features associated with rhythms (e.g., privileging their quantifiable vs. qualitative properties). On the one hand, research in chronobiology assumes the relevance of measuring and quantifying physiological rhythms; related advances in medicine, pharmacology, chronopsychology and even in education prove to some extent the legitimacy of such a quantitative approach to interpret specific temporal constraints inherent to physiological functions. On the other hand, such a conception also contributes to an understanding of the human body – and beyond the self – according to principles and symbols that limit the social imaginary of time. The current trend labelled as 'quantified self' illustrates well the ambiguity of this phenomenon.[4] What emerges from those considerations is the necessity to critically reflect on the relevance and the limitations inherent to the quantification of embodied rhythmic phenomena, considering both the functional as well as the symbolic effects it may carry.

The temporal double binds of formal education

The concept of double bind was first introduced by Bateson, Jackson, Haley, & Weakland (1956) in their contribution to a communicational theory of schizophrenia. Beyond its application in psychotherapy, it is commonly used to refer to everyday situations characterized by three components: first, the involvement of an individual in an intense relationship, characterized by the strong necessity to respond appropriately to the situation; second, the individual caught in a situation in which the other member of the relationship expresses two orders of message, and one of these denies the other (typically, the contradictions occurs at two different levels of communication, e.g., verbally and nonverbally); third, the individual unable to comment or act to clarify or correct the expressed contradiction. Double binds are common in family and organization communicational patterns. Their repetition may induce defensive responses, confusion, helplessness or even psychosis (Bateson, Jackson, Haley, & Weakland, 1956).

The use of this concept appears particularly relevant to analyze the nature of the temporal constraints experienced in the contemporary context of formal education. Considering the pedagogical tensions described previously, educators appear to be systematically confronted to injunctions and prescriptions that are contradictory at different levels. Their practice is thus caught into a succession of unsolvable contradictions: on one side, teachers' activity is constrained by a temporal framework, defined by calendars and schedules, that aims at homogenizing the school organization to make it more efficient; on the other side, they have to respond to a democratic and humanistic ideal prescribing the respect of equity and adjustment to individual rhythms. With their students, the dilemma appears between the desire to accommodate the individual learning pace and the wish to maintain cohesion and meaningful socialization within an age cohort. Moreover, school time may be perceived simultaneously as a 'safe environment' protecting slowness and as a place where students should learn to adapt to the quick and ever-changing rhythms characterizing the temporal pressures of 'real life'. From a pedagogical perspective, educators are caught having to take into consideration the temporal adjustments between students (within the classroom and a cohort), between students' rhythms and the curriculum's sequences and between the school and society's temporalities.

The concept of double bind appears also relevant to analyze the temporal contradictions that characterize the professional and organizational dimensions inherent to formal education. For instance, the contradiction between the long-term temporal requirement (involved by the introduction of school reform) and the short-term reality (manifested by high turnover and the lack of temporal availability provided for professional support and training opportunities) typically constitutes a 'mixed message' that reveals itself as a source of confusion and disempowerment. In the same way, the prescription of contradictory requirements, such as programmatic expectations (e.g., requests to plan actions in advance) and strategic necessities (e.g., injunctions to respond instantaneously to unexpected situations) constitutes another form of double bind. From a professional point of view, the experience of time finally reveals the latent contradictions among values, experiences and positions inscribed in the everyday life. From an epistemic perspective, double binds are also inherent to the way time is symbolized and conceived. In spite of the humanistic values that move their proponents, the relevance of instructional time, differentiated curricula or chronobiological research is still 'measured' based on quantitative criteria; learning, inclusion or social justice remain conceived through 'rates' of success. Educators are therefore constrained by the paradoxical injunction to keep quantifying the temporal qualities of education.

From differentiated times to defragmented times

The contributions introduced in this chapter let us believe that throughout the second half of the 20th century, a significant shift occurred in the conception of the relationship between time and the politics of education. The emancipatory aim expressed through the development of rhythmic education at the turn of the 20th century faded away, replaced by the micropolitics of temporal autonomy. The imposition of temporal standards is no longer only a matter of rhythmic patterns imposed by an institution (e.g., church, trade or industry) onto another (e.g., schools). Within a system where people have internalized different temporal norms and expectations, struggles appear within the educational organization itself between professionals but also through inner conflicts experienced individually. Such tensions display a triple feature: they are located at the core of the everyday practice of education; they demonstrate deep contradictions; and they are internalized as being tacit characteristics of this environment. Such temporal constraints may therefore be interpreted as double binds leading to increased defensiveness, confusion or helplessness. As it will be discussed in the following chapter, such a movement has also been reinforced, throughout the century, by the social and cultural transformations that led to the defragmentation of formal education and the increased need to embrace the temporal discontinuities characterizing formal, nonformal and informal education.

Notes

1 As noted by Drazin (1940, pp. 105–106), Rabbis of the Tannaitic period (520 BCE to 200 BCE) already used to classify "individual differences" based on temporal criteria: "They are four type among pupils; swift to hear and swift to lose – his gain is cancelled by his loss; slow to hear and slow to lose – his loss is cancelled by his gain; swift to hear and slow to lose – this is a happy lot; slow to hear and swift to lose – this is an evil lot (Aboth, 5, 12)."
2 As shown by the titles of many references published at that period, the new trend was to criticize the lack of time experienced by educators: *Stop the Clock*; *Breaking the Tyranny of Time*; *Racing with the Clock*; *So Much to Do, so Little Time* (Aronson, 1985; Edelman, Walking Eagle, & Hargreaves, 1997; Livingston, 1994; Rose, 1998; as cited in Chopin, 2010, para. 19).
3 According to Testu (2008, p. xi), the notion of "school rhythm" carries two definitions: "[First] the regular alternance of moments of rest and activity imposed to students by the [institution] . . . It refers to daily and weekly schedules, vacations and school calendars. Such a rhythmicity is environmental or socioecological. Managed by adults and society as a whole, it regulates our mental, psychic and sociological life. [Second] school rhythms are understood as periodic, physiological, physical and psychological variations characterizing the child and the teenager located in school environment. It is then a matter of biological and psychological rhythms."
4 The expression refers to an emerging form of everyday habits and self-awareness, fed by the increasing ubiquity of technologies (e.g., wearable sensors) that make possible

'self-measurement' (e.g., body functions, physical performances). If such a trend presents some interest (e.g., increased awareness of one's physical activity or lack of), the underlying consequence associated with its development is that it shapes a social imaginary of human rhythms as discrete features that can be isolated, abstracted, quantified and measured. Accordingly, it promotes conceptions of health, well-being and personal efficiency grounded into an interpretation of the human body and the self, understood as a 'cyber organism' that could ultimately be managed, controlled and optimized, following strictly rational and measurable principles similar to those regulating instrumental demands. Such a rhythmic conception appears not so distant from the human machine metaphor, developed during the Industrial Age; to some extent, it may represent its updated version, ready to be used for people to internalize sharper rhythmic forms of control, promoted by contemporary industries.

References

Anderson, R.H. (1992, April). *The nongraded elementary school: Lessons from history*. Paper presented at the Annual Meeting of the American Educational Research Association, San Francisco, CA.
Bateson, G., Jackson, D.D., Haley, J., & Weakland, J. (1956). Toward a theory of schizophrenia. *Behavioral Science*, 1(4), 251–254.
Ben-Peretz, M. (1990). Perspectives on time in education. In M. Ben-Peretz, & R. Bromme (Eds.), *The nature of time in schools: Theoretical concepts, practitioner perceptions* (pp.64–77). New York: Teachers College, Columbia University.
Berliner, D.C. (1990). What's all the fuss about instructional time? In M. Ben-Peretz, & R. Bromme (Eds.), *The nature of time in schools: Theoretical concepts, practitioner perceptions* (pp.3–35). New York: Teachers College, Columbia University.
Bloom, B.S. (1968). Learning for mastery. *UCLA-CSEIP Evaluation comment*, 1(2), 1–12.
Carroll, J. (1963). A model of school learning. *Teachers College Record*, 64(8), 723–733.
Cavet, A. (Ed.). (2011). Rythmes scolaires: Pour une dynamique nouvelle des temps éducatifs. *Dossier d'actualité de l'Institut National de Recherche Pédagogique*, 60.
Chevallard, Y. (1991). *La transposition didactique: Du savoir savant au savoir enseigné*. Grenoble, France: Éd. La Pensée Sauvage.
Chevallard, Y., & Mercier, A. (1987). *Sur la formation historique du temps didactique*. Marseille, France: IREM d'Aix-Marseille.
Chopin, M.-P. (2010). Les usages du 'temps' dans les recherches sur l'enseignement. *Revue Française de Pédagogie*, 170, 87–110. Retrieved December 5, 2014, from http://rfp.revues.org/1614
Chopin, M.-P. (2011). *Le temps de l'enseignement: L'avancée du savoir et la gestion des hétérogénéités dans la classe*. Rennes: Presses Universitaires de Rennes.
Connelly, F.M., & Clandinin, D.J. (1990). The cyclic temporal structure of schooling. In M. Ben-Peretz, & R. Bromme (Eds.), *The nature of time in schools: Theoretical concepts, practitioner perceptions* (pp.36–63). New York: Teachers College, Columbia University.
Delhaxhe, A. (1997). Le temps comme unité d'analyse dans la recherche sur l'enseignement. *Revue Française de Pédagogie*, 118, 107–125.
Denham, C.D., & Lieberman, A. (Eds.). (1980). *Time to learn*. Washington, D.C.: National Institute of Education.
Fotinos, G., & Testu, F. (1996). *Aménager le temps scolaire: Théories et pratiques*. Paris: Hachette.
Fraisse, P. (1957). *Psychologie du temps*. Paris: Presses Universitaires de France.
Hall, E.T. (1989). *The dance of life: The other dimension of time*. New York: Anchor Books.

Hargreaves, A. (1994). *Changing teachers, changing times: Teachers' work and culture in the postmodern age*. London: Cassell.
Husti, A. (1999). *La dynamique du temps scolaire*. Paris: Hachette.
Jackson, P. (1968). *Life in classrooms*. New York: Holt, Rinehart and Winston.
Koukkari, W.L., & Sothern, R.B. (2006). *Introducing biological rhythms*. New York: Springer.
Lafleur, C. (2001). A court de temps: Perspectives temporelles dans l'éducation en Ontario. In C. St-Jarre, & L. Dupuy-Walker (Eds.), *Le temps en éducation: Regards multiples* (pp. 193–218). Sainte-Foy, QC: Presses de l'Université du Québec.
Mercier, A. (1995). La biographie didactique d'un élève et les contraintes temporelles de l'enseignement. *Recherches en didactique des mathématiques*, *15*(1), 97–142.
Michon, P. (2012). *Notes éparses sur le rythme comme enjeu artistique, scientifique et philosophique depuis la fin du XVIIIème siècle*. Retrieved December 12, 2013, from http://rhuthmos.eu/spip.php?article540
National Education Commission on Time and Learning. (1994). *Prisoners of time*. US Department of Education. Retrieved September 20, 2009, from http://www2.ed.gov/pubs/PrisonersOfTime/index.html
Perrenoud, O. (2005). *Les cycles d'apprentissage: Vers une nouvelle organisation au service des élève* (Cahiers de la Section des Sciences de l'Education, n°105). Genève, Suisse: Université de Genève.
Perrenoud, P. (2001). Gérer le temps qui reste: L'organisation du travail scolaire entre persécution et attentisme. In C. St-Jarre, & L. Dupuy-Walker (Eds.), *Le temps en éducation: Regards multiples* (pp. 287–316). Sainte-Foy, QC: Presses de l'Université du Québec.
Pineau, G. (2000). *Temporalités en formation: Vers de nouveaux synchroniseurs*. Paris: Anthropos.
Reinberg, A. (1979). *Des rythmes biologiques à la chronobiologie*. Paris: Bordas.
Reviol, A. (2001). Enseigner en Suisse: Un rapport au temps empreint de tensions spécifiques. In C. St-Jarre, & L. Dupuy-Walker (Eds.), *Le temps en éducation: Regards multiples* (pp. 163–192). Sainte-Foy, QC: Presses de l'Université du Québec.
Slattery, P. (1995). A postmodern vision of time and learning: A response to the National Education Commission Report 'Prisoners of time'. *Harvard Educational Review*, *65*(4), 612–633.
Sue, R., & Caccia, M.-F. (2005). *Autres temps, autre école: Impacts et enjeux des rythmes scolaires*. Paris: Retz.
Sue, R., & Rondel, Y. (2001). Rythmes de vie et éducation: Education et modes de vie. *Les Cahiers Millénaire*, *3*(24), 25–53. Retrieved November 20, 2014, from http://www.millenaire3.com/content/download/6992/129867/version/2/file/Millcahier24.pdf
Testu, F. (2008). *Rythmes de vie et rythmes scolaires*. Issy-les-Moulineaux, France: Masson.

Chapter 7

The rhythms of lifelong learning, between continuity and discontinuity

Acknowledging discontinuities

There is a proximity between the ideas of order and continuity. Social order may thus be conceived as an expression of the continuity of institutions and culture. The integrity of the self, as another expression of order, can also be interpreted as a form of continuity, sustained by the capacity to avoid ruptures or the ability to resolve crisis. To some extent, the history of education can be interpreted as a constant search for increasing order, either organizationally (e.g., school's efficiency) or from a social and normative point of view (e.g. equity and justice). Both conservative and progressive functions associated with education may therefore be understood as requiring some form of continuity. If such an assumption probably remains dominant in the social imaginary, another paradigm started, however, emerging a century ago, acknowledging discontinuity as a constraining feature characterizing progress and growth.

The aim of this chapter is to illustrate how educational praxis and theories have been transformed throughout the 20th century by the necessity to take into consideration temporal discontinuity as a specific form of disorder contributing to their organization. At every level of the educational praxis, discontinuity has emerged as a key aspect to be taken into consideration, both from a practical and theoretical point of view. Such a position is going to be developed throughout this chapter considering the activity of learning itself (Whitehead's rhythmic theory of education), the temporal features that characterize respectively the evolution of vocational education (*alternance*), the relationship between formal and informal education (lifelong learning, *tiers-temps scolaire*) and the temporal dimensions inherent to one's existence as they get translated through life histories (schizochrony, epiphanies and *épreuves*). Theories introduced in the following sections were selected because of the importance they give to the temporal and rhythmic aspects of education. Taken as a whole, they demonstrate the role played by the concept of rhythm as a privileged resource to conceive the organization of the temporal complexity inherent to the continuities and discontinuities of educational phenomena.

Continuity, discontinuity and the emergence of the concept of rhythm in modern philosophy

Since the debate that opposed Eleatics to the Pythagoreans 25 centuries ago, the philosophical study of time has been animated by ongoing considerations around the continuous and discontinuous nature of time (Gonord, 2001, p. 217). At the end of the 19th century, influenced by recent scientific discoveries (e.g., evolutionary theory, quantum physics and the theory of relativity), the cultural transformations affecting the subjective experience of time, and in reaction to the classical conceptions of time found in philosophy, such debates gained a new traction, especially through the contributions of philosophers such as Bergson (1859–1941), Whitehead (1861–1947) and Bachelard (1884–1962). Considering the aim of our reflection, their work appears indeed particularly relevant to locate and understand how the concept of rhythm emerged in the contemporary field of philosophy – even if it remained at its margins – and contributed to renew the modern reflection around the experience of time.

Bergson's duration and the creative aim of education

Criticizing the tendency to reduce time to its spatial and homogeneous representation, Bergson (1888/1970) developed a conception privileging the qualitative and heterogeneous aspects of "duration". For him, the experience of duration was at the core of the experience of time. Time was not however a smooth and empty form of perception, as suggested by the Kantian view. Duration – as the fabric of reality – referred to a succession of qualitative changes that merge and penetrate each other without clear borders (Bergson, 1888/1970). Like a melody translates a temporal synthesis between the different notes that compose it, duration was for Bergson a creation, a process of invention and growth, that was fundamentally indivisible and continuous. It could not therefore be reduced to a succession of instants (Sauvanet, 2000). However, Bergson never conceived the idea of continuity on its own. He rather envisioned an experience of continuity – neither static nor linear – that suggested some form of rhythmicity (Worms & Wunenburger, 2008). If the creative tension between continuity and discontinuity was a core feature of Bergson's philosophy, it did not lead him to theorize further the temporal dynamics of education. For him, education had to be conceived through the balance between fidelity to one's cultural inheritance and rupture as a way to promote change and progress. Education was therefore understood through its creative function as a means to transcend habits to accomplish a creative gesture (Lombard, 1997, p. 162).

Bachelard's rhythmanalysis

Bachelard's epistemology was grounded in the idea of crisis. His study of the history of sciences showed indeed how the evolution of rationality and the progress of scientific knowledge were built around the capacity to negotiate epistemological obstacles. For him, the time of scientific discoveries was therefore fundamentally discontinuous (Bachelard, 1931). Accordingly, his conception of *formation* privileged a time made of ruptures (Fabre, 1995). Bachelard (e.g., 1931, 1950) published several writings on time and rhythms, developing his critique of Bergson's philosophy of duration (e.g., Worms & Wunenburger, 2008). Unlike Bergson, he believed that the experience of discontinuity constituted the privileged way to access the understanding of time. The problem for him was no longer to explain the appearance of discontinuity of time in the continuity of duration but rather to explain the appearance of continuity in the discontinuity of lived instants (Sauvanet, 2000, p. 99). Thus, the main divergence between Bergson and Bachelard was that, for the former, temporality was defined as a succession of intertwined qualitative changes that were not distinguished from each other, and for the later, it was defined by the fundamental distinction between discontinuous instants that could be a posteriori reconstructed into a coherent whole (Sauvanet, 2000, p. 99). Bachelard's (1950) view grounded the concept of rhythm against the concept of substance. Like a photon or a chemical substance, he conceived the self as temporal being that 'vibrates', locating the experience of discontinuity at its core (e.g., the divided time of one's action and the fragmented time of one's consciousness). If the life course of the individual is fundamentally divided, rhythm was conceived as what articulates the discontinuity of lived instants (Sauvanet, 2000, p. 110). Bachelard envisioned the self not by its nature but rather through the formative impulse that leads it to renew itself (Fabre, 1995). Repetition and renewal, habit and progress, were all conceived in a philosophy privileging an ongoing effort (Fabre, 1995). The progress of one's own development follows a movement going from an external and contingent to an internal and necessary temporal order (Bachelard, 1950). Progress was always linked to a resourcing, a return to oneself (*reprise de soi*) (Fabre, 1995, p. 164). Bachelard's metaphysics of time opened up a way of living. Thus, he developed an ethic based on the capacity to care and create, through and for the subject, the continuity of one's individuality (Bachelard, 1950; Sauvanet, 2000). His contribution privileged a mode of analysis based on the study of rhythms to provide individuals with a resource to develop balance and coherence (Bachelard, 1950). His philosophy of rest led him to conceive the principles of a rhythmanalytical method, considered nowadays by some authors (e.g., Pineau, 2000) as particularly relevant to envision the temporal aspects of education. This approach will be introduced and discussed in Chapter 10.

Alfred Whitehead's process philosophy

Inspired by Bergson's contribution, Whitehead provided another philosophical ground to conceive the relations between continuity and discontinuity. Like Bachelard, he was influenced by the theoretical advances emerging in physics that were raising ontological questions about the organization of phenomena characterized by instability, unpredictability and ongoing movement (Michon,

2012). In *The Principles of Natural Knowledge*, Whitehead (1919) referred to "objects" and "events" as the two irreducible categories required to develop scientific knowledge; objects were characterized by "sameness", and events displayed "novelty". The concept of rhythm was then introduced to refer to living phenomena that cut across this separation: "the essence of rhythm is the fusion of sameness and novelty" (Whitehead, 1919, p. 198). Later, in *Process and Reality*, Whitehead (1929) elaborated the assumption that "process", rather than substance, should be taken as the most fundamental metaphysical constituent of the world. The idea that "all things flow" would therefore constitute for him a generalization around which philosophical systems should be weaved (Whitehead, 1919, p. 208).

Whitehead's rhythmic theory of education

Based on his own interest for questions of education, Whitehead (1929/1967) applied his process-oriented approach to build up a critique of traditional pedagogy (Riffert, 2005; Woodhouse, 2014). Accordingly, he criticized postulates assuming that pupils' progression should be uniform, steady and linear; learning should follow mechanist and cumulative principles; or education should be compartmentalized and hierarchized. In *The Aims of Education*, Whitehead (1929/1967) defined the terms of a rhythmic theory of education to describe his conception of children's development and the role that teachers may play. For him, the pace of a child's progress and mental development is unsteady and must be differentiated. It varies depending on the periodicity of social life (e.g., alternance between work–play, activity–sleep, seasons and holidays). It also displays "subtler periods of mental growth, with their cyclic recurrences, yet always different as we pass from cycle to cycle, though the subordinate stages are reproduced in each cycle" (Whitehead, 1929/1967, p. 17). Specifically, the concept of rhythm conveys the idea of "difference within a framework of repetition" (Whitehead, 1929/1967, p. 17).

Whitehead grounded his educational theory in two principles, "freedom" and "discipline", whose alternance constitutes the fundamental rhythm of education. For him, the dominant note of education, at its beginning and at its end, is freedom, but there is also an intermediate stage of discipline with freedom in subordination. Such a "threefold cycle of freedom, discipline, and freedom" constitutes a pattern whose repetition composes all mental development. Analyzing such a pattern, Whitehead calls the first period of freedom the "stage of romance", the intermediate period of discipline "stage of precision", and the final period of freedom "stage of generalisation" (Whitehead, 1929/1967, pp. 30–31). The stage of romance referred to the stage of first apprehension: the subject matter has the "vividness of novelty"; it is unexplored yet and exhibits a "wealth of material"; at this stage, knowledge is not dominated by systematic procedure (Whitehead, 1929/1967, p. 17). In the stage of precision, the "exactness of formulation" dominates; it is the "stage of grammar": "It proceeds by forcing on the students' acceptance a given way of analysing the facts, bit by bit" (Whitehead, 1929/1967, p. 18). The stage of generalization was "a return to romanticism with added advantage of classified ideas and relevant technique" (Whitehead, 1929/1967, p. 19). The distinction established by Whitehead was one of emphasis: "romance, precision, generalisation, are all present throughout. But there is an alternation of dominance, and it is this alternation which constitutes the cycle" (Whitehead, 1929/1967, p. 28). According to Whitehead's view, "Education should consist in a continual repetition of such cycles" (Whitehead, 1929/1967, p. 20).

Whitehead's rhythmic theory of education formalized important insights about the temporal nature of learning and autonomy and the way they can be fostered within a formal educational setting. It introduced a model to represent both the pattern and the periodicity constitutive of the rhythmic aspect of education (cf. Chapter 9). Furthermore, it constitutes an innovative attempt to describe the rhythmic aspects that may characterize the relationship between autonomy and dependency in education. To some extent, Whitehead's rhythmic theory provides us indeed with a first attempt to formalize one of the paradoxes of emancipatory education: the fact that the capacity to build up autonomy is embedded into an educational process that is necessarily experienced, at some point, as constraining (cf. Chapter 8).

The rhythms of vocational training

Whitehead's theory located rhythms at the core of the learning process, abstracting from it an ideal conception of educational temporality, mainly conceived within a formal context of transmission of knowledge. The history of vocational learning provides us with a second entry point to envision the continuity and discontinuity of educational praxis beyond the classroom. The following sections illustrate more specifically the crucial role played by the notion of alternance to conceive another rhythmic aspect of education.

From the organization of guilds' apprenticeship to alternance and dual education

In Europe, since the 11th century, guilds – through which artists and craftspeople were professing their art – were perpetuating professional training. The cultural model of apprenticeship and mentorship (*compagnonnage*) privileged experiential training based on both the observation and imitation of the master's gestures and a process of trials and errors in real-life situations (Geay, 1998). During the 13th century, with the expansion of universities, a distinction emerged between the professions relying on liberal arts and those based on mechanical arts. It contributed to the rupture between two forms of temporality: the time of action and production, and the time of study and the mind (Geay, 1998, p. 14). During the 16th century, to avoid wasting material, losing time, or hindering the relationship with the client, night courses were introduced. They constituted the very first form of alternance between work and study. Such a time was enabling the possibility to make mistakes; it was also favoring a didactic progression and taking distance with productive work, which was promoting reflection (Geay, 1998, pp. 16–17). It provided the first basis to conceive a form of education stressing the articulation between two specific moments – one theoretical, one practical – characterized by two distinctive temporalities (Geay, 1998, p. 18) Considering vocational training and technical teaching, the temporal organization of educational practices evolved in Europe following the relationships instituted in each country between apprenticeship and school.

In France, for instance, during the first half of the 20th century, the first forms of alternance involving vocational training for apprentices were organized in the continuation of the *école de demi-temps* (training school for workers created at the beginning of the Industrial Revolution) and the establishment of the new laws regulating apprenticeship (Geay, 1998, pp. 23–25). The word 'alternance' appeared in 1946 in the charter of a movement of rural education to designate the alternance of stays between the family house and the farm (Geay, 1999, p. 108). With the surge of the 'all school' (*tout-école*) principle, the practice of apprenticeship was progressively discontinued, unlike Germany, which kept its 'dual system'. A second period started at the end of the 1960s. The notion of "alternated education" (*éducation alternée*) was then introduced to describe the discontinuities associated with the activity of study, conceived as part of *éducation permanente* (Geay, 1999, p. 108). In Europe, this discourse became part of Organization for Economic Cooperation and Development's (OECD's) policy and triggered the utopia of "another school" (Schwartz, 1977, as cited in Geay, 1999, p. 108) entirely structured and organized according to an alternated form, conceived as a pedagogical rupture aiming at sustaining students' motivation. Starting during the 1970s, in a difficult economical context, alternance was conceived as a new form of relationship between vocational training and employment (Geay, 1998, 1999).

Systemic-institutionalist and cognitivo-institutional approaches to alternance

During the past 40 years, the idea of alternance has been conceptualized and inspired by various theoretical backgrounds (Geay, 1998, 1999; Pineau, 2000). Among the models developed in France, Bourgeon's (1979) contribution theorized the rhythmic organization of systems of alternance, taking explicitly into consideration their systemic and institutional features. His contribution distinguished three forms of social settings based on specific organizational temporalities. The first one, "juxtapositive alternance" refers to two periods of different activities (e.g., work and study) without any connection between them (Bourgeon, 1979, p. 35). The training setting relies on the creation of learning spaces and times autonomous from each other (e.g., evening classes or training courses organized at the end of the day). Through institutional standards (e.g., laws regulating continuing education and credits management), school and professional organizations impose a temporal framework to the different actors involved without considering their learning strategies or the means required to foster the integration of knowledge (Geay, 1999, p. 113). As teaching units remain homogenized, such a format privileges bureaucratic organization; it does not however favor people's capacity to self-organize their learning (Pineau, 2000, p. 157). "Associative alternance" constitutes a second form of temporal organization which relies on the association between general and vocational training (Bourgeon, 1979, p. 36). The educational system acknowledges the role played by professional practice, and participants' agency is taken into consideration. It requires both an adjustment between training's offer and demand and a temporal organization based on time units that are longer than traditional hours of course (e.g., full day or weekend) (Pineau, 2000, p. 157). The possibilities of encounter between different partners (e.g., students, mentors and internship supervisors) opens up a network of relationships that goes beyond the standardizing effects inherent to a centralized educational system; however, considering the singularity of the different environments through which each person evolves, the institutionalization of such relationships remains precarious (Geay, 1999, p. 114). Finally, Bourgeon (1979, p. 37, my translation) defined a third kind of alternance, called "copulative". It suggests an "effective compenetration of the socio-professional and school environments within a formative temporal unit". In this type of setting, the power of the instituted forces (e.g., vocational school and work environment) is limited to the organization of the training time and space (e.g., training sessions), the definition of the learning objectives and the organization of certifying assessment. The learning strategies and the conditions of alternance remain for the most part negotiated between the partners themselves, as individuals, networks or groups (Geay, 1999). The privileged temporality is no longer the one characterizing the administrative time unit of the institution; it is rather the persons who participates in the training. Such a system privileges therefore the time of *auto-formation* (Pineau, 2000, p. 157).

To theorize further the relationships developed between people's autonomy and institutional structures, Bourgeon's contribution was eventually enriched by alternative conceptions articulating his model with a cognitivist perspective, inspired by Piagetian theory (e.g., Lerbet, 1981, as cited in Geay, 1998, 1999; Pineau, 2000). Such an approach led to the study of the relationships existing between institutional temporalities and the regulatory rhythms that characterize the cognitive development of learners (Geay, 1999; Pineau, 2000, p.156). Such theories provide scholars with additional resources to conceive the functions and the conditions required for the experience of discontinuity to be part of an educational rhythm that benefits the learners and contributes to their professionalization (Alhadeff-Jones, 2014; Roquet, 2007; Zaid & Lebeaume, 2015). The change of environment and the succession of heterogeneous tasks introduce discontinuities. Those are negotiated according to a design and a setting that translates various types of temporal constraints (e.g., political, social and technical), learning results therefore from the modalities according to which they are negotiated, reproduced or imposed among the actors involved. Learners' capacities to increase their autonomy also depends on the psychological processes involved and how their individual rhythms match the collective organization. The learners' autonomy appears finally as an emergence, conditioned by hybrid rhythmic patterns (e.g., training's organization and succession of cognitive operations) and periodicities (e.g., training's frequency and tasks' repetitions) whose regulation is at the core of the experience of temporal constraints.

The rhythms of formal and informal education

With the case of alternance, we have explored how vocational training may be shaped by the rhythmic constraints that unfold at the junction between two systems (school and work) and two levels of organization (individual and institutional). A third way to conceive the dialogical relationships between the continuity and discontinuity of education suggests one take into consideration the rhythms that pace the alternance between formal and informal learning throughout the life span. To contextualize this observation, the next section briefly locates some of the social and cultural changes that significantly affected the experience of time in Western countries throughout the 20th century. With the recognition of the ideas of *éducation permanente* (Delors, 1996, as cited in Fourcade, 2009) and lifelong learning, the following section describes the emergence of a new paradigm that acknowledges and expresses a new understanding of the heterogeneity of formative places and times. If education is now conceived as an ongoing process, it remains that such a 'duration' is organized around rhythms that integrate the discontinuity inherent to the increased heterogeneity of learning experiences and settings. To illustrate such a phenomenon, the discontinuities of compulsory education will be then considered more specifically.

The increased differentiation of social times, the invention of the everyday life and the individualization of the life course

Throughout the 19th century, the genesis of industrial time contributed to the regularization of working conditions, the division of labor and the exercise of new forms of temporal discipline. This emerging order contributed to the reorganization of the entire rhythm of Western societies, influencing deeply other temporalities, such as those shaping religious, family or personal life (Pronovost, 1996). Throughout the 20th century, such an institutional and organizational order came to be challenged by the progressive transformations that affected the organization of the state, work and economy and the way their influence was experienced in the every day. During the period between the two world wars, time dedicated to leisure started to expand among workers and the experience of freed time emerged, providing them with an increased sense of autonomy. Such a movement grew after 1945, in parallel with the development of leisure activity and the rise of a consumerist society (Pronovost, 1996). Throughout the second half of the 20th century, a new way of perceiving one's own time emerged in the Western world. In parallel with the institutionalization of the life course (e.g., childhood and school, adulthood and work, and old age and retirement), the 'everyday life' became the temporal reference point. As analyzed by Nowotny (1994, pp. 102–103), the tensions lived around daily tasks became the locus of temporal conflicts involving the value and the quality of people's "proper time".

Toward the end of the 20th century, the relationship between working time and free time evolved: on the one hand, regular and standard working time ceased to be the compulsory model implemented within professional environments; on the other hand, people were increasingly looking for self-determination in the way they were organizing the temporalities of the heterogeneous spheres of their life (Nowotny, 1994, pp. 108–109). Today, within postindustrial societies, the notion of a consistent working life has lost its consistency: "Average employment . . . involves alternating phases of work and further training, voluntary and involuntary discontinuities of occupation, innovative career switching strategies, and even self-chosen alternation between employment and family centered phases (Arthur, Inkson, & Pringle, 1999)" (Alheit & Dausien, 2007, p. 59). Such changes have affected people's expectations and made individual life planning a much riskier enterprise (Alheit & Dausien, 2007, p. 59). For employment agencies, social and pension institutions or the educational system, the deregulation and increased flexibility characterizing the contemporary evolution of the labor market introduced new challenges related to the necessity to regulate the increasing amount of discontinuity (e.g., personal or professional transitions and reorientations) and unpredictability experienced (e.g., due to a larger number of options available); such phenomena eventually contributed to a greater sense of "individualization" marking people's life trajectories (Alheit & Dausien, 2007, p. 59).

Permanent education and the continuity of lifelong learning

To some extent, expressions such as '*éducation permanente*' and 'lifelong learning' represent semantic markers whose frequency in the rhetoric of education demonstrates the rising awareness of the qualitative discontinuities shaping educational praxis and individual existence. Rooted in the first efforts made to promote universal instruction during the 19th century, those notions were initially found during the 20th century in both the development of technical or scientific education for adults and in popular education initiatives that aimed at transmitting cultural inheritance and developing collective actions (Fourcade, 2009; Pineau, 2000).

In the 1960s, the notion of *éducation permanente* was developed in France to include the whole of the training actions found in the school and higher and professional education. It was conceived as "total education concerned by all the dimensions of personality, all the phases of individual existence and all the social categories" (Fourcade, 2009, p. 919, my translation). In the 1970s, international organizations, such as United Nations Educational, Scientific and Cultural Organization (UNESCO) or OECD, contributed to the recognition of those notions. The expressions "lifelong learning" or "recurring education" were introduced in a social context characterized by the general calling into question of educational systems (Fourcade, 2009). The report titled *Learning to Be. The World of Education Today and Tomorrow* (Faure, 1972, as cited in Fourcade, 2009) recommended the integration of formal and informal contexts of education and a fair distribution of the resources allocated to both of them as well as to educational activities occurring throughout the different ages of life. During the 1990s, the notion of lifelong learning reappeared in a context interpreted through the lenses of the "knowledge economy" and the "learning society" (Fourcade, 2009). Its use stressed at that time the necessity to implement the social and political conditions required to allow everyone to pursue one's own education in a formal environment (e.g., school system and adult education), nonformal context (e.g., outside formal systems but within civil society's organizations) or informally (e.g., everyday learning, self-directed learning and *auto-formation*).

For Pineau (2000), the emergence of *éducation permanente*, as a movement, and *a fortiori* lifelong learning should be interpreted as an attempt to reply to the 'temporal crisis' that marked the end of the 20th and the beginning of the 21st century.

> Educational time is no longer seen exclusively as the one that precedes the other times (initial education), or the one that is inserted in between them (recurring education and alternance), but as the one that results from their change.
> (Pineau, 2000, p. 35, my translation)

Thus, the critical aim of *éducation permanente* would be grounded in the transgression of the discontinuity instituted between "educational time" and "non-educational time" (Pineau, 2000, p. 35).

The discontinuities of compulsory education and the rise of educational third-time

Traditionally, when envisioning the formative years that constitute the first period of life, school time appears as the core 'duration' taken into consideration. As such, it is however neither smooth nor continuous (Sue & Rondel, 2001). Besides instructional time – itself divided – school time also includes breaks, time required to transfer between classrooms, transition times between activities and so on (Sue & Rondel, 2001). Since the 1980s, the assumption that school time constitutes the continuity located at the core of the educational experience of children started to be challenged, even if it still remains largely dominant

(Sue & Rondel, 2001). Extracurricular time (e.g., mealtime or nursery), out-of-school time (e.g., weekends and vacations) and more broadly free time, as it is experienced at any age, but especially during childhood and adolescence, became central issues that could no longer be conceived as "residual time" or marginal discontinuities within the continuum of someone's education (Sue & Rondel, 2001, pp. 27–28).

For Sue and Rondel (2001, p. 32), the progressive decrease of the amount of school time observed in France throughout the 20th century contributed to the emergence of what those authors have labeled "educational third-time" (*tiers-temps éducatif*): "the whole of educational actions that happen during the time available for children between school, family and personal time, when all the other physiological functions are fulfilled" (Sue & Rondel, 2001, p. 32, my translation). The emergence of educational third-time contributed to the implementation of innovative educational practices, letting more room for the individualization of learning (Sue & Caccia, 2005, p. 25). Such periods being under the responsibility of families, situations remain, however, contrasted depending on parents' financial resources, culture, professions, educational options chosen, place of residency, proximity and availability of close family or friends (Sue & Rondel, 2001, p. 28). Depending on the way such free time is used (e.g., after-school programs), it can contribute to reproduce or even increase social inequalities and fragmentation; it can also become an educational time if the child has the capacity required to master it (Sue & Caccia, 2005, p. 26).

For Sue and his collaborators, conceiving free time as an educational time challenges the status of school time as it can no longer be considered as exclusive educational time. Such an evolution requires that children learn earlier to anticipate and exercise some form of control over the temporal organization of their everyday lives to integrate better the discontinuities of their formative time. It may also require the valorization of educational resources associated with extracurricular and out-of-school time and the search for new synergies with school time as well (Sue & Caccia, 2005, p. 26). What remains at stake is the capacity to establish connections between knowledge acquired within and outside school and to develop a "time of educational connection" (*temps de reliance éducative*) among school, family and leisure, susceptible to foster the development of transversal competencies. For Sue and Caccia (2005, p. 124), establishing some form of continuity for the learners, rather than transforming the institution, finally requires one to acknowledge the role of such discontinuities to erase the discriminatory bias associated with extracurricular and out-of-school practices where irreducible inequalities are produced.

Reconfiguring the rhythms of existence

Conceiving education as an ongoing process, unfolding through formal and informal spaces and times at every age of life has consequences that go far beyond curricular and organizational preoccupations. It carries an existential weight that fundamentally affects the way adulthood itself is conceived. Like the institution of school time contributed to redefine the meaning of childhood, the institution of permanent education and lifelong learning contributed to redefine the status of adulthood and the perception of its development. From the modernist interpretation of the adult, conceived as the "norm" defining maturity, characterized by the completion of a full growth to which other age categories (e.g., children or elderly) were compared, one started acknowledging since the end of the 1970s the "incompletion of adult age" (Lapassade, 1963) or its "immaturity" (Boutinet, 1998). Adulthood appeared then as characterized by an identitary malaise and precariousness – especially emotional and economical – that may eventually be tackled by lifelong learning efforts (Boutinet, 2007). Among the training and research trends that have emerged as a response to the new challenges associated with the reconfiguration of adulthood, educational practices grouped under the umbrella of life history and biographical approaches appear as particularly central. They provide us with a fourth and last entry point to study the rhythmic aspects inherent to the continuity and discontinuity of one's existence.

Life history, biographical approaches and the work of time in adult education

Considering the relationship between biography and education, the activity of narrating one's own life is inscribed in a long tradition made of practices and writings (e.g., autobiography, *Bildungsroman*) through which philosophers, thinkers, or authors, have represented and narrated one's existence as a way to develop oneself (Delory-Momberger, 2003). In the contemporary field of education, the use of life history and biographical methodologies emerged during the 1980s, reinforcing an existing trend already present in social science (e.g., Chamberlayne, Bornat, & Wengraf, 2000; Pineau & Le Grand, 1993). In adult education more specifically, such approaches have privileged an understanding of personal development, growth, or manifestations of human agency as experienced by subjects located in specific historical and social contexts (West, Alheit, Andersen, & Merrill, 2007). Conceiving learning as a process rather than a product, biographical approaches have contributed to the development of a broad range of research and training practices focusing on the dynamic aspects of education.

From a temporal perspective, the implementation of life history and biographical methods by adult educators constitutes a resource helping individuals shaping the temporalities constitutive of their own lives. It provides them with an opportunity to gather and organize heterogeneous experiences, moments and aspects of their existence to elaborate, through the formulation and the sharing of a (written and/or oral) narrative, a more or less cohesive whole giving a specific consistency to their history. The time of one's life constitutes therefore the raw material used within a process of self-construction to unify the temporality of the self and reinforce one's identity (Alhadeff-Jones, Lesourd, Roquet, & Le Grand, 2011; Lesourd, 2006). According to Ricoeur (1990), the evasive character of real life requires indeed people to use narratives to organize retrospectively the meaning given to their own experiences. The capacity to elaborate such a 'plot' (*intrigue*) is therefore located at the core of the linguistic, psychological and social processes through which one learns to develop a "narrative identity". For McAdams (1993), the genesis of such a capacity appears as the condition required for someone to appropriate the meaning of one's own time and historicity. From a sociological perspective, Alheit (1992, as cited in Alheit & Dausien, 2007, p. 66) refers to the notion of "biographicity" to describe the ability to reconfigure the meaning of one's lifeworld in such a way that self-reflexive activities begin to shape the way one relates to a given social context (e.g., increased capacity to make purposeful life choices). The reinterpretation of one's biography provides therefore individuals with the resource to reshape the contours of their lives within the limits of the social context that bounds their trajectory (Alheit & Dausien, 2007, p. 66).

Through their multiple expressions, educational practices that privilege the use of biography or life history assume the potential benefits inherent to the organizing effects, catalyzed by the production and the sharing of a narrative. For Dominicé (2000), such a formative dimension meshes with participants' quests for *complétude* as an expression of the human need to unify the plural facets – often lived as divided – of one's own personal existence (e.g., professional life, family, culture, political commitment and spirituality). From a temporal perspective, such a divide relates to an experience of fragmentation and discontinuity that can be apprehended through at least two different perspectives. Considering the simultaneous presence of heterogeneous times, fragmentation may appear through the difficulty to maintain cohesion between the multiple intertwined temporalities (e.g., physical, biological, psychological and social) that are constitutive of the fabric of everyday life. Considering the diachronic aspect of time, discontinuity may appear as an emergence (e.g., crisis or bifurcation) breaking through and disrupting what would have been otherwise experienced as a more or less ordered sequence of actions (e.g., life course).

Fragmentation and intertwined temporalities

Dominicé (2007) evokes the notion of "double belonging" to characterize the personal tensions inherent to the divide between complementary and antagonistic aspects of one's life: family versus working life; social background versus professional career; urban life versus rural roots; conflicting traditions; cultural, linguistic or racial mix and so on. Those aspects of one's life express and evolve through different rhythms and temporalities. Therefore, whenever they appear as too divergent from each other, they may be experienced as fragmented. This reinforces a feeling of being split between caring and being productive, the history of one's family and one's own trajectory, the rhythms that characterize the places where one comes from versus where one lives, the rhythms of one's verbal expression versus the rhythms of one's thinking and so on. Because it may limit one's sense of agency, the lack of congruence between concomitant facets of one's life, as they may be experienced or reflected at a specific time, may therefore represent a significant source of temporal constraint.

Adopting a broader perspective, Pineau (2000) proposed the neologism "schizochrony" (from the Greek *schizo-*, meaning divide, and *chronos*, time) to refer to the various forms of temporal divide that are experienced and eventually lead individuals to the feeling of being temporally alienated. Such divides occur for instance between the qualitative aspects of lived time (e.g., the feeling of flow) and the social necessity to remain temporally oriented and therefore quantify and measure one's time (e.g., checking the hour or the date). The reference to chronological time and the prescription to objectivize one's temporal experience may thus split the subject's experience of time (e.g., the flow that emerges from within the course of action), leading discontinuity to take over the creative experience of duration. At the opposite, the absence of temporal markers, or the impossibility to relate one's own rhythm to a collective time, may also lead to a feeling of exclusion or "temporal exile" (Lesourd, 2006, p.21); for instance, the experience of being unemployed may lead one to lose track of social rhythms, such as those prescribed by working schedules, and suffer from such a lack of temporal structure (Demazière, 2006). Schizochrony also appears through the desynchronization that happens between the experience of the social times that shape everyday activity (e.g., work, rest and consumption) and the physical time that paces natural phenomena (e.g., circadian or seasonal cycles); it prevents then people to connect their daily existence to broader cycles, including the symbolic or metaphysical meanings they may carry. Schizochrony is also manifest when a divide occurs between social times and biological rhythms: it can either emerge when an individual is led to neglect one's own inner rhythms to follow the pace given by external temporalities or when, due to physiological constraints (e.g., health issues or aging), someone cannot keep up with external temporal expectations.

Discontinuities within the life course

A second kind of temporal disorder can be identified when the experience of the life course is disrupted by an event that disorganizes what would have been otherwise experienced as a more or less ordered sequence of actions and eventually provokes deeper transformations of the self. Such discontinuities have been conceptualized referring to various ideas, depending on the disciplinary and theoretical framework mobilized to interpret their formative effects. The notions of epiphany and *épreuve* concentrate well the meaning that may be associated with discontinuities occurring throughout the life course.

The use of the notion of epiphany tends to stress the psychological dimensions associated with the experience of discontinuity. The term itself derives from the Greek word '*epiphainesthai*' meaning 'to appear' or 'to come into view'; it generally refers to an experience of great revelation and a catalyst for personal growth (McDonalds, 2005, p. 11). In human sciences, Denzin (1989, 1990, as cited in McDonalds, 2005) has defined epiphanies as interactional moments that leave a mark on people's lives and have the potential to create transformational experiences for the person. They are related to existential crises whose effects may be both positive and/or negative. Epiphanies reveal someone's character and alter the fundamental meaning structures in a person's life. They also catalyze the perception of a new identity. According to McDonalds's (2005, p. 45) extensive literature review, the use of the notion of epiphany (or similar notions found in the literature, such as "vital moment", "nuclear episode", or "quantum change") seems to gather six core characteristics: (a) antecedent states (e.g., periods of depression, anxiety and inner turmoil); (b) suddenness; (c) personal transformation (e.g., transformation in self-identity); (d) illumination or insight (i.e., acute awareness of something new); (e) meaning making (i.e., profound and significant insights); and (f) enduring nature (i.e., while the actual epiphany is a momentary experience, the personal transformation that results is permanent and lasting).

The notion of *épreuve* provides us with additional meanings. As noted by Baudouin (2014), the notion of *épreuve* appears closely related to those of "bifurcation" or "event" frequently used in social theory. It tends to orientate the reflection toward the linguistic and sociological aspects inherent to the description of formative discontinuities within the life course rather than their psychological dimensions. From a semiotic perspective, an *épreuve* is what defines the core of a narration, the basic unit that enables the configuration and the structuration of the plot that organizes a narrative (Baudouin, 2014). The role played by *épreuves* within a narration explains why, from a methodological perspective, the collection of a life history tends to systematically highlight critical episodes and discontinuities rather than the redundancy of everyday routines. The notion of *épreuve* emerged in social theory during the 1980s (Baudouin & Frétigné, 2013). For Boltanski and Thévenot (1991/2006), the notion is used to refer to situations of conflict or disputes that disrupt the normal course of events and everyday routines. *Épreuves* may be experienced as critical because they test and reveal the values and qualities of the subjects involved within a situation whose outcome remains fundamentally uncertain. Following a different perspective, Martuccelli (2006) conceives the succession of a series of *épreuves* as what constitutes the subjective experience and the singularity of someone's life. They cannot be separated from the history of the subject, and at the same time, they constitute some kind of test through which the individual's supports and resources are evaluated within a socially and historically determined situation (e.g., at school, at work and in the family). *Épreuves* appear de facto as challenges and operations of selection. They articulate the social and contextual order that defines for instance an institution or a specific historical period with the singular history of a person.

The experience of temporal fragmentation and discontinuity as engines for growth

With the research conducted in the field of life history and biographical approaches, the meaning of an existential temporality appears through the elaboration of one's own historicity and the singularity of one's life trajectory. Education is no longer only conceived as a matter of everyday routines and habits that require acknowledgment and organization on a daily basis. Because existence is fragmented and divided by heterogeneous temporalities (e.g., schizochrony) and because it is organized around events experienced as challenging discontinuities (e.g., epiphanies or *épreuves*), it requires an effort to be lived as a more or less coherent whole. As suggested by Bachelard (1931), the feeling of continuity experienced by the self is not a given; it is work (*oeuvre*). Considering the practices described in this section to be conceived as formative, such work has been envisioned through the elaboration and socialization of a narrative that brings a person or a group to reconstruct their experience of time. As long as they can be reflected and elaborated, temporal fragmentation and lived discontinuities may appear as engines for growth and transformation. From this perspective, the experience of alienation would come from the inability to elaborate new or alternative meanings to gather into a coherent story what would be otherwise experienced as an unrelated aggregate of heterogeneous rhythms belonging to disparate domains of one's life or a succession of separate events or crises challenging the long-term cohesion of the self. Emancipatory education would emerge therefore as an organizing process through which one learns to relate what constitutes the fragments and discontinuities of one's own life.

From the experience of discontinuity to the educational power of rhythmic organization

Whitehead's rhythmic theory of education and theories of alternance, or *tiers-temps scolaire*, provide us with models to conceive the articulation between the continuity and discontinuity of educational experiences. They organize continuity and discontinuity around specific temporal patterns and periodicities highlighting respectively the repetition of cycles alternating freedom and constraint, study and work, individual and organizational requirements or formal and informal learning. Taking into consideration the idiosyncrasy of life histories, another aspect of the rhythmicity of education emerged. What we will define in Chapter 9 as the 'rhythmic movement' of education reveals thus a third criterion defining educational temporalities: their organization around the unique configuration of single events located at the junction between one's life history and the social and historical contexts within which they unfold. As shown with the problematic of *épreuves*, such singularities carry meanings that are socially constructed. The rhythmic movement of education is therefore revealed through the way discontinuities are experienced individually and collectively. At the same time, the meanings of such discontinuities depend on their inscription within the historical movement of education as an institution evolving through its own temporality. Finally, the emergence of contemporary practices focusing on the importance to relate discontinuous rhythms (within a learning task, between institutions or between heterogeneous spheres of one's life) demonstrates the educational power inherent to the capacity to elaborate resources and narratives that participate to the individual and collective construction of temporal cohesion. The third part of this book will question and explore further this idea, focusing more specifically on the emancipatory dimension of a rhythmanalytical framework as initially conceived by Bachelard.

References

Alhadeff-Jones, M. (2014). Pour une approche réflexive et critique des rapports entre temporalités et professionnalisation. *Revue Phronesis, 3*(4), 4–12.

Alhadeff-Jones, M., Lesourd, F., Roquet, P., & Le Grand, J.-L. (2011). Questioning the temporalities of transformative learning in a time of crisis. In M. Alhadeff-Jones, & A. Kokkos (Eds.), *Transformative learning in time of crisis: Individual and collective challenges. Proceedings of the 9th International Transformative Learning Conference* (pp.394–407). New York & Athens: Teachers College, Columbia University & The Hellenic Open University.

Alheit, P., & Dausien, B. (2007). Lifelong learning and biography: A competitive dynamic between the macro- and the micro level of education. In L. West, P. Alheit, A.S. Andersen, & B. Merrill (Eds.), *Using biographical and life history approaches in the study of adult and lifelong learning: European perspective* (pp.57–70). Berlin: Peter Lang.

Bachelard, G. (1931). *L'intuition de l'instant.* Paris: Stock.

Bachelard, G. (1950). *La dialectique de la durée.* Paris: Presses Universitaires de France.

Baudouin, J.M. (2014). La phrase qui tue: La notion d'épreuve, de la dissémination à la conceptualisation. In J. Friedrich, & J.C. Pita Castro (Eds.), *La recherche en formation des adultes: Un dialogue entre concept et réalité* (pp.223–251). Dijon, France: Raison & Passions.

Baudouin, J.M., & Frétigné, C. (2013). La question des épreuves et la recherche en formation d'adultes: Quelques éléments prospectifs. *Savoirs, 33,* 95–104.

Bergson, H. (1970). *Essai sur les données immédiates de la conscience.* Paris: Presses Universitaires de France. (Original work published 1888)

Boltanski, L., & Thévenot, L. (2006). *On justification: Economies of worth* (C. Porter, Trans.). Princeton: Princeton University Press. (Original work published 1991)

Bourgeon, G. (1979). *Socio-pédagogie de l'alternance.* Paris: UNMFREO.

Boutinet, J.-P. (1998). *L'immaturité de la vie adulte.* Paris: Presses Universitaires de France.

Boutinet, J.-P. (2007). Les temporalités de la vie adulte en context postmoderne, un changement de perspective. *Carriérologie, 11*(1), 23–32.

Chamberlayne, P., Bornat, J., & Wengraf, T. (Eds.). (2000). *The turn to biographical methods in social science.* London: Routledge.

Delory-Momberger, C. (2003). *Biographie et éducation: Figures de l'individu-projet.* Paris: Anthropos.

Demazière, D. (2006). Le chômage comme épreuve temporelle. In J. Thoemmes, & G. De Terssac (Eds.), *Les temporalités sociales: Repères méthodologiques* (pp.121–132). Toulouse: Octarès.

Dominicé, P. (2000). *Learning from our lives: Using educational biographies with adults.* San Francisco: Jossey-Bass.

Dominicé, P. (2007). *La formation biographique*. Paris: L'Harmattan.
Fabre, M. (1995). *Bachelard éducateur*. Paris: Presses Universitaires de France.
Fourcade, B. (2009). La formation tout au long de la vie. In J.-M. Barbier, E. Bourgeois, G. Chapelle, & J.-C. Ruano-Borbalan (Eds.), *Encyclopédie de la formation* (pp.915–955). Paris: Presses Universitaires de France.
Geay, A. (1998). *L'école de l'alternance*. Paris: L'Harmattan.
Geay, A. (1999). Actualité de l'alternance (note de synthèse). *Revue Française de Pédagogie*, *128*, 107–125.
Gonord, A. (2001). *Le temps*. Paris: Flammarion.
Lapassade, G. (1963). *L'entrée dans la vie: Essai sur l'inachèvement de l'homme*. Paris: Editions de Minuit.
Lesourd, F. (2006). Des temporalités éducatives: Note de synthèse. *Pratiques de Formation / Analyses*, *51–52*, 9–72.
Lombard, J. (1997). *Bergson: Création et éducation*. Paris: L'Harmattan.
Martuccelli, D. (2006). *Forgé par l'épreuve*. Paris: Armand Colin.
McAdams, D.P. (1993). *The stories we live by: Personal myths and the making of the self*. New York: Guilford Press.
McDonald, M.G. (2005). *Epiphanies: An existential philosophical and psychological inquiry*. Doctoral dissertation, University of Technology, Sydney.
Michon, P. (2012). *Notes éparses sur le rythme comme enjeu artistique, scientifique et philosophique depuis la fin du XVIIIème siècle*. Retrieved December 12, 2013, from http://rhuthmos.eu/spip.php?article54
Nowotny, H. (1994). *Time: The modern and postmodern experience*. Cambridge, MA: Blackwell.
Pineau, G. (2000). *Temporalités en formation: Vers de nouveaux synchroniseurs*. Paris: Anthropos.
Pineau, G., & Le Grand, J.-L. (1993). *Les histoires de vie*. Paris: Presses Universitaires de France.
Pronovost, G. (1996). *Sociologie du temps*. Bruxelles: De Boeck.
Ricoeur, P. (1990). *Soi-même comme un autre*. Paris: Seuil.
Riffert, F.G. (Ed.). (2005). *Alfred North Whitehead on learning and education: Theory and application*. Newcastle, UK: Cambridge Scholar Press.
Roquet, P. (2007). La diversité des processus de professionnalisation: Une question de temporalités? *Carriérologie*, *11*(1), 195–207.
Sauvanet, P. (2000). *Le rythme et la raison (vol.2): Rythmanalyses*. Paris: Kimé.
Sue, R., & Caccia, M.-F. (2005). *Autres temps, autre école: Impacts et enjeux des rythmes scolaires*. Paris: Retz.
Sue, R., & Rondel, Y. (2001). Rythmes de vie et éducation: Education et modes de vie. *Les Cahiers Millénaire*, *3*(24), 25–53. Retrieved November 20, 2014, from http://www.millenaire3.com/content/download/6992/129867/version/2/file/Millcahier24.pdf
West, L., Alheit, P., Andersen, A.S., & Merrill, B. (2007). *Using biographical and life history approaches in the study of adult and lifelong learning: European perspectives*. Frankfurt am Main: Peter Lang.
Whitehead, A.N. (1919). *The principles of natural knowledge*. London: Cambridge University Press.
Whitehead, A.N. (1929). *Process and reality*. New York: The Free Press.
Whitehead, A.N. (1929/1967). *The aims of education and other essays*. New York: The Free Press.
Woodhouse, H. (2014). Alfred N. Whitehead. In D.C. Phillips (Ed.), *Encyclopedia of educational theory and philosophy* (pp.849–852). London: Sage.
Worms, F., & Wunenburger, J.-J. (Eds.). (2008). *Bachelard et Bergson: Continuité et discontinuité*. Paris: Presses Universitaires de France.
Zaid, A., & Lebeaume, J. (Eds.). (2015). *La formation d'ingénieurs en alternance: Rythmes et temporalités vécus*. Villeneuve d'Ascq, France: Presses Universitaires du Septentrion.

Part III

Theorizing the rhythms of emancipation in education

Chapter 8

The meanings of emancipation within a context of temporal alienation

As it appeared throughout the previous chapters, the relationship between temporal constraints and autonomy is shaped by multiple logics. On the one hand, the prescription of temporal norms and the implementation of temporal discipline reduce individuals' margins of freedom: power is exercised through the imposition of fixed schedules, sequences of actions or the influence of specific rhythms to regulate what would be otherwise perceived as asynchronous, unpredictable or uncontrollable behaviors. On the other hand, the increased confusion and disorder inherent to conflicting temporal demands, as well as the fragmentation and the discontinuities that punctuate the life course, emerge as disorganizing factors that tend to increase uncertainty and instability: temporal double binds or schizochrony constitute thus disempowering experiences that prevent one to develop a genuine sense of autonomy. In the contemporary societal context – at least in Western countries – the effects of such dynamics have become more intense, influenced by the increased preponderance of 'speed' within our society. Such phenomena have brought scholars to focus more specifically on how people experience and eventually suffer from a greater sense of urgency, a more intense pace of life and a sustained (sometimes unsustainable) feeling of acceleration of their everyday lives.

In this temporal environment, what does it mean to be emancipated, and what does a process of emancipation involve? To address such questions, the aim of this chapter is to frame how emancipation can be theorized, from a temporal and rhythmic perspective, and identify the issues that such an attempt may raise from an epistemological and educational point of view as well. At the core, it is assumed that a process of emancipation should be conceived as a temporal phenomenon, composed through specific rhythms, and that it must be contextualized in relation to specific forms of temporal alienation. This chapter is organized around four sections. The first one discusses the emancipatory aim of education and some of the paradoxes characterizing the implementation of critical pedagogies. Considering such contradictions from an epistemological point of view, the next section reinterprets the relationship between autonomy and dependence from a dialogical and process-oriented rhythmical perspective. To locate our contribution in relation to contemporary reflections around the disempowering experience of time in Western societies, the third section explores the meaning of temporal alienation, focusing in particular on phenomena such as social acceleration and urgency. In the final section, the impact of those phenomena is considered in education through two emerging trends (accelerated learning and slow education). Identifying some of their limitations, we will stress the importance to define a theoretical framework within which the relationship between pace of change (i.e., the experience of time) and autonomy could be theorized more systematically.

The emancipatory aim of education

Defining emancipation

The concept of emancipation stems from Roman law, where it referred to the act through which a slave or a child was given the right to become a free man (Bouillet, 1859, as cited in Institut National de la Langue Française, 2005, *émancipation*). In modern civil law, it refers to a solemn act or a benefit resulting from marriage through which a minor child is freed from the father's authority and/ or guardianship. Emancipation literally means to give away ownership (*ex*: away; *mancipum*: ownership). More broadly it means to relinquish one's authority over someone (Biesta, 2010, p. 41). By extension, the term refers to the action of freeing or liberating (oneself) from a state of dependency or the state that results from such an action. In the figurative sense, the expression evokes the freeing from a moral dependency or from the prejudices from one's time (e.g., emancipation of thought or political, intellectual and sexual emancipation) (Institut National de la Langue Française, 2005, *émancipation*). During the 17th century, emancipation came to be used in relation to religious toleration, during the 18th century in relation to the emancipation of slaves, and during the 19th century, in relation to the emancipation of women and workers (Biesta, 2010, p. 42). Inspired by Vico's historical reflections about the transition from family to political order during the Roman period, Navet (2002, p. 8) stresses the fact that emancipation is rooted in the refusal of an established order (*état de fait*). It designates the opening of a space and time of rupture. It also constitutes an effort and a movement that reciprocally carry on the subject that exercises them (Navet, 2002, p. 9). Any movements of emancipation aim at modifying fundamental relationships between humans and affect them by their very existence (Navet, 2002, p. 10). Emancipation is inscribed between the forces tearing away from an established order, appearing as natural, and the threat of renaturalization consecutive to the increased influence of contingent forces. Such a movement is linked to a critical moment through which the social and political organization of the city appears through its arbitrary power and contingency (Navet, 2002, p. 10).

Emancipation and educational theory

As stressed by Biesta (2010, p. 42), during the 18th century, emancipation became intertwined with the Enlightenment. For Kant (1784, as cited in Biesta, 2010), it entailed a process of becoming independent or autonomous, based on the proper use of one's reason. Thus, the "propensity and vocation to free thinking" (Kant, 1803, as cited in Biesta, 2010, p. 42) was an inherent part of human nature that required education to emerge. Kant's position exemplifies what Biesta (Biesta, 2010, p. 42) refers to as "the modern educational nexus", a set of interlocking ideas that characterizes modern educational thinking and connects it with the question of freedom. The idea that education is not about the insertion of the individual into existing order, but entails an orientation toward autonomy and freedom, played indeed an important role in its establishment as an academic discipline toward the end of the 19th century and the beginning of the 20th century (e.g., *Reformpädagogik*, New Education and Progressive Education) (Biesta, 2010, p. 43). Throughout the 20th century, emancipation appeared as an ideal for critical contributions in education, suggesting at least two intertwined aims: the elaboration of discourses, methods and actions challenging traditional and mainstream educational theories or practices and the production of discourses describing or interpreting the stakes inherent to the development of a critical capacity (e.g., critical thinking and critical self-reflection). The institutionalization of critical pedagogies progressively raised new concerns from practical, theoretical and epistemological perspectives as well. Their contemporary contributions remain therefore problematic and even paradoxical (Alhadeff-Jones, 2007, 2010; Biesta, 2010).

The paradoxes of emancipatory education

The contradiction between the finality of education and its means appears very early in the history of education as a matter of theoretical concern. In Greek antiquity for instance, the antagonism between the ideal of autonomy and the passivity instilled by the act of subordination and subjectification, located at the core of the educational praxis, was already tackled by Socrates's ethical reflection and Aristotle's political philosophy (Jeanmart, 2007, p. 8). As suggested by Biesta (2010), such a contradiction still characterizes the contemporary development of critical pedagogies whose emancipatory interests focus on the analysis of oppressive structures, practices and theories. Biesta identifies at least three contradictions regarding the way those theories relate to learners' autonomy and freedom. The first contradiction is that although emancipation is oriented toward equality, independence and freedom, critical pedagogies actually install dependency at the very heart of the act of emancipation. The pedagogical intervention is thus based upon a knowledge considered as fundamentally inaccessible to the one to be emancipated, which supposes the paradoxes that "[w]hen there is no intervention, there is, therefore, no emancipation"

(Biesta, 2010, p. 45). The second contradiction is that emancipatory education is also based upon a fundamental inequality between the emancipator and the one to be emancipated: "the emancipator is the one who knows better and best and who can perform the act of demystification that is needed to expose the workings of power" (Biesta, 2010, p. 45). Finally, the third contradiction has to do with the fact that although emancipation takes place in the interest of those to be emancipated, it is based upon a fundamental "distrust" of and "suspicion" about their experiences: "The logic of emancipation dictates . . . that we cannot really trust what we see or feel, but that we need someone else to tell us what it is that we are really experiencing and what our problems really are" (Biesta, 2010, pp. 45–46).

Considering emancipatory education according to a complexivist and rhythmic perspective

Such contradictions between the aim of emancipatory education (autonomy vs. dependence), the status of the subjects involved (equality vs. inequality) and the method implemented (trust vs. suspicion) raise questions that can be treated at the theoretical level. For instance, Biesta's (2010) argument, inspired by Rancière's stance on emancipation and pedagogy, follows this path by redefining the aim of emancipatory education (cf. Chapter 10). Such contradictions may also appear at the epistemological level. They would therefore require one to focus on the assumptions that define the logic according to which legitimate knowledge can be produced about emancipation. Indeed, such contradictions appear as paradoxical as long as their terms are considered as mutually exclusive according to a classical and identitary logic: the value of a proposition cannot be simultaneously A and non-A, and contradictions have to be solved to formulate a claim that can be considered as 'true'. From an ontological perspective, those contradictions are also based on the assumption that we are operating with distinct, stable and substantial entities (e.g., individuals) that can be objectively distinguished and differentiated. From a complexivist and rhythmic perspective, the validity of those two principles (logical exclusion and essentialist ontology) remains however problematic.

Toward a dialogical conception of the relationship between autonomy and dependence

One of the core contributions of Morin's *Method* (1977–2004/2008) is the formulation of principles of thought whose adoption allows one to complexify the interpretations provided to grasp human's problems. With the second volume of *Method*, Morin (1980) was among the first scholars to explore systematically the epistemological and theoretical impacts of discoveries made in life sciences (e.g., self-organization, *autopoïesis*). Theorizing the principles required to conceive living organizations (from cells to human societies and cultures), his inquiry brought him to reframe notions such as control and autonomy based on observations made in biology, social sciences and anthropology of knowledge. If the three orders of reality evolve according to distinct rules, they share however common features and require similar logical principles to be conceived from a complexivist perspective. Thus, at every level, autonomy and dependence appear as two intertwined qualities that cannot be separated from each other because they are inscribed simultaneously within complementary, antagonistic and contradictory relationships.

For instance, at the biological level, the emergence – throughout the evolution of life – of the nervous system appears as an adaptive feature that increased the capacity for animals to get around (unlike plants); at the same time, it also corresponds with the emergence, from within the organism, of a new apparatus (e.g., brain, nerves and synapses) characterized by new forms of control, reducing the autonomy of the other organs. At the level of society, the evolution of political systems (e.g., democracy) toward more sophistication reinforced innovative and open forms of governance associated with broader political rights but also new duties and constraints (e.g., administrative apparatus and the political elite) with their own liability. At the level of ideas, the development of science participated in the increased mastery of humans over their environment as well as it brought new forms of reliance (e.g., to expertise and technology) and potentially alienating risks (e.g., nuclear destruction, health issues and natural disasters).

According to Morin, emancipation has therefore to be conceived with caution, especially considering the failure of political utopias that have shown throughout the recent history that "subjectification (*assujettissements*) is henceforth grounded in principles of emancipation, rather than principles of enslavement (*asservissement*)" (Morin, 1980, p. 447, my translation). Emancipation and enslavement rather appear through their dialogical relationship. Thus, they require the adoption of a principle of thought that goes beyond dualistic oppositions and binary logic. In congruence with the logic of the "middle third" conceived by Lupasco, the "autonomy-dependence" principle formulated by Morin (1990/2008) focuses therefore on the property that what makes a system (e.g., a living organism, a person, a group, a theory, etc.) self-sufficient and autonomous is also what makes it dependent. Accordingly, it appears as misleading to conceive freedom without reflecting on the constraints or dependency it involves. Applied to education, Morin's autonomy-dependence principle encourages one to systematically consider emancipatory practices as a manifestation of the complex interplay among complementary, contradictory and antagonistic forms of self- and mutual control (embedded in organisms, individuals, groups, institutions, etc.) rather than considering them as separated and mutually exclusive (Alhadeff-Jones, 2007, 2012). Considering the theme of our reflection, such considerations raise questions not so much related to the possibility to eradicate or dominate temporal constraints but rather linked to the capacity to purposefully regulate the trade-off that may always exist between rhythmic autonomy and temporal constraints.

Toward a rhythmical conception of the relationship between autonomy and dependence

Another binary opposition that frames critical theories in education is found with the distinction established between individuals (e.g., emancipator vs. person emancipated) or between individuality and collectivity (e.g., individual change vs. collective transformation). Inscribed in a filiation embedded in Plato's idealism and Aristotle's ontology, the individual or collective subject of education is primarily conceived through the stability of its attributes and the order that must characterize their development. In congruence with modern psychological and sociological theories, such individuals (e.g., baby, child, parent and teacher) and collectivities (e.g., family, class, group, school, organization, nation and society) are conceived as separated, distinct and interacting with each other according to a more or less stable and structured system of interrelations. From a structuralist perspective they are perceived as static entities; from a systemic perspective, they may be understood as the stable products of dynamic processes (Michon, 2005, p. 421).

However, if one chooses to privilege an interpretation favoring process and flow over substance, conceiving an individual or a collectivity as an emergence, rather than as an essence, such 'atomizing' interpretations become problematic. After Elias (1970, as cited in Michon, 2005), Michon suggests for instance to replace those traditional conceptions by an approach that conceives individuals in permanent interaction with each other. Rather than considering the existence of "beings" as a prior condition to study their interactions, the movement of their corporeal and discursive interrelations is conceived as the primary locus of analysis to understand how "psychic beings" (i.e., what we usually call "individuals") and "social beings" (i.e., what we usually call "groups" or "collectivities") are formed (Michon, 2005, p. 422). Such a process-oriented approach is congruent with a dialogical conception of the relationship between autonomy and dependence; those features appear thus located within relationships at least as much as they may pertain to subjects themselves. It also suggests one to consider emancipation as an ongoing movement, built up through always evolving interactions, as much as it may be conceived as a discontinuity that affects the essence of an individual (i.e., being or not being emancipated). Michon (2005, p. 423) – who privileges the term "individuation" to describe such a dynamic – stresses the fact that such a movement is neither static nor totally erratic. The dialogic between emancipation and alienation, autonomy and dependence, must therefore be conceived neither as fully ordered nor as fully disordered. It is constituted by evolving forms organized through time – "forms in movement" that we can conceive, based on the etymology of the term (cf. Chapter 4) as the expressions of a *rhuthmos* (Michon, 2005, 2007).

Michon's notion of individuation is embedded, among other references, in Mauss's anthropology and Meschonnic's historical anthropology of language. Accordingly, the rhythmicity that characterizes the tensions between psychic and social beings (or between autonomy and dependence) appears through the evolving expressions taken by bodies, discourses and social configurations as three main aspects constitutive of the process of individuation and emancipation. For Mauss, bodies evolve through forms of movement and rest, socially determined by "body techniques" that define what Michon (2007, p. 47) calls "corporeity". Any human activity (e.g., meals, sleep, walk, play, care, work or sex) is thus always accomplished according to principles that are socially determined and embodied through socialization and education. Language, too, is shaped by expressions that display rhythmic features – what Michon suggests to call "discursivity" (Michon, 2007, p. 55). Thus, lexical meaning, semantics, syntax and accentuation, among other features, display forms that are inscribed – through enunciation as well as through history – in an ongoing movement. Poetry and singing, as well as chats, blogs or propaganda, rely on linguistic activities organized through techniques that determine what humans may express, how they may proceed and therefore how they may organize and conceive their own subjectivity. Thirdly, Michon (2007, p. 65) refers to "sociality" to conceive the rhythms that organize the variations of intensity that characterize human interactions – what Mauss conceived as "morphological variations". Thus, sociality refers to the rhythms that shape daily, weekly or yearly, the ways humans gather with each other; they include, for instance, the alternance between being lonely or within a group, gathering through low or high intensity (e.g., so-called low vs. high season or critical events such as elections or periods of negotiation). In the next chapter, those three aspects of individuation (corporeity, discursivity and sociality) will serve to describe further the rhythmic dimensions of emancipatory education.

The contemporary experience of temporal alienation

Following Morin and Michon's contributions, the previous section has introduced a conception of emancipation, envisioned as an emergence and grounded in an ongoing dialogical process between autonomy and dependence, that occurs through corporeal, discursive and social interactions and displays the features of a rhythmic phenomenon. To contextualize such a reflection, this section is going to focus on the temporal context within which emancipation may occur. To proceed, we are going to explore more specifically how the idea of temporal alienation may be conceived.

Defining alienation

The term "alienation" originally (13th century) designates the action of transferring legal ownership of something to another (Oxford English Dictionary, 2015, *alienation*). With Rousseau (1762, as cited in Bensussan & Labica, 1982, p. 16), the term takes a political and anthropological meaning and is used to refer to the essence of the social contract (i.e., each individual is totally alienated to the whole community). Hegel (1820, as cited in Bensussan & Labica, 1982) further distinguishes two specific meanings associated with the term. The first one (*Entäusserung*) refers to an action that contributes to the construction of a rational reality (i.e., the alienation of an ownership as a way to confer an objective existence to one's will). The second meaning (*Entfremdung*), alluding to the Latin etymology of the word (*alienation*: derangement of mental faculties), evokes the idea of instability, separation and the state of being estranged; in this sense, the concept of alienation expresses a form of loss of the self (Bensussan & Labica, 1982, pp. 16–17). This second meaning inspired Feuerbach's thesis on 'religious alienation' (i.e., people alienate their essential being by attributing their human qualities to a god who is then worshipped on account of these qualities). According to this second meaning, the concept evokes "a loss, a severance from a part that becomes alien, as well as to the independent power that such a lost part acquires over one's own existence" (Martineau, 2015, p. 14). Marx used almost indistinguishably both meanings defined by Hegel but privileged the connotations associated with *Entfremdung* (Bensussan & Labica, 1982, p. 17). Thus, Marxian theory (e.g., Marx, 1932/1959) conceives alienation as a condition of workers in a capitalist society: with alienated labor, work turns into a mere means of subsistence rather than being an end in itself; it prevents producers from fulfilling their capacities, reaching their human potential and interacting meaningfully with their fellow human beings (Martineau, 2015, p. 15).

Marx's (1847/1955) reflections on time are thus associated with considerations around the value of merchandise and labor. Working time required to produce merchandise is alienating because it is based on an abstract estimate opposed to the concrete time experienced by workers. The rationalization of work contributes to the reification of time, which loses its qualitative, changing and flowing attributes and becomes rigid, delimited, quantified and objectified, according to a mechanical logic, detached from the subjective experience (Lukacs, 1960, p. 101). Furthermore, working time is alienating because it determines and constrains individual actions (Postone, 1993, p. 215). The tyranny of time in capitalist society remains therefore a central dimension of Marxian analysis (Postone, 1993, p. 214) and a recurring theme in sociological studies focusing on the role played by the rigidity, the coercion and the regularity imposed through the temporal framework of industrialization (e.g., Friedmann, 1956/1964; Grossin, 1969, 1996; Naville, 1972). During the past decades, many authors have revisited this problematic, exploring the effects of temporal alienation through specific notions such as "speed" (e.g., Eriksen, 2001; Hassan, 2009; Virilio, 1977, 1995), "urgency" (e.g., Aubert, 2003; Bouton, 2013; Carayol & Bouldoires, 2011; Finchelstein, 2010) and the "acceleration" of the everyday life (e.g., Rosa, 2005/2013, 2010). Doing so, they provided interpretations to grasp the cultural shift that seems to have marked late modernity and currently affects people's experiences and struggles with time. Work remains to be done to critically assess such contributions and discuss how their commonalities and divergences may be articulated. Not everyone is indeed equally equipped to cope with temporal tensions; gendered inequalities and differences related to class, ethnicity or age have to be considered to fully grasp the extent to which temporal alienation is experienced. Considering the aim of this chapter, it appears relevant to limit our analysis to two contributions, respectively related to social acceleration (Rosa, 2005/2013, 2010) and the experience of urgency (Bouton, 2013), as they encapsulate significant issues related to the experience of temporal alienation in the current debate around the politics of time.

The hegemony of social acceleration

Rosa (2005/2013, 2010) studies the logic of acceleration as a unifying concept to examine the structure and the quality of our lives through their temporal patterns. His thesis is that the concept of social acceleration is relevant to analyze how and why late modernity's structures of recognition (Honneth) and communication (Habermas) are distorted, contributing to new forms of alienation. Rosa distinguishes three categories constitutive of social acceleration. First, "technical acceleration" refers to the intentional acceleration of goal-directed processes (Rosa, 2005/2013, p. 74) (e.g., transportation, communication, production and new forms of organization and management). From this perspective, time appears more and more as an element of compression, or even annihilation, of space; it seems like increased speed of transportation and communication bring things and people closer to each other. Secondly, the "acceleration of social change" (Rosa, 2005/2013, p. 76) refers to the increased rhythms of change affecting attitudes, values, fashion, life style and services but also relationships and obligations among groups, languages, practices and habits. At the core, the acceleration of social change affects the sense of stability felt toward one's life as everything seems to be changing faster. Thirdly the "acceleration of the pace of life" (Rosa, 2005/2013, p. 78) appears objectively through the shortening or condensation of episodes of action such as mealtimes, amounts of sleep, time spent communicating in the family and so on. It is also expressed subjectively through the growing sense that one lacks time or is pressed for time as well as in anxiety about 'not keeping up'.

At the core of his critique, Rosa denounces the fact that social acceleration participates in the increase of a sense of alienation as it affects the ways one relates to the physical and material environment, things and information; one's actions and experiences; as well as the way we relate to ourselves and others. Considering the modernist idea of emancipation, Rosa observes that the contemporary temporal norms violate the ethical project of autonomy and self-determination located at the core of modernity. Thus, the compulsion to accelerate "forces people, organizations, and governments into a *reactive situational attitude* instead of a self-determining conduct of individual and collective life" (Rosa, 2005/2013, p. 295, stressed by the author). Self-determination and autonomy are threatened because the stability they require is by itself jeopardized. For Rosa, social acceleration must therefore become a matter of social critique because it constitutes a totalitarian phenomenon: (a) it exerts a pressure on the subjects' wills and actions; (b) it affects everyone and cannot be escaped; (c) it influences every single aspects of social life; and (d) it is very difficult to criticize and fight against it (Rosa, 2010).

The generalization of urgency as temporal social norm

Bouton (2013) locates the notion of "urgency" at the core of his sociological and philosophical analysis of the current experience of time. Because of its normative value, the use of this term appears for him more heuristic than referring to the notions of speed (Virilio, 1995) or acceleration (Rosa, 2005/2013). Urgency is not limited to the sensation of being in the hurry, stressed or abused; neither is it only a simple subjective matter. Urgency appears in any aspect of social life and can be located geographically (e.g., industrialized countries) and historically (e.g., starting with the end of the 18th century). Assuming the normative aspect of social time, Bouton questions the legitimacy of its contemporary expressions. Rather than being just a technical or a psychological issue, the problem with the contemporary experience of urgency is that it comes from the generalization to the entire society of a norm that existed before but was limited to specific environments (e.g., hospital or fire emergency). The extension of the domain of urgency spread out to economy, work, everyday life, law, politics, environment, education and media. Considering the densification and the compression of time imposed at work, Bouton (2013, p. 49) points out the loss of satisfaction inherent to the "work well done", a feeling of distress at work, tiredness, exhaustion, depression, burnout or even suicide. Adopting a Marxian perspective, Bouton also develops a classical critique because time of urgency and time of 'good work' (*oeuvre*) are incompatible; what is produced does not have the qualities that could make it sustainable. Urgency produces idleness (*désoeuvrement*) and dispossesses paid work of its style and its creative drive (Bouton, 2013, p. 178). From this perspective, the spread of urgency means the end of a specific culture where having a vocation and lifelong personal or professional project was the norm. Such phenomena drive psychological changes that affect what Levine (1997) describes as the "time-urgent personality". Urgency provokes discordance between the subjective time of the individual and social time (Bouton, 2013, p. 139). Such discrepancy appears at least at three intertwined levels: in the everyday life (e.g., temporal tensions); when lifetime perspective is reduced to the experience of the present (e.g., incapacity to envision one's future or to give meaning to one's past); and when the time of history loses its dynamics and orientation (e.g., individuals dissociate themselves from present history) (Bouton, 2013). Urgency finally involves a drastic limitation of freedom: "Schedule, work rhythm, project organization escape more and more from the control of those it concerns. . . . Urgency is the negation of time for oneself" (Bouton, 2013, p. 187, my translation).

Temporal alienation as the disconnection between the experience of time and its meanings

One of the common features identified by authors referring to the idea of temporal alienation appears with the disconnection, the "distorsion" (Rosa, 2010) or the "decoupling" (Thompson, 1967) that occurs between the "qualitative" time experienced as meaningful by people, and the quantitative, standardized and abstract time imposed onto their activity through social dynamics favoring speed, acceleration or the generalization of temporal norms such as urgency. According to Postone's (1993) reinterpretation of Marx's critical theory, one of the specificities of capitalism is that people are dominated by abstractions rather than by other individuals or groups. Capitalism throws people into abstract time and work that become the measure of everything (e.g., labor time as an objective temporal norm) (Postone, 1993, p. 215). Such disconnection and abstraction echo Castoriadis' (1975/1997, p. 115) considerations around alienation, defined as the "autonomization" of an institution (cf. Chapter 3). From this perspective, what appears to be at stake is the individual and collective capacity to relate and articulate heterogeneous experiences and conceptions of time, especially as they may be conceived as disjointed, contradictory or antagonistic with each other.

Rosa evokes Taylor's (2006, as cited in Rosa, 2010) idea of "resonance" to envision an existentialist and emotional strategy of emancipation centered on the way people relate to the world around them. From an epistemic perspective, following Morin's ethic (1977–2004/2008), we could also refer to the notion of "reliance" as a capacity to articulate ideas and experiences which would remain otherwise disconnected, disjointed, fragmented or compartmentalized. To resist against the autonomization of an abstracted and generalized conception of time, that imposes itself onto people's life and contributes to a feeling of *Entfremdung*, strategies of reliance should be found and promoted. Such strategies should help people to relate and interpret the heterogeneous experiences and meanings of time constitutive of their lives, including those lived as temporal constraints.

What is at stake in such an emancipatory process relies on a capacity to organize heterogeneous experiences of time (e.g., quantitative, qualitative, fast and slow). The term 'organization' does not refer here to the instrumental notion of 'time management' as a set of skills required to arrange one's commitments according to a schedule or a calendar. It rather refers to the ability to articulate meanings translating complementary, contradictory and antagonistic experiences, such as those associated with the multiple rhythms that shape everyday life and the experience of temporal constraints. Such an approach suggests that to conceive emancipatory education in regard to a context of temporal alienation, one must challenge the way time is experienced and meanings constructed around it. To engage in this direction, the next section will describe how the ideas of speed and acceleration have been envisioned in education.

Speed and education

Contributions such as those from Bouton (2013) and Rosa (2005/2013) highlight some of the dynamics through which the prevalence of speed, acceleration or urgency may spread among every single aspect of society and influence significantly everyone's everyday lives, at least in some parts of the world. Those descriptions are useful to identify and evaluate the possible impacts of such phenomena on education and the recent evolution of educational praxis and research. It remains that sociological research in education has not yet integrated those perspectives to analyze the current evolution of temporal experience and the way it may influence learning and development. Critical considerations about speed and the increased pace of social temporalities remain indeed scarce in this field (Plumb, 1999). References to social theory of time are marginal in educational theory, and so far, empirical research is limited to higher education (e.g., Clegg, 2010; Vostal, 2015). Such a theoretical deficit is problematic because practices continue to evolve in reaction to such social and cultural influences. As a consequence, the transformations that occur in education in response to the effects of social acceleration remain only superficially understood and therefore more susceptible to perpetuate weakly argued positions about what to do or not. Among such transformations, two types of responses deserve to be briefly introduced at this point to illustrate what may be at stake at both ends of the educational spectrum.

Accelerated learning

On one side, the notion of acceleration[1] emerged in the field of adult and higher education with the development of "accelerated learning programs" (Wlodkowski, 2003) during the 1970s. The implementation of those programs, usually targeting adult and 'nontraditional' learners, represents a growing phenomenon characterized by organizational structures designed for students to take less time than conventional programs to attain university credits, certificates or degrees. In this context, "accelerated courses" (often referred to as "intensive courses") are presented in less time than the conventional number of instructional contact hours (e.g., 20 hours of class time vs. 45 hours) and for a shorter duration (e.g., five weeks rather than 16 weeks) (Wlodkowski, 2003, p. 6). For Wlodkowski and Kasworm (2003, p. 93), such programs took hold in higher education because of the demographic momentum of adults whose numbers and demand for continuing education could not be ignored. Often perceived as 'moneymakers', assimilated to 'McEducation' or 'Drive-Thru U' in reference to fast food, such programs remain however controversial. Perceived by some authors as a symptom of the commodification of learning (Brookfield, 2003), they are indeed criticized for stressing convenience over substance and rigor and for being too compressed to produce consistent educational value. In addition, the fact that such programs often rely on affiliate or adjunct faculty, and usually apply a standardized and predesigned curriculum, raises questions about their quality (Wlodkowski, 2003, p. 6). At the same time, the proponents of such practices also claim that accreditation standards, learning assessments, student satisfaction and alumni attitudes, as well as the persistence and success of some categories of students involved, provide researchers and practitioners with evidences that demonstrate the value and benefits of such programs (Wlodkowski, 2003).

Slow education

On the other end of the educational spectrum, one finds practices labelled as "slow education" in reference to the "slow movement" that emerged in the filiation of the "slow food movement" launched during the 1980s (Eriksen, 2001; Honoré, 2005, 2009; Parkins, 2004). As summarized by Parkins (2004, p. 364),

> Slow living involves the conscious negotiation of the different temporalities which make up our everyday lives, deriving from a commitment to occupy time more attentively.... [S]lowness is constructed as a deliberate subversion of the dominance of speed. By purposely adopting slowness, subjects seek to generate alternative practices of work and leisure, family and sociality.

The idea according to which "losing one's time" may be the most valuable rule for education was first formulated by Rousseau (1762/1966) in *Emile*. Almost three centuries later, references to "slow education" emerge inspired by the analogy with the slow-food movement (Domènech Francesch, 2009, 2010; Holt, 2002, 2007; *L'éducation lente*, 2010; Zavalloni, 2009). Accordingly, the expression 'slow education' is used to rally educators around a critique of standards-based measurement and performativity promoted in mainstream education. Contesting values associated with speed, standardization and the quantification of life and learning, slow education prescribes principles[2] and pedagogical strategies[3] favoring the adaptation of children's and educators' pace of activity as a way to subvert the perverse and alienating effects of "school deregulation" (*L'éducation lente*, 2010, p. 15), conceived as a by-product of the application of capitalistic values to mainstream education.

Lack of theoretical grounds

Both accelerated learning and slow education are based on principles (e.g., increased efficiency and humanistic ideals) that are not specific to the current social and cultural context. To some extent, a parallel could be drawn with the study of time and rhythms conducted in education in the early 20th century (e.g., the quest for efficiency associated with the development of research on instructional time and the hope invested in the critical – sometimes reactionary – aim of rhythmic education) (cf. Chapter 5). From a theoretical perspective, the emerging literature on accelerated learning and slow education remains however quite unelaborated and does not display the theoretical audacity expressed by scholars a century earlier.

At least three limitations deserve to be mentioned. The first one is that both accelerated learning and slow education – even if their proponents acknowledge the relative value of speed – contribute through their semantic to dichotomize its appreciation, depending on the underlying ideology that justifies their development. The reason why, and this constitutes the second limitation, is that they do not rely on any elaborated temporal or rhythmic theory to nuance, explain and justify the conceptualization of speed and its correspondence to learning and development. In other words, the ratio 'educational action/time unit' that defines the pace considered as legitimate by educators (either fast or slow) is either conceived based on general assumptions (e.g., education is a slow activity) or correlated with field observations and empirical inquiry (e.g., Wlodkowski, 2003) without any theoretical framework legitimizing the specific tempo required for a given educational activity. Thus, from a theoretical point of view, such contributions appear as uncritical because they do not question the assumptions that frame the way time and rhythms are conceptualized and relate to the experience of the educational process, neither from a sociological nor from a psychological perspective, for instance.

Notions such as speed or acceleration remain difficult to define and tend therefore to become either metaphors or catch-all concepts (Maccarini, 2014, p. 61). As such, they limit the type of analysis that can be conducted. It is thus difficult to establish the actual relationships that exist among learning, education, and the specific pace of an activity. To develop such an understanding, what is required is the possibility to describe and interpret the evolution of the causes and effects associated with the tempo of an activity. Thus, to reflect on the relationship between the experience of time and education, such a relationship must be by itself contextualized and inscribed within a larger framework. Furthermore, the type of activity (e.g., verbal, nonverbal, individual or collective) and the variables (e.g., individual or systemic) that influence it need to be differentiated and contextualized. Then only can values be applied and judgment pronounced about the legitimacy of specific educational practices, taking into consideration the specificity of the psychological and social environments where they unfold.

Theorizing the rhythmic dimensions of emancipatory education

To discuss the meanings associated with a process of emancipation, and the forms of temporal constraint that determine the milieu within which it may unfold, this chapter has explored two of its facets. The first one relates to the temporality of emancipation itself; it suggests one to conceive it through the fluidity – the *rhuthmos* – that characterizes both the aim (autonomy and dependence) and the nature (process and steady state) of the changes it may carry. The second facet relates the necessity to adopt an approach that privileges the contextualization of emancipation, taking into consideration the experience of temporal alienation. It implies the development of an ability to articulate complementary, contradictory and antagonistic meanings associated with the multiple rhythms that shape the everyday life and experience of temporal constraints. In education, such a position requires one to nuance discourses and values associated with specific 'paces' (e.g., fast or slow). It finally leads to the formalization of the relationship between the experience of time, autonomy dependence and the emancipatory aim of education, according to a rhythmic perspective, rather than based on the hypothetical, normative and decontextualized value of a specific tempo. To envision the rhythmicity of emancipatory education, the next chapter is going therefore to consider how temporal constraints relate to autonomy and dependence, according to their specific rhythmic features.

Notes

1 The term "acceleration" appeared for the first time in the education of the "gifted and talented" (e.g., Brody, 2004), a field that has grown since the 1960s, especially in the United States. Accordingly, the notion of 'acceleration' refers to pedagogic strategies that are supposed to serve gifted students who need more challenge than the typical age-in-grade curriculum can provide. In this context, the use of the term 'acceleration' is thus inscribed in the debates that emerged in educational psychology around the differentiation of the curriculum (cf. Chapter 6); it does not refer to the social and cultural changes that later came to the center of sociologists' attention.
2 Domènech Francesch (2010, my translation) suggests for instance to promote slow education based on fifteen principles: (a) education is a slow activity; (b) educational activities define by themselves the time they require; (c) in education, less is more; (d) education is a qualitative process; (e) educational time is global and interrelated; (f) the construction of an educational process must be sustainable; (g) every child, and every person, needs one's proper time for one's learning; (h) each learning has its moment; (i) take the most advantage of time – define and hierarchize the finalities of education; (j) education requires time without time; (k) give back to the learner the control of time; (l) rethink the time of the relationship between adults and children; (m) redefine the time of the educators; (n) school must provide education about time; (o) slow education belongs to pedagogical reform.
3 Zavalloni (2009, my translation) suggests for instance methods such as: (a) to lose time when speaking; (b) to go back to handwriting and calligraphy; (c) to wonder and walk around; (d) to draw rather than photocopy; (e) to look at clouds in the sky through the window; (f) to write real letters and postcards; (g) to learn to whistle in school; (h) to garden in school.

References

Alhadeff-Jones, M. (2007). *Education, critique et complexité: Modèle et expérience de conception d'une approche multiréférentielle de la critique en sciences de l'éducation*. Lille, France: Atelier National de Reproduction des Thèses.
Alhadeff-Jones, M. (2010). Challenging the limits of critique in education through Morin's paradigm of complexity. *Studies in Philosophy and Education, 29*(5), 477–490.

Alhadeff-Jones, M. (2012). Transformative learning and the challenges of complexity. In E.W. Taylor, P. Cranton (Eds.), *Handbook of transformative learning: Theory, research and practice* (pp.178–194). San Francisco: Jossey-Bass.
Aubert, N. (2003). *Le culte de l'urgence: La société malade du temps*. Paris: Flammarion.
Bensussan, G., & Labica, G. (1982). *Dictionnaire critique du Marxisme*. Paris: Presses Universitaires de France.
Biesta, G. (2010). A new logic of emancipation: The methodology of Jacques Rancière. *Educational Theory*, 60(1), 39–59.
Bouton, C. (2013). *Le temps de l'urgence*. Lormont, France: Le Bord de l'eau.
Brody, L.E. (Ed.). (2004). *Grouping and acceleration practices in gifted education*. Thousand Oaks, CA: Corwin Press.
Brookfield, S.D. (2003). A critical theory perspective on accelerated learning. *New Directions for Adult and Continuing Education*, 97, 73–82.
Carayol, V., & Bouldoires, A. (Eds.). (2011). *Discordance des temps: Rythmes, temporalités, urgence à l'ère de la globalisation de la communication*. Bordeaux: Maison des Sciences de l'Homme d'Aquitaine.
Castoriadis, C. (1997). *The imaginary institution of society* (K. Blamey, Trans.). Malden, MA: Polity Press. (Original work published 1975)
Clegg, S. (2010). Time future: The dominant discourse of higher education. *Time & Society*, 19(3), 345–364.
Domènech Francesch, J. (2009). *Elogio de la educación lenta*. Barcelona: Grao.
Domènech Francesch, J. (2010). Quinze principes. *Revue Silence*, 382, 11–12. Retrieved April 12, 2015, from http://www.education-authentique.org/uploads/PDF-DOC/SEL_Silence_Education_lente.pdf
Eriksen, T.H. (2001). *Tyranny of the moment: Fast and slow time in the information age*. Sterling, VA: Pluto Press.
Finchelstein, G. (2010). *La dictature de l'urgence*. Paris: Fayard.
Friedmann, G. (1964). *Le Travail en miettes: Spécialisation et loisirs*. Paris: Gallimard. (Original work published 1956)
Grossin, W. (1969). *Le travail et le temps*. Paris: Anthropos.
Grossin, W. (1996). *Pour une science des temps*. Toulouse, France: Octares.
Hassan, R. (2009). *Empires of speed: Time and the acceleration of politics and society*. Leiden: Brill.
Holt, M. (2002). It's time to start slow school movement. *Phi Delta Kaplan*, 84(4), 265–273.
Holt, M. (2007, January). The case for the slow school (Nuffield Review Discussion Paper 41). *The Nuffield Review of 14-19 Education & Training*. Retrieved October 24, 2010, from http://www.nuffield14-19review.org.uk
Honoré, C. (2005). *In praise of slowness: Challenging the cult of speed*. San Francisco: Harper-Collins.
Honoré, C. (2009). *Under pressure: Rescuing our children from the culture of hyper-parenting*. San Francisco: Harper-Collins.
Institut National de la Langue Française. (2005). "émancipation, n.". In *Le trésor de la langue française informatisé* [Electronic resource]. Paris: Centre National de la Recherche Scientifique & Editions Gallimard. Retrieved September 5, 2005, from http://atilf.atilf.fr/tlf.htm
Jeanmart, G. (2007). *Généalogie de la docilité dans l'Antiquité et le Haut Moyen Âge*. Paris: Vrin.
L'Education lente. (2010). *Revue Silence*, n°382. Retrieved April 12, 2015, from http://www.education-authentique.org/uploads/PDF-DOC/SEL_Silence_Education_lente.pdf
Levine, R. (1997). *A geography of time*. Oxford: OneWorld.
Lukacs, G. (1960). *Histoire de conscience de classe*. Paris: Editions de Minuit.

Maccarini, A. (2014). The emergent social qualities of a 'morphogenic' society: Cultures, structures, and forms of reflexivity. In M.S. Archer (Ed.), *Late modernity, trajectories towards morphogenic society* (pp. 49–76). London: Springer.

Martineau, J. (2015). *Time, capitalism and alienation: A socio-historical inquiry into the making of modern time*. Boston, MA: Brill.

Marx, K. (1955). *The Poverty of philosophy* (Institute of Marxism-Leninism, Trans.). Moscow: Progress Publishers. (Original work published 1847)

Marx, K. (1959). *Economic and philosophic manuscripts of 1844* (M. Mulligan, Trans.). Moscow: Progress Publishers. (Original work published 1932)

Michon, P. (2005). *Rythmes, pouvoir, mondialisation*. Paris: Presses Universitaires de France.

Michon, P. (2007). *Les rythmes du politique*. Paris: Les Prairies Ordinaires.

Morin, E. (1980). *La méthode (vol.2): La vie de la vie*. Paris: Seuil.

Morin, E. (2008). *La méthode*. Paris: Seuil. (Original work published 1977–2004)

Morin, E. (2008). *On complexity* (S.M. Kelly, Trans.). Cresskill, NJ: Hampton Press. (Original work published 1990)

Navet, G. (Ed.). (2002). *L'émancipation*. Paris: L'Harmattan.

Naville, P. (1972). *Temps et technique, les structures de la vie de travail*. Genève, Suisse: Librairie Droz.

Oxford English Dictionary Online. (2015). "alienation, n.". Retrieved October 4, 2015, from http://www.oed.com/view/Entry/4999?redirectedFrom=alienation&

Parkins, W. (2004). Out of time: Fast subjects and slow living. *Time & Society*, *13*(2/3), 363–382.

Plumb, D. (1999). Adult education in a world 'on speed'. *Studies in Continuing Education*, *21*(2), 141–161.

Postone, M. (1993). *Time, labor and social domination: A reinterpretation of Marx's critical theory*. Cambridge, UK: Cambridge University Press.

Rosa, H. (2010). *Alienation and acceleration: Towards a critical theory of late-modern temporality*. Svanesund, Sweden: Nordic Summer University Press.

Rosa, H. (2013). *Social acceleration: A new theory of modernity* (J. Trejo-Mathys, Trans.). New York: Columbia University Press. (Original work published 2005)

Rousseau, J.-J. (1966). *Emile ou de l'éducation*. Paris: Flammarion. (Original work published 1762)

Thompson, E.P. (1967). Time, work-discipline and industrial capitalism. *Past and Present*, *38*, 56–97.

Virilio, P. (1977). *Speed and politics*. Los Angeles: Semiotext(e).

Virilio, P. (1995). *Open sky*. New York: Verso.

Vostal, F. (2015). Speed kills, speed thrills: Constraining and enabling accelerations in academic work-life. *Globalisation, Societies and Education*, *13*(3), 295–314.

Wlodkowski, R.J. (2003). Accelerated learning in colleges and universities. *New Directions for Adult and Continuing Education*, *97*, 93–97.

Wlodkowski, R.J., & Kasworm, C.E. (2003). Accelerated learning: Future roles and influences. *New Directions for Adult and Continuing Education*, *97*, 5–15.

Zavalloni, G. (2009). *La pedagogia della lumaca: Per una scuola lenta e nonviolenta*. Bologna, Italy: EMI.

Chapter 9

Toward a rhythmic theory of emancipation in education

Formalizing the rhythmic features of education

The aim of this chapter is to articulate a conceptual framework to conceive the relationship between the rhythms of education and the constraints inherent to them. The approach developed in this chapter is inspired by Sauvanet's (2000a, 2000b) research, especially the criteria he defines to organize the heterogeneity of theories of rhythm formulated in philosophy and human sciences and his appreciation of their philosophical and ethical contributions. It is also inspired by Michon's (2005, 2007) reflections on the relationships among discursive, corporeal, social rhythms and processes of individuation. According to Sauvanet (2000a, p. 155), three main obstacles appear when one tries to define the idea of rhythm: first, there is at the same time a plethora of definitions and no real one; second, using the same word in very heterogeneous domains remains challenging; and third, because only things or objects can be defined with rigor, it seems that the idea of rhythm cannot be rigorously defined. Considering such difficulties, Sauvanet's contribution relies on the definition and the articulation of three criteria that may be used to identify and characterize rhythmic phenomena: pattern, periodicity and movement. Those criteria are introduced in this chapter to frame how the rhythmicity of emancipation can be theorized from an educational perspective. Accordingly, the exploration of the rhythmic patterns of education leads to focus on the temporal organization that shape sociality, discursivity and corporeity and their effects on autonomy. Studying the periodicity of educational rhythms suggests one to question the relationship between the nature of repetition and the experience of alienation. Finally, investigating what constitutes the singularity of a rhythm – its movement – brings one to interrogate the disruptive as well as the regenerative and transformative roles played by the experience of discontinuities in the process of emancipation.

Temporal constraints, autonomy and the rhythmic patterns of education

This section explores educational temporalities through the analysis of the patterns they display as a first criterion to identify and qualify rhythmic organizations. After having defined the notion, rhythmic patterns are then considered in regard to social, discursive and corporeal forms of organization to describe expressions of temporal constraints and autonomy.

Structure, pattern and rhythm

Structure (or *skhêma* in Greek) is the first criterion used by Sauvanet (2000a, p. 168) to define a rhythm: rhythm is not a structure or only a structure, but structure can be an element of a rhythm. As used by Sauvanet (2000a, p. 168), the term stresses the idea of construction, layout (*agencement*), composition or imbrication. Its meaning highlights an interdependency between each element, structurally constitutive of a whole: "Structure is the principle of unity and organization of a rhythmic phenomenon; it is the *motif* that gives it its own configuration" (Sauvanet, 2000a, p. 168). In French, Sauvanet uses the word "structure", without referring to a structuralist approach; thus, he suggests that the most appropriate translation in English would be the word "pattern" (in German: *Gefüge* or *Gestalt*) (Sauvanet, 2000a, p. 168). What distinguishes the structure, or pattern, from the form is the fact that it designates an ephemeral configuration or setting (*disposition*) rather than the form constitutive of the essence or existence of a being (Sauvanet, 2000a, p. 168). A rhythmic pattern is created by the combination of stresses (*accents*) standing out from an unstressed background; it appears as a principle of identification of rhythmic phenomena. For instance, with auditory stimuli, structure refers to four components: duration, intensity, timbre and height; with visual stimuli, it is associated with dimension, intensity, material and color (Sauvanet, 2000a, p. 168). This criterion provides us with a first entry to conceptualize the rhythmicity of the social, discursive and corporeal phenomena that determine the experience of autonomy and constraint from an educational perspective.

Rhythmic patterns and the social organization of education

Emancipation determines, as well as it is embedded in, social dynamics that regulate the ways people relate and exercise influence over each other. Such dynamics can be envisioned through specific rhythmic patterns that shape the evolution of changes and transformation as they appear at the level of social institutions and organizations, in people's individual trajectories and through everyday activities. Considering social institutions (e.g., state education), socio-historical studies such as the one conducted by Archer (1979) have established how dynamics of social change can be interpreted according to specific patterns that express some form of rhythmicity. Archer's study of the emergence of states' education systems throughout the last centuries, in four countries, provides us with a detailed illustration of the patterns that determined the history of educational systems and the political dynamics that shaped the evolution of educational policy. According to her study, centralized systems (e.g., France and Russia) used to follow a "stop-go pattern" due to the specificity of the process of interaction they privileged (e.g., demands for change had to be accumulated, aggregated and articulated at the political center before being negotiated and eventually transmitted downward). Decentralized systems (e.g., England and Denmark) were characterized by an "incremental pattern of change", due to the fact that social and political transactions did not have to be passed upward and could therefore be negotiated autonomously and incrementally. From this perspective, the cycles through which an institution evolves express a form of organization that can be represented according to specific regularities. Without entering here into the details of Archer's morphogenetic theory, the interest of such an approach, from an emancipatory perspective, is that it defines through time the presence or absence of features that constrain individual agency based on the specificities of the social structures and cultural patterns of change within which they are inscribed.

Rhythmic patterns are also found at the organizational level. As suggested for instance by Ben-Peretz's (1990) analysis, schools' sequential structures (e.g., learning cycles), calendars or planning (e.g., annual and daily cycles) are constitutive of temporal modes of organization that impose a specific order and coherence to the rhythms of interactions (cf. Chapter 3). In the same way, the different forms of alternance that characterize the sequence between vocational training and work in dual education (Geay, 1999), or between formal education and *tiers-temps scolaire* (Sue & Rondel, 2001), also constitute patterns that condition the relative level of autonomy lived from childhood to adulthood (cf. Chapter 7). Such organizational patterns shape the ways people relate to each other and translate tensions between autonomy and dependence because they express the interplay between various forms of temporal constraints (e.g., individual vs. social, formal vs. informal and personal vs. professional). From the perspective of individuals' lives, phenomena related to the chronologization, institutionalization and standardization of the life course (Settersten, 1999) are also constitutive of schemes that shape how people are grouped (e.g., age cohorts and graded schools) and how they evolve according to educational opportunities provided within a specific culture (cf. Chapter 3). Such patterns – typically formulated through laws, rules or policies – define the legitimate entry and exit points for someone to get into a specific grade or formal education or to transition between study and work. Hence, they organize and constrain people's opportunities of belonging to specific groups or communities. At the same time, the contemporary study of adult lives brings one to relativize the ordering function played by such institutionalized schemes, stressing the increased importance taken by discontinuous life events in people's social trajectories (cf. Chapter 7).

At the level of the activity, the organization of instructional time and more broadly the routines and rituals that punctuate schools' everyday life (e.g., Jacklin, 2004; Quantz & Magolda, 1997) provide us with additional examples. Rhythmic patterns of action appear thus through the scripts that structure, regulate and eventually constrain the gathering of students and educators (e.g., individual vs. group activities and teaching vs. recess). From an educational perspective, autonomy and dependence are therefore shaped by the patterns that condition the learning setting (cf. Chapters 4 to 7); recursively, the experience of autonomy also shapes how learning activity may unfold. As suggested by Whitehead's (1929/1967) educational cycles, the pattern constituted by the three stages he defined (romance, precision and generalization) may thus determine the succession of interactions between educators and learners as well as their different qualities (e.g., level of intellectual freedom or constraint experienced by pupils) (cf. Chapter 7).

Rhythmic patterns and the discursive organization of education

Autonomy and dependence are determined, as well as they determine, the way people can express themselves, including verbally. As discussed by Michon (2005), discursive rhythms play a central role in the process of individuation. Thus, language and texts provide the educational praxis with an additional layer imposing its own rhythmic organization onto people's learning experiences. For instance, as discussed in Chapter 4, Jewish traditional education demonstrates the role played by linguistic patterns (e.g., oral tradition and the absence of vowel system) in the implementation of learning techniques (Morris, 1937). With Plato's musical education, the pattern of speech flow appears at the core of the individual's moral development (Adamson, 1903). As shown with the case of monastic education, discursive techniques and the rigor of their applications (e.g., praying, reciting, singing and copying) reveal their disciplinary function and their contribution to the imposition of obedience as a specific way of learning (Jeanmart, 2007). In a similar way, the organization of the texts studied (e.g., biblical, epic, philosophical or scientific) also constrains, within each formal system, the structure of its curriculum: it was the function of *ordines legendi* in the transmission of knowledge throughout the Renaissance; it is also found when contemporary textbooks are used as synchronizers to organize the succession of teaching units according to a specific pattern. In an analogous way, the use of new technologies provides learners and educators with alternative formats of verbal interactions (e.g., synchronous and asynchronous), imposing their own structure and logic to the educational process. The linguistic features that shape the production and the sharing of life histories, used for instance in higher and adult education to help learners increase their sense of agency (cf. Chapter 7), constitute another example of how language's structuration (e.g., the necessity to elaborate a plot according to a specific succession of actions to build up the coherence of a narrative) may determine the formative outcome associated with educational practices (Baudouin, 2010).

Rhythmic patterns and the corporeal organization of education

Autonomy and dependence are also fundamentally experienced through the level of freedom experienced within one's body. Considering the dynamics shaping corporeity, the history of education provides numerous examples of rhythmic schemes imposed to constrain, rule and control bodies through their movements: musical education in Sparta aimed at reinforcing cohesion and discipline among soldiers (Marrou, 1948/1981); the imposition of the *sequela Christi* in monastic education reinforced the docility and the order required within Christian communities to counter the individualistic aspects of idiorhythmy (Jeanmart, 2007). Since the Early Modern period, the increased codification of children's gestures in schools aimed at enforcing the discipline that supported the emerging industrial order (Foucault, 1975/1995) (cf. Chapter 4). Later, it was therefore through physical movement that the proponents of rhythmic education (e.g., Bode, 1920/2014; Jaques-Dalcroze, 1921) conceived the possibility to resist against the new forms of hegemony inherent to the Industrial Revolution; the goal was then to provide learners with the opportunity to develop a more fluent way of moving rather than being subjugated by the rigidity imposed by the educational system and the society more broadly (Hanse, 2007). Jaques-Dalcroze's or Bode's methods were thus focusing on the reorganization of movement's schemes and corporeal rhythms as an interface between individual autonomy and social constraints (cf. Chapter 5). Nowadays, the patterns producing – and produced by – our biological rhythms (e.g., attention and exhaustion), objectivized through scientific measurement (Testu, 2008), constitute another source of struggle in the political arena that determines the terms of the debates around school organization, educational policy and learners' autonomy (cf. Chapter 6).

Quality, quantity and the periodicities of education

The heterogeneity of rhythmic patterns illustrated here leads us to the core of the temporal complexity of education: they illustrate the diversity of 'temporal units' that may define educational temporalities and the changes they carry. To precisely detail how their qualities may interact with the experience of temporal constraints and emancipation, a second criterion has to be introduced: their periodicity.

Periodicity and repetition

Periodicity is the second criteria identified by Sauvanet (2000a, p. 177) to define rhythmic phenomena. The term comes from the Greek *periodos*, which designates a circuit, a circular march or a traveler returning to its starting point (Sauvanet, 2000a, p. 177). Periodicity covers all the rhythms that are perceived or conceived as cycles, returns, alternances, repetitions, cadences and so on. According to Sauvanet (2000a, p. 179), not every rhythm is periodicity, but there may be periodicity in a rhythm. Furthermore, rhythms that are considered as influential always involve periodicities (Sauvanet, 2000a, p. 179). Period or cycle refers to the time spent between two limits of the same interval. The tempo is the relative speed of a rhythmic phenomenon. The period is not enough to determine periodicity; the frequency of the repetition of the period is also required (Sauvanet, 2000a, p. 179). Thus, this criterion provides us with a second entry to conceptualize the rhythmicity of educational phenomena and determine more specifically their value.

The periodicity of educational rhythms

To be sustained, emancipation requires not only a rupture with an existing order, experienced as constraining or alienating, but also the reproduction, through time, of the features that characterize an emerging mode of organization (e.g., a way of living or a culture). Thus, the history of education can be seen as a succession of ruptures and the repeated efforts implemented to institutionalize and sustain new forms of social organization characterized by their own rhythms. From an institutional perspective, the repetition of specific (social, discursive and corporeal) patterns plays a central role in the reproduction of what constitutes the dominant features of a society (e.g., modes of production, values, norms and artifacts) at a given time. As shown in the second part of this book, reproduction is located at the core of any form of education (e.g., traditional, aristocratic, monastic education or modern education), whose function is to guarantee the subsistence of a group or a community, materially and symbolically (cf. Chapter 4). In addition, from an organizational perspective, the autonomy of a system (e.g., school or dual education) is sustained by the more or less uniform rates of occurrence that characterize the repetition of the temporal patterns organizing its structure: sequences, cycles, alternances and so on. Repetitions also characterize actions at a smaller scale, such as "organizational routines" (Sherer & Spillane, 2011) that participate in the constancy of the work practice in schools. Likewise, repetitions apply to rituals and ritualizations constitutive of everyday life, within formal settings, such as classrooms (e.g., Jacklin, 2004), or throughout informal activities, such as those through which one learns to take care of oneself (Pineau, 2000). From the point of view of the individual, repetitions characterize every aspect of one's own experience, including one's biorhythms (e.g., the frequency of sleep, digestion or sexual activity), cognitive functions (e.g., techniques of memorization) and movements and behaviors (e.g., cadences of gestures and frequency of interactions) (cf. Chapters 4 to 6). Every level of the educational praxis appears therefore characterized not only by the periodicity that characterizes the repetition of an organizational or learning pattern but also by the specific frequency and pace through which it is reproduced.

Learning theories usually involve the reiteration of social, discursive or corporeal features – traditionally represented as a loop or a cycle – whose regulation is at the core of the educational apparatus. The most basic example remains Pavlov's model, according to which the acquisition of conditional reflexes requires the successive repetition of a simple pattern of association between an absolute stimulus and a conditional stimulus. More elaborated contributions include Dewey's educational theory, especially his views on the formation of habits as repeated processes through which the meaning of experience is reconstructed through self-reflection (Lamons, 2012). More recent models also include Argyris and Schön's (1974) "double loop learning" theory. With those two contributions, the periodic aspect of education and learning appears through necessity to restore continuity within a context affected by changes (whether individual, organizational or societal). Hence, education evolves through periodic efforts that relate to struggles, tensions and ruptures experienced individually or collectively (e.g., Archer, 1979; Morris, 1937). Thus, the repetition of marking events (e.g., epiphanies, *épreuves* and bifurcations) reveals significant individual or systemic transformations that may lead to a greater sense of autonomy or dependence (cf. Chapter 7).

The relationship between emancipation and periodicity has therefore to be conceived dialogically. Associated with the conservative function of education, repetition remains equivocal; the periodicity of specific pedagogical patterns (e.g., teaching methods) or organizational configurations (e.g., *tiers-temps scolaire*) may contribute to the reproduction of social inequalities (e.g., Sue & Rondel, 2001). At the same time, repetition may also participate in the emergence of new features. Considering for instance Whitehead's (1929/1967) rhythmic theory of education, or the principles of alternance found in vocational training (Geay, 1999), periodic repetition may be conceived at the core of learning processes that eventually contribute to an increased capacity to generalize knowledge or principles assimilated under the constraint of formal study but contributing nevertheless to a greater sense of autonomy. To analyze more thoughtfully the bivalence of repetition in regard to autonomy and emancipation, it appears particularly relevant to turn to Lefebvre's (1961/2002, 1992/2004) reflection on the relationship between repetition and alienation.

Repetition and the experience of alienation

The relationship between alienation and periodicity is both a matter of quality and quantity. As discussed by Lefebvre (1961/2002, p. 340), different types of repetition have to be distinguished (i.e., taking into consideration the level of difference and creativity they involve) to analyze their value and meaning. Working on an assembly line, or repeating every day the same routines within a classroom, may be experienced as alienating because repetition is lived as a source of monotony, tiredness, consumption or exhaustion (Jacklin, 2004). It dispossesses therefore the person from one's own embodied experience. It does not let room for self-creation, plenitude or harmony with oneself and with the world. From this angle, the redundancy of the pragmatic demands of everyday life may constitute a source of detachment that separates daily actions (e.g., at work, in school or in the family) from what generates them (e.g., impulse or desire), resulting in an emptying out of meaning and the banality of the quotidian (Lefebvre, 1961/2002, 1992/2004). Alienation may come therefore from the separation between creative impulses and the repetitive rhythms of life (Lefebvre, 1992/2004). This is one of the reasons why Lefebvre's rhythmanalytical project was grounded in the study of the rhythmic dimensions of the every day as potential sources of alienation.

In education, such a phenomenon has motivated curricular reforms (e.g., Husti, 1999) and has been studied empirically. For instance, research such as that conducted by Jacklin (2004) demonstrates how repetition and differences are regulated in classroom practice, leading to a more or less "arid pedagogic experience" that impacts negatively learners' achievement. It develops further the initial insight formulated a century earlier by scholars such as Jacques-Dalcroze, Bode or Steiner and their critique of the cadence imposed by the new industrial and capitalist order (Hanse, 2007). As discussed in the previous chapter, alienation also appears to be associated with the quantitative dimension of repetition. The feeling of urgency or acceleration may thus be experienced as alienating because it involves actions (e.g., routines, organizational changes and learning performances) that are conducted at a tempo or a speed that may be experienced as inappropriately high; such a critique is at the core of the slow school movement's raison d'être (cf. Chapter 8). The opposite may also be true; the reason why the experience of boredom in the classroom has led to the promotion of accelerated learning for gifted students, or the perceived lack of institutional reforms, regularly constitutes a matter of preoccupation.

Evolution, singularity and the movement of education

For Sauvanet (2000b, p. 126), the periodicity of a rhythm corresponds to an attempt to assimilate through repetition what may at first be conceived as a unique experience. If patterns provide rhythms with a structure, and periodicity describes the modalities according to which they are reproduced, the necessity remains to recognize what singularizes the form taken by their evolution through time; this includes the events or the discontinuities that shape the evolution of a rhythm. To proceed, Sauvanet's (2000a) introduced a third criterion that he designated as "movement".

Movement and transformation

For Sauvanet (2000a, p. 188), the idea of movement constitutes the third criteria that defines rhythmic phenomena, even if the movement is what resists the most to the rational analysis of rhythms. The movement refers to the "particular way of flowing" evoked by Benveniste (1951/1966), which distinguished the *rhuthmos* from a simple repetition (Sauvanet, 2000a, p. 188). The idea of movement evokes the transformative aspect of rhythmic phenomena. Referring to the etymology of the term (from the Greek *metabolè*), Sauvanet (2000a, p. 189) stresses its "transformative" connotation, which can be perceived negatively (inconsistency or inconstant) or positively (renewal or exchange). Conceiving rhythms through their movement highlights the assumption according to which a rhythm goes beyond mere repetition and remains fundamentally shaped through the indeterminacy of an irregular configuration: "the rhythmic phenomenon must be at the same time foreseeable (it is peculiar to its regularity, it is here the periodicity of its structure) and unforeseeable (this is precisely the movement)" (Sauvanet, 2000a, p. 190, my translation). The movement of a rhythm is therefore located at the core of its temporal and historical configuration. The movement refers to the "entropic" aspect of a rhythm, what is constitutive of its complexity and irreversibility (Sauvanet, 2000a, p. 193).

The movement of educational rhythms

As already suggested, at the core, emancipation involves some form of rupture that disturbs a social and symbolic order. Traditionally, it is conceived as an event or a series of distinct events – interpreted either from the point of view of a life history (e.g., breakthrough, crisis or bifurcation) or through the lens of collective history (e.g., revolution) – that leads to the increased independence of a person or a community. From an institutional and organizational perspective, the movement that characterizes the rhythms of emancipatory education belongs to the history of education and the political struggles that shape it. From a biographical perspective, it appears through the singularity of a life history and the unique path through which one builds up a greater sense of autonomy, including through adversity (cf. Chapter 11). Such a movement fundamentally relates to the subject's capacity to control and negotiate the tensions existing between one's own rhythms and the constraints or regulations imposed by social temporalities throughout the life span. In adult education, the capacity to negotiate and give meaning to the events that punctuate one's life (e.g., disorienting dilemma) can become a matter of critical self-reflection that may carry transformative and emancipatory effects (Mezirow, 1991). From an emancipatory perspective, the ability to reconfigure the meaning of one's lifeworld is thus becoming a critical skill to increase one's capacity to make purposeful life choices (including educational ones) and sustain a sense of agency (cf. Chapter 7).

Beyond the discontinuities that shape individual and collective history, the dynamics of emancipation are also embedded in the uniqueness of the events that shape quotidian actions. Their movement appears indeed through the specific "ways of flowing" (*manières de fluer*) that characterize the discursive, corporeal and social features forming both individual and collective organizations (Michon, 2005, 2007). From this angle, the movement of emancipation appears therefore through the affirmation of one's own ways of speaking, moving or gathering with each other as well as it is constitutive of every single event when autonomy and dependence are negotiated, consciously or not. At the level of everyday actions, the movement of a rhythm appears through what provides a subject's activity its singularity. It is constitutive for instance of those phenomena through which people aim at finding and following a particular rhythm, where individual freedom is understood as the conquest of one's own rhythms (Jeanmart, 2007, pp. 139–141).

From the point of view of sociality, it requires that the collectivity is able to compose with rhythmic singularities to accommodate them. When it succeeds, individual autonomy is increased. However, as discussed by Jeanmart (2007, pp. 139–141) with the example of monastic education, idiorhythmy may eventually appear as a threat that requires to be strictly controlled by the collectivity (e.g., through discipline and obedience). Considering today's compulsory education system, issues related to idiorhythmy are linked to the capacity of the system to implement a differentiated pedagogy. As discussed in Chapter 6, it may lead to a greater fluidity within the movement that composes the formation of classrooms and grades to favor exchanges and accommodate the pace of each student. More radically, it is also found in debates surrounding the project of autonomy claimed by families who defend the values and the lifestyle associated with 'home education'.

Considering discursive and corporeal rhythms, particular examples such as stuttering, a physical disability, or the behavioral flow that characterizes so-called attention deficit disorder illustrate well what is in fact constitutive of anyone's expression or gesture: those idiosyncrasies that confer something unique to the way people express themselves through language and embodiment. In formal settings, when such idiosyncrasies are experienced as disrupting or disorganizing the 'average' collective rhythms, they tend to justify the adoption of measures that either ignore, stigmatize or isolate those who express such 'arrhythmic' behaviors. From the perspective of the subject, they may become a source of exclusion and alienation. If, at the opposite, they are acknowledged, respected and taken into consideration within the collective flow of a group, they may contribute to the recognition of the subject's own singularity and participate to one's own movement of emancipation. Emancipatory education may appear therefore as the process through which one's rhythmic movement is negotiated and eventually asserted for one's own *rhuthmos* to be recognized and acknowledged.

Emancipation and the experience of syncope

Questioning the movements that shape the rhythms of one's life, and conceiving them as something that is neither regular nor measured, requires one to question the meaning of events or discontinuities and the ways it can be qualified. One way to explore further the relationship among rhythm, movement and emancipation is to explore the experience of what Sauvanet (2000b, p.114) groups under the term "syncope", conceived as a suspended time that recalls a rhythm. From an existential perspective, Sauvanet's use of the term "syncope" appears close to notions such as interval, *kairos*, crisis or leap (Sauvanet, 2000b, p. 126). The phenomena they describe may have freeing effects because they momentarily liberate from the pattern and the strict repetition that characterize a rhythmic experience to renew them. Recursively, because emancipation involves some form of rupture, it may also be interpreted as the emergence of a syncope within what would have been otherwise conceived as a regular repetition. The experience of a crisis is probably the type of syncope most often associated with an emancipatory process. As shown by the etymology of the term (*krisis*, the moment of decision), emancipation is thus embedded in the experience of a more or less intense state of rupture that requires a critical capacity involving – according to the Greek root *krinein* – the ability to sort, separate, organize, decide and judge what has to be done (Rey, 2000, pp. 953–954). Such a critical experience shares also a proximity with Kierkegaard's notion of leap as a passage from an order of existence to another, which contributes to produce significant change within the self (Sauvanet, 2000b, p. 114).

Emancipation can also be conceived through the more casual and everyday forms of syncope it involves. For instance, the daily experience of intervals opens up an "art of living" (e.g., tea time as a break within the flow of the every day) that displays valorized qualities and contributes to sustain some form of balance (Sauvanet, 2000b, p. 126). It provides one with an opportunity to find a sense of rhythm based on the capacity to make a break to enjoy a specific time. Another way to conceive such an experience would be to refer to the notion of *kairos* (Sauvanet, 2000b, p. 126) as a qualitative time through which the self emerges and reveals itself (cf. Chapter 11). From this perspective, alienation may occur whenever the ability to make a break is hindered, as illustrated and denounced by the proponents of the slow movement (cf. Chapter 8).

As it is the case with periodicity, the relationship between emancipation and movement has to be conceived as a dialogical one. Discontinuity may thus be experienced as a source of disorder that disorganizes the pattern and the regularity of one's activity: stuttering, having an accident and losing someone constitute many experiences that may be lived as constraining or alienating because they disorganize respectively the flow of speech, the course of life, or the ongoing development of a relationship. Because they are unpredictable or unique, discontinuities and events are destabilizing and create an experience of uncertainty that appears as critical, especially when its outcome remains undetermined (e.g., *épreuves*). At the same time, the experience of a syncope can also be conceived as an opportunity to resource or reinvent oneself and renew a rhythm that would have been otherwise lived as too regular or monotonous. Someone who heavily stutters in one's mother tongue can eventually find the right discursive flow when using another language.[1] The experience of a catastrophe may untie attachments that used to constitute constraints. The good timing or the right opportunity (*kairos*) may provide the occasion to relate or 'be in synch' with a new situation or a new relationship in a way that reveals itself as creative and original.

From the perspective of its movement, emancipation can therefore be interpreted through the tension between constancy or continuity (monotonous and potentially alienating but also reassuring) and inconstancy or discontinuity (threatening but potentially stimulating) (Sauvanet, 2000a, p. 139). The ruptures it involves may reveal themselves as constructive; they may contribute to one's development or progression. They may as well appear as destructive: the lack of rhythm that characterizes arrhythmia becomes a source of alienation, regression or even death. Acknowledging the movement through which autonomy and emancipation emerge, considering what goes beyond patterns and repetitions finally involves a reflection on the irreversibility of one's existence, its *sens* (as direction and meaning) and therefore its finitude.

Interrogating what grounds the pattern, periodicity and movement of emancipatory education

Theorizing emancipation from a rhythmological perspective does not solve the ambiguities or the contradictions that characterize its relationship to education. It rather provides us with a framework to represent and organize the tensions they reveal from a temporal perspective. Rhythmic patterns shape – from the perspective of discourse, corporeity and sociality – the dialogical relationship between autonomy and dependence. They do not define alienation or emancipation per se, although they provide a form that determines their expression at the micro level of social interactions and at the macro level of the history of institutions as well. To grasp how rhythmic patterns interact with emancipation, it seems rather critical to consider how they evolve on the continuum between rigidity and fluidity. None of those two polarities carries an intrinsic value. From a rhythmic perspective, considering the patterns of emancipation requires one to question why and how they appear as more or less rigid or fluid at a specific time and in a specific context. Furthermore, they question who has the capacity and what are the resources required to define or impose such patterns. From an educational perspective, it is important to conceive what justifies the rigidity of a temporal pattern of change and transformation or the absence of a rhythmic structure organizing one's experience.

Emancipation involves both a rupture with an existing order and the reproduction through time of the features that characterize an evolving pattern of organization. Whether they are conceived from an institutional perspective or from the point of view of everyday life, repetitions define every aspect of one's own temporal experience. Their periodicity concerns therefore both redundant operations and the reiteration of periods or episodes of rupture as well. Periodicity appears at the core of conservative dynamics as much as it participates in the emergence of new qualities. When considering the relationship between periodicity and temporal constraint, the bottom line may be to determine the value associated with the level of redundancy (monotonous vs. generative) or the value of the pace or tempo (faster vs. slower) through which sequences or cycles are repeated. Exploring the periodical aspect of educational rhythms raises many questions. What are the sources of change or innovation within daily routines? What has to be repeated or not? Where does the pace of the activity come from? And more fundamentally, what are the criteria that define the 'right' periodicity, tempo or speed within a specific context, and who has the capacity to define, legitimize or impose them?

Finally, the rhythmic movement of education, whether conceived through the history of an institution, the life course of a person or their mutual relationships, involves a tension between continuity and discontinuity. Emancipation is traditionally envisioned through the punctual events that introduce a rupture within a continuum. However, it should not be reduced to the emergence of a discontinuity as the experience of discontinuity itself may appear as an alienating feature of post-modern life trajectories. Emancipation appears therefore through the capacity to negotiate the meanings, and balance the tensions, that characterize the relationship between continuity and discontinuity. Autonomy and freedom relate to the conquest of what constitutes the singularity of one's own *rhuthmos*, one's own way of flowing through the discursive, corporeal and social movement, that shapes quotidian actions. It also involves the capacity to experience or provoke a syncope (e.g., break, crisis or *kairos*) as an opportunity to resource or reinvent oneself and renew a rhythm that would have been otherwise lived as too regular or monotonous. Considering the rhythmic movement of education also raises a series of questions. What does justify the continuity or the discontinuity of a movement? How to conceive its interruption? What are the resources required to articulate continuity and discontinuity?

The aim of this chapter has been to articulate a framework to theorize the rhythmic dimensions of emancipation from an educational perspective. In the next chapter, we are going to explore how this framework may feed a reflection on the temporal dimensions of critical pedagogies and how it may enrich emerging educational practices referring to rhythmanalysis. In Chapter 11, this framework will be mobilized to interpret how the biographical movement through which someone increases one's autonomy is organized around patterns and periodicities that reveal the rhythmicity of emancipation.

Note

1 A participant of one of my seminars who suffered from stuttering in his childhood excelled later in his life in public speaking contests organized in another language.

References

Adamson, J. (1903). *The theory of education in Plato's 'Republic'*. London: Swan Sonnenschein & Co.

Archer, M.S. (1979). *Social origins of educational systems*. London: Sage.

Argyris, M., & Schön, D. (1974). *Theory in practice: Increasing professional effectiveness*. San Francisco: Jossey-Bass.

Baudouin, J.M. (2010). *De l'épreuve autobiographique: Contribution des histoires de vie à la problématique des genres de texte et de l'herméneutique de l'action*. Bern: Peter Lang.

Ben-Peretz, M. (1990). Perspectives on time in education. In M. Ben-Peretz, & R. Bromme (Eds.), *The nature of time in schools: Theoretical concepts, practitioner perceptions* (pp.64–77). New York: Teachers College, Columbia University.

Benveniste. E. (1966). *Problèmes de linguistique générale* (vol.1). Paris: Gallimard. (Original work published 1951)

Bode, R. (2014). Rhythm and its importance for education (P. Crespi, Trans.). *Body & Society*, *20*(3/4), 51–74. (Original work published 1920)
Foucault, M. (1995). *Discipline and punish: The birth of the prison* (A. Sheridan, Trans.). New York: Vintage Book. (Original work published 1975)
Geay, A. (1999). Actualité de l'alternance (note de synthèse). *Revue Française de Pédagogie*, *128*, 107–125.
Hanse, O. (2007). *Rythme et civilisation dans la pensée allemande autour de 1900*. [Electronic version]. Doctoral dissertation, Université Rennes 2, France. Retrieved January 15, 2014, from https://tel.archives-ouvertes.fr/tel-00204429
Husti, A. (1999). *La dynamique du temps scolaire*. Paris: Hachette.
Jacklin, H. (2004). *Repetition and difference: A rhythmanalysis of pedagogic practice*. Unpublished doctoral dissertation, University of Cape Town, South Africa.
Jaques-Dalcroze, E. (1921). *Rhythm, music and education* (H.F. Rubinstein, Trans.). London: Putnam's Sons.
Jeanmart, G. (2007). *Généalogie de la docilité dans l'Antiquité et le Haut Moyen Âge*. Paris: Vrin.
Lamons, B.N. (2012). *Habit, education, and the democratic way of life: The vital role of habit in John Dewey's philosophy of education*. Doctoral dissertation, University of South Florida. Retrieved September 24, 2015, from http://scholarcommons.usf.edu/etd/4118
Lefebvre, H. (2002). *Critique of everyday life (vol. 2)* (J. Moore, Trans.). London: Verso. (Original work published 1961)
Lefebvre, H. (2004). *Rhythmanalysis: Space, time and everyday life* (S. Elden & G. Moore, Trans.). London: Continuum. (Original work published 1992)
Marrou, H. (1981). *Histoire de l'éducation dans l'Antiquité. Le monde grec (vol. 1)*. Paris: Seuil. (Original work published 1948)
Mezirow, J. (1991). *Transformative dimensions of adult learning*. San Francisco: Jossey-Bass.
Michon, P. (2005). *Rythmes, pouvoir, mondialisation*. Paris: Presses Universitaires de France.
Michon, P. (2007). *Les rythmes du politique*. Paris: Les Prairies Ordinaires.
Morris, N. (1937). *The Jewish school*. London: Eyre & Spottiswoode.
Pineau, G. (2000). *Temporalités en formation: Vers de nouveaux synchroniseurs*. Paris: Anthropos.
Quantz, R.A., & Magolda, P.M. (1997). Nonrational classroom performance: Ritual as an aspect of action. *The Urban Review*, *29*(4), 221–238.
Rey, A. (Ed.). (2000). *Le Robert – Dictionnaire historique de la langue française*. Paris: Dictionnaires Le Robert.
Sauvanet, P. (2000a). *Le rythme et la raison (vol. 1): Rythmologiques*. Paris: Kimé.
Sauvanet, P. (2000b). *Le rythme et la raison (vol. 2): Rythmanalyses*. Paris: Kimé.
Settersten, R.A., Jr. (1999). *Lives in time and place: The problems and promises of developmental science*. Amityville, NY: Baywood Publishing Co.
Sherer, J.Z., & Spillane, J.P. (2011). Constancy and change in work practice in schools: The role of organizational routines. *Teachers College Record*, *113*(3), 611–657.
Sue, R., & Rondel, Y. (2001). Rythmes de vie et éducation: Education et modes de vie. *Les Cahiers Millénaire*, *3*(24), 25–53. Retrieved November 20, 2014, from http://www.millenaire3.com/content/download/6992/129867/version/2/file/Millcahier24.pdf
Testu, F. (2008). *Rythmes de vie et rythmes scolaires*. Issy-les-Moulineaux, France: Masson.
Whitehead, A.N. (1929/1967). *The aims of education and other essays*. New York: The Free Press.

Chapter 10

Facilitating emancipatory education, from critical pedagogy to rhythmanalysis

Establishing the relevance of a rhythmanalytical approach to critical education

The reflections conducted throughout this book point toward the critical role played by the capacity to symbolize, relate and organize heterogeneous, complementary, contradictory and antagonistic experiences of time. In the previous chapter, a conceptual framework has been formulated to conceive the relationships among emancipation, the rhythms of education and the constraints inherent to them. This chapter explores how such a resource may enrich reflections that frame the development of pedagogical approaches aiming at emancipation. The reflection is divided in two parts. The first one focuses on existing educational theories. It questions some of the limitations inherent to contemporary critical pedagogies from a temporal perspective (Freire's pedagogy of the oppressed, Rancière's view on emancipation and pedagogical practice and Mezirow's conception of emancipatory and transformative learning) to analyze more systematically their temporal assumptions and specificities. The second part of this chapter focuses on emerging educational conceptions that illustrate and open up new possibilities for the development of rhythm-centered pedagogical approaches. To locate their origins, it briefly introduces the contributions proposed by Bachelard and Lefebvre around the idea of rhythmanalysis. Their influence on educational theory is then illustrated through the contributions of two generations of French scholars (Pineau and Hess, as pioneers, and Galvani and Lesourd, among other innovative followers) who explicitly refer to rhythmanalysis in the field of adult and higher education. Their respective approaches are discussed to identify possible orientations as well as existing limitations.

Critical pedagogies: Their rhythmic features and their temporal assumptions

The following sections explore the contributions of three educational theories carried by an emancipatory ideal to explore how they relate to time and the questions they raise from a rhythmological perspective. Considering the multiplicity of critical theories and pedagogies developed in the field of education (e.g., Alhadeff-Jones, 2007, 2010), the selection of those contributions is based on both their relevance in regard to the development of critical discourses in education and the fact that each one tends to privilege a specific rhythmic feature (movement, periodicity or pattern). Those three contributions have therefore been chosen for their illustrative value: they exemplify rhythmic attributes that may be privileged by different pedagogical approaches as much as they trigger questions about the relevance of their own temporal assumptions.

Freire and the movement that orientates radical pedagogies

For Freire (1970/2005), in congruence with his Marxist background, the overcoming of oppression and the process of liberation are conceived first and foremost as an historical movement. The pedagogy of the oppressed takes therefore people's historicity as its starting point (Freire, 1970/2005, p. 84). Its transformational character necessitates that education be conceived as an ongoing activity (Freire, 1970/2005, p. 84). Understood as such, the "revolutionary" aim of education suggests an irreversible transformation of concrete situations of oppression, a transformation of reality that constitutes in itself a "historical task for humanity" (Freire, 1970/2005, p. 51). Such a movement is articulated through the discontinuity that occurs between two distinct stages: "In the first, the oppressed unveil the world of oppression and . . . commit themselves to its transformation. In the second stage . . . this pedagogy . . . becomes a pedagogy of all people in the process of permanent liberation" (Freire, 1970/2005, p. 54). Those two moments are characterized by distinctive temporal references. For the "naïve thinker", "historical time" is perceived as a constraint:

> [It is] 'a stratification of the acquisitions and experiences of the past,' from which the present should emerge normalized and 'well-behaved.' For the naïve thinker, the important thing is accommodation to this normalized 'today'. . . . By thus denying temporality, it denies itself as well.
> (Freire, 1970/2005, p. 92)

For the critic, "transformation of reality" is rather an ongoing movement that remains paramount (Freire, 1970/2005, p. 92). The transition from the 'naïve' to the 'critical' stage is envisioned as an irreversible movement. Thus, raising consciousness suggests a shift in one's perspective on inequalities and oppression. However, before and after such an irrevocable move occurs, Freire's theory also suggests implicitly that those two moments revolve around the repetition of specific situations. During the first stage, oppressed people are animated by their struggle to detach themselves from oppressors' views of the world. Because it requires a sustained effort, the liberation from the "oppressor–oppressed" contradiction (Freire, 1970/2005, p. 49) involves the repetitive experience of situations constitutive of some form of cycle – grounded in the present – through which people learn to eventually extract themselves to become more "authentic". During the second stage, the emancipatory aim of education – which becomes future oriented – is "constantly remade in the praxis" (Freire, 1970/2005, p. 84). Education is thus understood through the repetitions of a pedagogical pattern conceived around dialogue and problem-solving activities. In spite of the fact that Freire explicitly discusses the "duration" (Freire, 1970/2005, p. 84) of the pedagogical process he theorized, the assumptions that legitimize it seem to remain taken for granted. At least three remarks can be formulated.

First, this approach relies on a chronosophy (i.e., a vision of how the present relates to the future) that locates the aim of education within a narrative privileging historical progression. Almost 50 years after its initial formulation, the relevance of such a vision appears however ambiguous. Such a narrative may indeed be more difficult to embrace, or may even no longer be appropriate, within a cultural context where the myth of progress became a source of suspicion and where society and education are characterized by new forms of temporal experiences, such as "presenteism" (loss of both a historical and future perspective), "changeability" (impermanence and ephemerality of realities), "non-progressiveness" (lack of coherence, consistency, as to what constitutes desirable change), "existential insecurity" (loss of continuity in one's reality) or "despair" (loss of faith in oneself as an agent of constructive change) (Bagnall, 1994).

Second, Freire's approach assumes that emancipation requires the experience of an irreversible discontinuity, marked by a shift within the learners' consciousness of oppression. Temporal constraints remain however diverse; their sources and effects cannot be reduced to simple expressions. Raising a rhythmic consciousness involves therefore multiple strategies unfolding through different temporalities (e.g., self-awareness, understanding of sociocultural or environmental dynamics) within heterogeneous contexts. Hence, such a critical process requires one to differentiate the various ways rhythmic awareness may be promoted and eventually linked to concrete, collective actions.

Third, even when awareness of temporal constraints may be quite developed, it is usually not enough to trigger effective transformations. From those who suffer from temporal pressures, solutions envisioned tend to be reduced to individual strategies (e.g., adoption of relaxation techniques, 'job-out', time management techniques) and psychologizing the interpretations of the problems encountered (e.g., as a matter of self-discipline); they may also paradoxically contribute to rehabilitate a capitalist logic (e.g., the emerging market of slowness) (Bouton, 2013). The ubiquity and self-reinforcing nature of phenomena of social acceleration (Rosa, 2005/2013) and the difficulty to envision collective actions (e.g., changing working laws relative to management techniques or temporal pressure and fiscal or economical mechanisms promoting sustainable shareholding) (Bouton, 2013) may therefore appear out of reach, not only due to the multiple layers they encompass but also because of the very temporality they require to be implemented. Freire's method – as most of those constitutive of critical pedagogies – relies on a pattern of activity (e.g., dialogue, self-reflection and collective gathering) that requires temporal resources that it is assumed people have (e.g., temporal availability and the capacity to synchronize and sustain collective action on the long run). In the contemporary environment, temporal pressures and the increased individualization of both everyday rhythms and lifelong trajectories tend to challenge such an assumption.[1]

Therefore, questions remain: what kind of chronosophy should be mobilized to integrate emancipatory education within a historical framework? Beyond 'quick-fix' solutions that provide learners with an illusion of control, how to promote a change of temporal consciousness that involves heterogeneous rhythms? How to conceive the temporality of the pedagogical process itself, considering the mismatch that may exist between the time required for sound judgment and collective actions, on the one hand, and the lack of availability and difficulties to synchronize and sustain collective efforts, on the other hand?

Rancière and the periodicity that paces emancipatory education

To some extent, Rancière's conception addresses some of those issues, focusing for instance on the present time and alluding to the fact that operations that enable emancipation may not require dedicated time. For Rancière, emancipation refers to a process of 'subjectification' that makes the appearance of subjectivity possible through a rupture in the order of things and a reconfiguration of the field of experience. It requires "the production through a series of actions of a body and a capacity for enunciation not previously identifiable within a given field of experience" (Rancière, 1999, p. 35). As stressed by Biesta (2010, p. 47), subjectification is therefore a supplement to the existing order because it adds something to this order by redefining the field of experience in a way that can be apprehended by the senses. Subjectification "decomposes and recomposes the relationships between the ways of *doing*, of *being* and of *saying* that define the perceptible organization of the community" (Rancière, 1995, p. 40, stressed by the author). It is therefore highly political because it intervenes in and reconfigures the existing order of things (Biesta, 2010, p. 47). For Rancière, "politics" refers to the mode of acting that perturbs – in the name of or with reference to equality – the "police", that is, the arrangement ruling the ways people find their place, their role or their position within a social order (Biesta, 2010, p. 48). According to this view, emancipation is not about raising awareness of oneself. It is rather about the "act" through which the subject "connects and disconnects different areas, regions, identities, functions, and capacities existing in the configuration of a given experience" (Rancière, 1999, p. 40). In this view, equality is not a goal that needs to be achieved through political or other means; it is rather an assumption that can be tested or verified in concrete situations (Biesta, 2010, p. 51). Emancipation is therefore based on a "transgressive act" that assumes equality as real and effectual. It is not about overcoming inequality (e.g., economical) but rather establishing a new social relation that reconfigures the social experience by reintroducing "dissensus" in the way it is interpreted (Biesta, 2010, p. 52). From a temporal perspective, such an action belongs to a movement that could be conceived as historical and therefore irreversible. However, by locating it in the everyday experience, and assuming its fragile and flowing nature, Rancière's conception rather stresses its recurring and periodical dynamics.

Suspicious about the attempts to use formal education to bring about equality, Rancière's project challenges the "progressive" views conceiving the role of the educator as a liberator (Biesta, 2010, p. 55). As long as it is based on the representation of inequality as a "delay" in one's development, education perpetuates the position held by the educator of always "being ahead" of the one who needs to be educated to be liberated (Biesta, 2010, p. 56). Rancière's conception of emancipation privileges therefore a temporal horizon focusing on the present situation rather than aiming at a hypothetic ideal future. As stressed by Biesta (Biesta, 2010, p. 57), as long as equality is projected into the future and perceived as something that has to be brought about through educational methods that aim to overcome existing inequality, educators cannot reach equality but simply reproduce inequality. In *The Ignorant School Master*, Rancière (1991) discusses his conception of emancipation from an educational perspective, exploring the method implemented by Joseph Jacotot (1770–1840). According to Jacotot's method, for education to be truly emancipating, it has to be based on the assumption of the "equality of intelligence" rather than distinguishing between an 'inferior intelligence' and a 'superior' one (e.g., Freire's 'naïve' vs. 'critical' subjects). Hence, the main educational "problem" becomes that of revealing "an intelligence to itself" (Rancière, 1991, p. 28). Following Jacotot's example, it does not require explication but attention. Two fundamental pedagogical acts are identified: "interrogating", that is, demanding speech to manifest one's intelligence, and "verifying" that the work of intelligence is done with attention (Rancière, 1991, p. 28). Unlike Socrates or Freire's methods that assume that the purpose of dialogue is already known by the educator, this conception does not privilege any predefined path to emancipation (Rancière, 1991, p. 29). According to Rancière (Rancière, 1991, p. 39), emancipation requires the constant verification of "what an intelligence can do when it considers itself equal to any other and considers any other equal to itself".

Such an approach reconfigures therefore how the temporality of the emancipatory aim of education is traditionally conceived. It is no longer located on a continuum distinguishing the learner's capacity based on a 'before' – equated with 'less' intelligence or critical capacity – and an 'after', characterized by 'more', a continuum that would suggest that emancipation can be reduced to a temporal gap filled by history. According to Biesta (2013), Rancière's contribution may lead to a conception of education that does not require time because its capacity to make subjectivity possible relies above all on the educator's acknowledgement of one's interlocutor (e.g., the child) as 'being there', an acknowledgement that, unlike the development of a specific competency, does not require time.

If Biesta (2013, p. 87) may be right to consider such acknowledgment as 'instantaneous', its temporality remains problematic for at least two reasons. First, acknowledgment should be understood within a field of tensions that determine why and how people – including educators – struggle to choose the ways they focus and dedicate their attention. Considering such tensions, the time for acknowledging someone's subjectivity may not only be scarce, but it is also unequally determined by logics that rule a specific form of economy – what Citton (2014) identifies as the "economy of attention"'. In addition, to be sustained, the emancipatory effects of Rancière's approach have to be inscribed in an ongoing loop, made of the constant act of 'testing' and 'verifying equality'. In other words, if the patterns of such an educational conception are made of acts of enunciation, verification or attentive acknowledgement, its unfolding is constituted by their ongoing periodical repetition. Its quality appears thus through the pattern and the frequency through which it is actualized. From a temporal perspective, the main limitation of this conception appears therefore with the fact that, by valorizing its discontinuous feature, the experience of subjectification is not conceived through its 'long-term' duration. By avoiding a projection of the aim of education into a hypothetical future, it misses a temporal framework to interpret how one elaborates on an empowering sense of self-cohesion through the succession of educational instants experienced in one's life.

Mezirow and the patterns that organize transformative learning

If both Freire and Rancière's approaches rely on specific patterns of emancipation, Mezirow's contribution explores further the role they may play within a theory of transformation. Influenced by heterogeneous theoretical traditions (e.g., pragmatism, symbolic interactionism, constructivism, hermeneutics, psychoanalysis and critical pedagogy), Mezirow's (1991, 2000) transformative learning theory provides adult educators with a model revolving around critical (self-)reflection and emancipatory learning. For Mezirow (2000, p. 5), learning can be understood as "the process of using a prior interpretation to construe a new or revised interpretation of the meaning of one's experience as a guide to future action." Transformative learning refers therefore to the process by which learners transform

> [their] taken-for-granted frames of reference (meaning perspectives, habits of mind, mind-sets) to make them more inclusive, discriminating, open, emotionally capable of change, and reflective so that they may generate beliefs and opinions that will prove more true or justified to guide action.
> (Mezirow, 2000, p. 7)

Considering the democratic aim of the educational praxis, this theory focuses in particular on how adults "learn to negotiate and act on [their] own purposes, values, feelings, and meanings rather than those . . . uncritically assimilated from others – to gain control over [their] lives as socially responsible, clear-thinking decision makers" (Mezirow, 2000, p. 8). Reinterpreting Habermas's contribution, Mezirow distinguishes two domains of learning: "instrumental learning" refers to the capacity to control and manipulate the environment or other people to improve performance; "communicative learning" relates to the ability to learn what others mean when they communicate, including their feelings, intentions, values and moral issues. Departing from Habermas' framework, Mezirow (2000, p. 10) envisions emancipation as the transformation process that pertains in both instrumental and communicative learning domains.

From a temporal perspective, the three aspects characterizing rhythmic phenomena are expressed to some extent in transformative learning theory. In comparison with Freire and Rancière's theories, one of the main characteristics of Mezirow's contribution is the fact that all the components of emancipatory education can be described (and even abstracted) as patterns susceptible to be repeated or generalized. For instance, the importance given to "meaning schemes" and "meaning perspectives" stresses the preponderant function played by cognitive, emotional and action patterns, as embodied and discursive phenomena shaping the learner's sense of autonomy and therefore the forms taken by one's own path toward emancipation. For Mezirow (2000, p. 16), a meaning perspective refers to "[t]he structure of assumptions and expectations through which we filter sense impressions. . . . It selectively shapes and delimits perception, cognition, feelings, and dissipation by predisposing our intentions, expectations, and purposes." Such frames of reference are thus made of 'habits of mind' and 'points of view' that mobilize meaning schemes, consciously or not, on an everyday basis. Therefore, in congruence with its cognitivist roots, transformative learning theory suggests – but does not develop the theoretical implications of – the presence of circular dynamics through which meaning schemes and meaning perspectives are produced, reproduced or eventually challenged and transformed. Following a hermeneutical influence, this theory also conceives the critical aim of educational praxis through the circularities involved in dialogical situations, organized around circles of interpretations challenging the meaning given to the learners' experience through activities of reflection or reframing. Finally, in congruence with Freire's critical pedagogy and the influence of developmental psychology, the process of transformation is generally conceived according to a developmental approach structured around a series of phases (e.g., disorienting dilemma, self-examination, critical assessment of assumptions, recognition that one's discontent and transformation are shared, exploration of new options, planning action, acquisition of knowledge and skills, trying new roles, building self-confidence, reintegration of the new perspective, etc.) constitutive at a broader scale of yet another pattern (Mezirow, 2000, p. 22). At the junction between the learner's everyday life and one's own lifelong development, the role played by the notion of "disorienting dilemma" – as common trigger for transformative learning – appears finally central to interpret both the discontinuous experiences that are constitutive of the learners' biographical paths and the ongoing reframing they require along the 'movement' of one's own transformation.

From a temporal perspective, at least two additional limitations deserve to be mentioned when considering this theory. First, as pointed by Taylor (2000), individual perspective transformation is most often explained as being triggered by a significant personal event in spite of the fact that there is still little understanding of why some disorienting dilemmas lead to a transformation and others do not. Thus, even if it acknowledges the role of circular dynamics involved for instance in dialogue, reflection or reframing, Mezirow's contribution does not theorize how repetition, retroaction (e.g., feedback loops) or recursion (e.g., generative loops), as periodic phenomena, contributes to a process of transformation. The fact that this theory does not explore systematically the qualities and occurrences of the repetitions and cycles involved in everyday life (e.g., positive or negative reinforcements leading to radicalization or inhibition) (Alhadeff-Jones, 2012) raises therefore questions regarding the way casual, ongoing periodic activities may relate to single discontinuous events (e.g., disorienting dilemma triggering a personal transformation). A second critique appears to be often formulated toward this theory: the mutual influences among context, culture and transformative learning remain only marginally looked at (Taylor, 2000); thus, it seems characterized by the lack of a sound connection between individual perspective transformation and social change. It seems assumed that perspective transformation will automatically lead to social action and social change (Finger & Asùn, 2001, p. 59). From a temporal perspective, such an assumption remains problematic. It questions the nature of the principles according to which an influence can be established between the rhythmic framework of personal transformation and the temporal context of social change.

Toward rhythmanalytical approaches to critical education

The examples provided by Freire, Rancière and Mezirow's contributions illustrate how existing emancipatory approaches do privilege specific temporal dimensions inherent to education (e.g., historical movement, everyday repetitions and learning patterns). The characteristics of such temporal features remain however mostly tacit, generally taken for granted or decontextualized. Temporal and rhythmic features are not conceived as an explicit matter of reflection and action. Freire, Rancière and Mezirow's critical contributions explore, to some extent, the historical, quotidian and biographical dimensions that are constitutive of educational temporalities. The forms of critical pedagogy they enable stress specific rhythmic features inherent respectively to the movement of emancipation, its periodicity and the patterns it may involve. However, such contributions do not refer to a systematic framework to conduct a temporal analysis of their own assumptions regarding educational rhythms. From that perspective, they remain literally "hypocritical" (Alhadeff-Jones, 2010, p. 488) as the complexity that characterizes the temporalities of their critical views remain largely unchallenged. Considering this limitation, the first aim of rhythmanalytical approaches in regard to critical education should be to ground and enrich existing critical pedagogies with conceptual resources to reframe how they approach contemporary experiences of time and the heterogeneous forms of temporal constraint lived nowadays.

The philosophical and sociological grounds of rhythmanalysis

To explore resources that may lead us to question how to explicitly conceive emancipatory education through a rhythmological lens, we need therefore to return to Bachelard's philosophical and ethical intuitions regarding the idea of rhythmanalysis, its sociological reinterpretation by Lefebvre and their respective influences on educational theory.

Bachelard's rhythmanalysis

The term "rhythmanalysis" was first introduced by Pinheiro dos Santos (1931, as cited in Bachelard, 1950), a Brazilian philosopher whose inaccessible writings remained largely unknown. According to Bachelard, Pinheiro dos Santos studied the phenomenology of rhythm from three points of view, respectively, material, biological and psychological. In *La Dialectique de la Durée*, Bachelard (1950) comments on this study to establish his own conception of the formative and healing work that he envisioned, based on his philosophy of instant. Bachelard's rhythmanalysis was conceived in opposition to two main references: Bergson's theory of time and Freud's psychoanalytical theory (Sauvanet, 2000). Unlike Bergson, Bachelard (1950) believed that the experience of duration is only an artificial continuity in the discontinuity of lived instants. Time is felt through the experience of rhythms as a flexible and subjective organization of systems of instants (cf. Chapter 7). Therefore, dealing with psychological suffering requires some form of rhythmanalytical work to reorganize the way the succession of instants and discontinuities are experienced, challenging inadequate feelings of "permanence", calming down "forced rhythms", stimulating "languishing rhythms" and regulating "temporal diversity" so that "the rhythms of ideas and songs could progressively command the rhythms of things" (Bachelard, 1950, pp. x–xi). Despite his interest for Freud's method, Bachelard was also criticizing its normative ground and the fact that psychoanalysis privileges a conception of the healthy being, based on dominant standards, conceived as static attributes of a determined social group (Sauvanet, 2000, p. 105).

Rather than considering the characteristics that are constitutive of people, Bachelard's rhythmanalysis focuses on those that make them evolve (Sauvanet, 2000, p. 165). Accordingly, the evolution of the self is conceived as "undulatory", as a fabric made of tensions (e.g., successes and mistakes or forgetting and remembering) (Bachelard, 1950, p. 142). Thus, rhythmanalysis aims at finding "patterns of duality" (*motifs de dualité*) for the mind to balance them (Bachelard, 1950, p. 141) beyond a dualistic logic. Doing so, it may carry some form of healing power. His approach aims therefore at freeing ourselves from contingent agitations through the analysis of lived temporalities and the purposeful choice of lived rhythms. As stressed by Sauvanet (2000, p. 107), rhythmanalysis does not involve for Bachelard a relationship between an analyst and a patient; it requires loneliness through which an individual self-analyzes through the use of media, such as literary works, which help symbolize and interpret one's own experience. If Bachelard was the first one to consider rhythm as a philosophical concept, his approach remains nevertheless mostly metaphorical (Sauvanet, 2000, p. 100). His main contribution is that it draws an ethical framework and formulates valuable intuitions regarding the role played by introspection in regard to rhythmic experience. As he never formalized it, Bachelard's rhythmanalysis is not a theory per se; it should rather be conceived as a "creative exercise" (Sauvanet, 2000, p. 101). The power of his intuitions relies on the assumption that the unicity of the self requires an ongoing work of self-elaboration that purposefully organizes lived instants into rhythms to tolerate and organize – rather than reduce – the tensions and contradictions they may carry.

Lefebvre's rhythmanalysis

Since the 1960s, Lefebvre took over Bachelard's initial use of the idea of rhythmanalysis and started conceiving it as a way to explore emancipatory strategies through the analysis of the experience of everyday rhythms (e.g., Lefebvre, 1961/2002, 1974/1991, 1992/2004).[2] His interest for rhythms was part of a broader concern regarding the quotidian, the banality and emptiness of everyday life within capitalist society. Because all human practices are constituted rhythmically, in terms of a relationship between repetition and difference (Lefebvre, 1992/2004), they provide grounds to study everyday interactions and understand how alienation and emancipation are embedded in quotidian rhythms. At first Lefebvre envisioned rhythmanalysis as a sociological method to study the fabric of relations and interactions between social time characterized by cyclic rhythms (e.g., circadian periodicities determined by cosmic rhythms) and linear processes (e.g., monotonous repetitions) inherent to techniques found in industrial society (Revol, 2014). Assuming that social space and time (e.g., urban city) produce, and are produced, through the experience of repetitions and rhythms, Lefebvre conceived quotidian spaces (e.g., streets, squares and working spaces) as the result of rhythmic activities that could become the focus of analysis (Revol, 2014). The emancipatory aim of rhythmanalysis came therefore from the possibility to interpret how space and time are socially produced; it had to unveil how they become a source of alienation. What was at stake remained the capacity to appropriate for oneself the experience of rhythms that shaped and was shaped by the spaces within which one evolves (Revol, 2014).

For that reason, Lefebvre conceived rhythmanalysis as an embodied approach through which the rhythmanalyst has to feel and to experiment empirically how rhythms are lived. The rhythmanalyst has therefore to "listen" to his or her body as a "metronome" and to "learn rhythm from it" to appreciate external rhythms (Lefebvre, 1992/2004, p. 19). Focusing on one's senses, breath, heartbeats and rhythmic use of one's limbs is required to feel and perceive lived temporalities and to apprehend how they relate to the temporal and spatial environment within which one evolves. It is a work of appropriation of one's own body as much as it may lead to the transformation of social praxis (Revol, 2014). Drawing a parallel with the practice of medicine, Lefebvre (1992/2004) suggests that the task of the rhythmanalyst is to identify social arrhythmia and transform the way it impacts social life. The approach also carries an esthetic function; to feel, perceive and be moved by rhythms, the rhythmanalyst must also focus on the sensible values of rhythms (Lefebvre, 1992/2004). From a philosophical and theoretical perspective, Lefebvre's conception of rhythm remains often unclear (e.g., the role of measure vs. its free-flowing features), and his interpretation of Bachelard's intuitions appears superficial (Sauvanet, 2000, p. 167). His main contribution, from an educational perspective, is that his conception of rhythmanalysis goes beyond the intimate and imaginary spaces envisioned by Bachelard to conceive its scope of action within the realm of concrete interactions within society (Revol, 2014). In comparison with Jaques-Dalcroze, Mandelstam's or Bode's rhythmic methods, Lefebvre's contribution fills a gap: by inscribing the experience of individual rhythms within the history of social spaces, and by showing how such spaces relate to the intimate experience of time, Lefebvre's rhythmanalysis provides us with a concrete path – and a medium –to envision how individual and collective rhythms may relate with each other beyond analogies and metaphors.

Rhythmanalysis and educational theory

The influence of rhythmanalytical conceptions on educational theory remains marginal. In English-speaking countries, interest for Lefebvre's contribution on rhythmanalysis starts emerging (e.g., Christie, 2013; Hopwood, 2013; Jacklin, 2004; Mathisen, 2015; Middleton, 2014), benefitting from the recent translation of his work. In France, Pineau (e.g., 1986, 2000) and Hess (e.g., 2004, 2006, 2009) were among the first ones to introduce theoretical reflections informed by Bachelard's and Lefebvre's contributions. Pineau's (2000) landmark book, *Temporalités et Formation*, constitutes probably the most significant attempt to develop a theory of education organized around the concept of rhythm, suggesting the idea of 'chronoformation' (later relabeled 'rhythmoformation') as a figure of emancipatory education. Inspired by Lefebvre's approach, Hess (e.g., 2004, 2006, 2009) privileged references to the concept of moment (cf. Chapter 11) to explore the strategies through which a subject may become more conscious of the whole rhythmic dynamics that organize the temporalities of one's life.

In France, Pineau's and Hess' contributions have inspired a new generation of scholars, mainly in adult and higher education (e.g., Galvani, 2004, 2011; Lesourd, 2004, 2009). Their interpretations of rhythmanalytical work appear through their efforts to question the strategies implemented, and the resources required for someone to build up the capacity to extract oneself from moments experienced as alienating, to facilitate transitions between moments or to create new liberating moments. Such contributions interrogate therefore the relationship between such a capacity and the processes and dynamics of self-development. Those approaches share common features: they express a hermeneutical, phenomenological and critical sensibility, and their focus revolves around issues related to self-development, transformative learning, or *auto-formation*.

Gaston Pineau's rhythmoformation

In the French-speaking field of adult education, Pineau's intuitions and research have been recognized since the 1990s for their significant contribution to the development of life history and biographical approaches as training and research methods. At the core of his educational project, Pineau's rhythmoformation refers to the individual capacity to learn and grow through the integration and the articulation of the plurality of biological, social and cosmic rhythms that compose one's life. From an emancipatory perspective, Pineau (2000, p. 105) locates, at the core of the relationship between autonomy and dependence, the capacity to set boundaries (*frontières*). Due to the impossibility to define objectively temporal boundaries (e.g., internal vs. external rhythms), what appears as crucial in his theory is the capacity for adults to define them subjectively (Pineau, 2000, p. 105). Accordingly, the aim of chronoformation is to bring people to learn how to distribute, combine and balance the rhythms and times that compose the historicity of their lives to fight against the experience of schizochrony (cf. Chapter 7). To theorize it, Pineau (2000, p. 120) borrows the concept of synchronization from chronobiology (cf. Chapter 6). Defining the borders of one's own time requires thus a process of adjustment based on the capacity to synchronize the heterogeneous rhythms that constitute one's life. Chronoformation's emancipatory aim requires therefore the capacity to take in charge the temporal conditions through which meanings emerge in everyday life as much as through the life span.

Pineau's (1986, 2000) educational theory articulates "educational temporalities", stressing in particular the relationships that exist between two times (day and night) and three movements (*auto-formation*, *hétéro-formation* and *éco-formation*) that characterize *éducation permanente*. For Pineau (1986, p. 100), the alienating dimension of the temporal organization imposed by society comes from both its homogeneous and homogenizing aspects and the fact that the monotony and the "mechanical succession" of days, nights, weeks, months and years erases, day after day, the qualitative differences of lived moments. If traditional educational theories conceive learning time as uniform and homogeneous (e.g., the course's hour or the daylong training), Pineau's approach, inspired among others by Durand's (1969, as cited in Pineau, 2000) anthropological contribution, stresses the role played by a basic temporal structure articulated around the alternance between day and night. Such a rhythm constitutes indeed an invariant that is not only essential from a cosmic, psychobiological and sociological perspective but also because it organizes cultures, everyday life and more broadly life trajectories from an educational point of view as well.

Noticing how nighttime "which brings sleep, dreams, pleasure, desires, love and crimes" remains excluded from dominant educational theories, including informal education, Pineau (1986, p. 104) considers that this "residuum" provides in fact the counterpart to daytime education, once it is no longer kept separate and lived as if it were a "free, private and autonomous time". Thus, Pineau associates the dynamics of "self-development" (*auto-formation*) to the "nocturnal" component of existence, conceived as the best place and time for the emergence and development of an autonomous individuality: "Just as the day is the realm of an education received from others [*hétéro-formation*], the nocturnal realm is that of self-development [*auto-formation*]" (Pineau, 2000, p. 105). Considering the nocturnal aspect of education leads him to question how the influence of *hétéro-formation* and society may decrease. Concretely, questioning the formative dimension associated with 'nighttime' brings Pineau to challenge the lack of research conducted on the different forms of *auto-formation* practiced in the margin of the day, depending on one's age, gender, social class and cultural environment. Through his reflection, he distinguishes for instance learning characterizing dusk, end-of-the-day transition, personal and social times experienced traditionally at the beginning of the evening, restful sleep and its unconscious component, waking time, sleeplessness and finally dawn time as the moments of confrontation between *auto-formation* and *hétéro-formation* (Pineau, 2000, p. 105).

Hess's study of educational moments

As a disciple of Lefebvre, Hess was the first one to explore the heterogeneity of 'moments' constitutive of one's own development and discuss this concept in relation to informal or nonformal education (e.g., dance, family, work, rest, sport, creation). According to Lefebvre (1961/2002, 2009), a moment designates a common form of experience that displays constancy and continuity within the course of one's life (e.g., the moment of love, play, art or formal education). At the same time, it emerges through the repetition of instants, events or circumstances that are discontinuous and never exactly similar to their previous occurrences (cf. Chapter 11). A moment is therefore not conceived as a short duration; it rather refers to a category of experience that is characterized by its own rhythmicity (e.g., eating, creating and practicing a sport constitute moments that have their own rhythms). Designating consciously a moment as such represents a critical operation. It provides the subject with a principle to explore a specific time of one's life to reflect on it and learn from the repetition of experiences that constitute it. Hess developed this idea through different themes. Among them, he discussed for instance the case of doctoral studies, associating the starting of the process of writing a doctorate to the creation of a singular moment within one's life (Hess, 2004) – a moment that appears as specific source of learning for the student as much as for the adviser (Hess, 2004).

Hess approached the various moments constitutive of one's biography from a phenomenological perspective, suggesting for instance that each one is associated with specific spaces. For him, journaling, autoethnography and biographical research appear as key methods favoring the conscientization of moments required to 'become author' of one's own life. For Hess, Lefebvre's theory of moments provides people with resources to transform the experience of dissociation and fragmentation – that characterizes the alienating effects of everyday life – into a constructive process. Such a process is at the core of his work in adult and higher education. Accordingly, the capacity to operate meaningful transitions from a moment to another remains crucial. Paying attention to the presence of a 'ritual of entrance' and a 'ritual of exit' in and out of each moment constitutes for instance a critical aspect of someone's development. Paying attention to those rituals allows the subject to focus or refocus on a moment to unfold it. Considering such transitions should also bring one to invent new rhythms to move from a moment to another (Hess, 2004). In addition, journaling constitutes a privileged research and educational tool as it provides a technique to conceive or create moments (Hess, 2009) based on the narrative reconfiguration of one's experience.

Lesourd's study of privileged moments

In the continuation of Pineau's project of *rythmoformation*, in affinity with Hess's contribution and based on his clinical experience, Lesourd (e.g., 2004, 2009) studied what he called "privileged moments", that is, moments characterized by intense transformations of the self. His work explores how the moment of transformation – as a form of 'meta moment' that relates to different forms of life experience – generates a specific 'know-how' (*savoir-passer*) required for people to negotiate the meaning of life transition. According to his research, privileged moments are characterized by an active reconfiguration of the temporalities (e.g., societal, institutional, interpersonal and intrapsychic) that shape the subject's experience. Changing the way heterogeneous and conflicting rhythms are conceived, the self operates, during those privileged moments, what may appear afterward as an 'existential transformation'. In his view, a privileged moment is also socially constructed. How the subject talks about it, and the way it is shared and acknowledged by others, participates thus to the validation of the meaning and relevance it takes for the person experiencing the transformation. Privileging the articulation between biographical work and the microanalytical recall of specific situations, Lesourd questions in particular how one learns to consciously perceive and move between distinctive moments in one's own field of attention. Assuming that the preponderance of a moment is a matter of being at the center (vs. the periphery) of one's attention, then the capacity to extract oneself from a moment becomes a matter of "mental gestures" (which include embodied experiences) that can be studied and developed. From this perspective, emancipation relies on the subject's ability to become more conscious of the mental gestures mobilized to focus on specific moments and one's capacity to purposefully transition from a moment to another.

Galvani's study of intense moments and kairos

In close proximity with the previous authors, Galvani's research (e.g., Galvani, 2004, 2011) explores people's "moments of *auto-formation*", defining several typologies to differentiate the ways people learn from their life experiences and eventually increase their margins of autonomy. For Galvani, emancipation comes from the individual's capacity to relate the different "levels of reality" (e.g., theoretical, practical and symbolic) that constitute *auto-formation*, especially as they are found in the study of "intense moments". Inspired by Jankélévitch's philosophical work, Galvani (2011, p. 75) designates such moments with the term *"kairos"*, originally borrowed from the Greek mythology,[3] to stress how much they constitute "opportune" moments when "everything is at stake". The *kairos* is a moment of inspiration, a time when meanings and new forms emerge. It is found for instance in the moments of the 'very first time' – all those times that inaugurate the emergence of a new kind of experience in someone's life (e.g., the first love, the first encounter with death or the first day of work). It also emerges through the paroxysm of 'great moments' characterized by the intensity of borderline situations when the experience of love, death, loneliness or the infinite dissolves usual landmarks and references. In those instances, the emancipatory impact of the experience of *kairos* can be related, to some extent, to the processes described by Mezirow's (1991) transformative learning theory. At another temporal scale, the *kairos* finally appears in the everyday repetition of daily activities, such as those exercised for instance by professional athletes or musicians. It designates then the spontaneous and non-reflected ability to operate the relevant move, or the correct judgment, at the right time. In this case, the notion is close to Csikszentmihalyi's concept of "flow" (Csikszentmihalyi & Selega Csikszentmihalyi, 1988). The *kairos* usually requires one to suspend discursive consciousness and intentionality for the self to spontaneously cope with the moment and be fully involved within it (Galvani, 2011). From an educational perspective, the emancipatory value of the *kairos*, as an intense moment, requires both the spontaneous capacity to be in the 'flow' and the retrospect ability to reflect on the theoretical meanings, practical effects and existential values it carries.

Contributions and limitations of rhythmanalytical contributions in education

The idea of emancipation is omnipresent in the rhythmic contributions introduced by Pineau, Hess, Lesourd and Galvani's contributions. In congruence with the theoretical filiations they belong to, their main contribution is that they ground the experience of emancipation both in the most existential aspects of one's life and the most casual ones too. Taken all together those contributions display a coherent framework to conceptualize the rhythmic dimensions that shape the intellectual, practical and existential moves that participate in a greater sense of autonomy through the distinctions they introduce (e.g., *hétéro-formation*/daytime, *auto-formation*/nighttime); the dynamics they privilege (production and transition between the moments of existence); the phenomena they study (privileged or intense lived moments); and the methods they implement (e.g., life history, journals of moments or *explicitation biographique*). Those contributions represent therefore stimulating resources to both enrich a theoretical reflection around the rhythms of emancipation and envision how it may be implemented in the educational praxis.

Two main limitations remain however. First, in spite of conceiving emancipation and autonomy from a rhythmical perspective, they do not explore more systematically how the concept of rhythm itself is theorized. For the most part, Bachelard and Lefebvre's rhythmanalytical references remain taken for granted, with their inspiring visions and their theoretical weaknesses as well. The tendency remains to conceive a broad range of rhythms without nuancing the patterns, the periodicities and the movements that distinguish their social, discursive and corporeal expressions. In addition, those contributions lack a reflective and contextual analysis of both the temporal resources they require to be implemented (e.g., time required for self-reflection, introspection or dialogue) and the way they conceive the temporal articulation between individual self-development and social transformation. Focusing mainly on individual's autonomy, they do not provide a framework to relate and interpret their actions in regard to collective changes.

Envisioning the careful, reflexive and rhythmically informed interpretation of life experiences

The reflection conducted in this chapter illustrates how existing critical pedagogies rely on tacit temporal assumptions that need to be challenged to be enriched. From this perspective, introducing a rhythmanalytical framework does not require one to reinvent critical pedagogy; it may rather constitute an additional resource to enhance existing theories and practices. Thus, we have explored the value of questioning the assumptions that frame how educators may interpret the movements, the periodicities and the patterns through which people may develop and increase their autonomy. Some of the hypotheses associated with the idea of rhythmanalysis, as it was originally imagined by Bachelard and later conceived by Lefebvre, have also been identified. They suggest that the experience of tensions through time reveals rhythms that can be taken as a matter of introspection and that their elaboration may contribute to self-development. The analysis of lived rhythms may also participate in the emergence of a specific set of skills required for someone to learn how to appropriate and transform the rhythms of one's individual and social life. Through the theoretical contributions of Pineau, Hess, Lesourd and Galvani, the possibility to implement a rhythmanalytical approach, from an educational perspective, emerges as an innovative path. Such reflections demonstrate the value inherent to educational efforts conducted around the rhythmicity of one's own *autoformation*. They appear therefore as an invitation to envision the development of a much-needed field of practice, characterized by the careful, reflexive and rhythmically informed interpretation of life experiences to increase autonomy and promote emancipation. The next chapter is going to engage further on this way by exploring how the biographical path, through which the movement of someone's autonomy is organized, displays patterns and periodicities that reveal the rhythmicity of emancipation.

Notes

1 One significant exception may be found with unemployed people, who suffer from the lack of temporal structures, which constitutes another form of temporal alienation (Demazière, 2006).
2 For a contextualization of the emergence of critical writings related to rhythm theories between 1970 and 1980 in France, see Michon (2011).
3 In the Greek mythology, several gods were associated with the idea of time: *Chronos* was the god of duration and irreversible time; *Aion* was a god of eternity, and *Kairos* was the god of the creative instant, the opportune time when everything is at stake.

References

Alhadeff-Jones, M. (2007). *Education, critique et complexité: Modèle et expérience de conception d'une approche multiréférentielle de la critique en sciences de l'éducation*. Lille, France: Atelier National de Reproduction des Thèses.
Alhadeff-Jones, M. (2010). Challenging the limits of critique in education through Morin's Paradigm of complexity. *Studies in Philosophy and Education*, *29*(5), 477–490.
Alhadeff-Jones, M. (2012). Transformative learning and the challenges of complexity. In E.W. Taylor, & P. Cranton (Eds.), *Handbook of transformative learning: Theory, research and practice* (pp. 178–194). San Francisco: Jossey-Bass.
Bachelard, G. (1950). *La dialectique de la durée*. Paris: Presses Universitaires de France.
Bagnall, R. (1994). *Educational research in a postmodernity of resignation: A cautionary corrective to utopian resistance*. Paper presented at the Annual Conference of the Australian Association for Research in Education. Retrieved December 20, 2015, from http://www.aare.edu.au/publications-database.php/968/educational-research-in-a-postmodernity-of-resignation-a-cautionary-corrective-to-utopian-resistance

Biesta, G. (2010). A new logic of emancipation: The methodology of Jacques Rancière. *Educational Theory, 60*(1), 39–59.
Biesta, G. (2013). Time out: Can education do and be done without time? In T. Szkudlarek, & R.G. Sultana (Eds.), *Education, politics, and disagreement: Theoretical articulations* (pp.75–88). Rotterdam: Sense.
Bouton, C. (2013). *Le temps de l'urgence*. Lormont, France: Le Bord de l'eau.
Christie, P. (2013). Space, place, and social justice developing a rhythmanalysis of education in South Africa. *Qualitative Inquiry, 19*(10), 775–785.
Citton, Y. (Ed.). (2014). *L'économie de l'attention: Nouvel horizon du capitalisme*. Paris: La Découverte.
Csikszentmihalyi, M., & Selega Csikszentmihalyi, I. (1988). *Optimal experience: Psychological studies of flow in consciousness*. Cambridge: Cambridge University Press.
Demazière, D. (2006). Le chômage comme épreuve temporelle. In J. Thoemmes, & G. De Terssac (Eds.), *Les temporalités sociales: Repères méthodologiques* (pp.121–132). Toulouse: Octarès.
Finger, M., & Asùn, J.M. (2001). *Adult education at the crossroads: Learning our way out*. New York: Zed Books.
Freire, P. (2005). *Pedagogy of the oppressed*. New York: Continuum. (Original work published 1970)
Galvani, P. (2004). L'exploration des moments intenses et du sens personnel des pratiques professionnelles. *Interaction, 8*(2), 95–121.
Galvani, P. (2011). Moments d'autoformation, kaïros de mise en forme et en sens de soi. In P. Galvani, D. Nolin, Y. de Champlain, & G. Dubé (Eds.), *Moments de formation et mise en sens de soi* (pp.69–96). Paris: L'Harmattan.
Hess, R. (2004). *Produire son oeuvre: Le moment de la thèse*. Paris: Téraèdre.
Hess, R. (2006). Rythmanalyse et théorie des moments. *Pratiques de Formation/Analyses, 51–52*, 127–149.
Hess, R. (2009). *Henri Lefebvre et la pensée du possible: Théorie des moments et construction de la personne*. Paris: Economica.
Hopwood, N. (2013). The rhythms of pedagogy: An ethnographic study of parenting education practices. *Studies in Continuing Education, 36*(2), 115–131.
Jacklin, H. (2004). Discourse, interaction and spatial rhythms: Locating pedagogic practice in a material world. *Pedagogy, Culture & Society, 12*(3), 373–398.
Lefebvre, H. (1991). *The production of space* (D. Nicholson-Smith, Trans.). Oxford: Blackwell. (Original work published 1974)
Lefebvre, H. (2002). *Critique of everyday life (vol.2)* (J. Moore, Trans.). London: Verso. (Original work published 1961)
Lefebvre, H. (2004). *Rhythmanalysis: Space, time and everyday life* (S. Elden & G. Moore, Trans.). London: Continuum. (Original work published 1992)
Lefebvre, H. (2009). *La somme et le reste*. Paris: Economica-Anthropos.
Lesourd, F. (2004). *Les moments privilégiés en formation existentielle: Contribution multiréférentielle à la recherche sur les temporalités éducatives chez les adultes en transformation dans les situations liminaires*. Doctoral dissertation, Université de Paris 8, Paris.
Lesourd, F. (2009). *L'homme en transition: Éducation et tournants de vie*. Paris: Economica-Anthropos.
Mathisen, A. (2015). Rhythms in education and the art of life: Lefebvre, Whitehead and Steiner on the art of bringing rhythmical transformations into teaching and learning – Part I. *Research on Steiner Education, 6*(2), 36–51.
Mezirow, J. (1991). *Transformative dimensions of adult learning*. San Francisco: Jossey-Bass.

Mezirow, J. (Ed). (2000). *Learning as transformation: Critical perspectives on a theory in progress.* San Francisco: Jossey-Bass.

Michon, P. (2011). *A short history of rhythm theory since the 1970's.* Retrieved December 12, 2013, from http://rhuthmos.eu/spip.php?article462

Middleton, S. (2014). *Henri Lefebvre and education.* London: Routledge.

Pineau, G. (1986). Time and lifelong education. In P. Lengrand (Ed.), *Areas of learning basic to lifelong education* (pp. 95–120). Oxford: UNESCO Institute for Education (Hamburg) & Pergamon Press.

Pineau, G. (2000). *Temporalités en formation: Vers de nouveaux synchroniseurs.* Paris: Anthropos.

Rancière, J. (1991). *The ignorant schoolmaster: Five lessons in intellectual emancipation* (K. Ross, Trans.). Stanford, CA: Stanford University Press.

Rancière, J. (1995). *On the shores of politics* (L. Heron, Trans.). New York: Verso.

Rancière, J. (1999). *Dis-agreement: Politics and philosophy* (J. Rose, Trans.). Minneapolis: University of Minnesota Press.

Revol, C. (2014). *La rythmanalyse lefebvrienne des temps et espaces sociaux, ébauche d'une pratique rythmanalytique aux visées esthétiques et éthiques.* Retrieved October 12, 2015, from http://rhuthmos.eu/spip.php?article1102

Rosa, H. (2013). *Social acceleration: A new theory of modernity* (J. Trejo-Mathys, Trans.). New York: Columbia University Press. (Original work published 2005)

Sauvanet, P. (2000). *Le rythme et la raison (vol.2): Rythmanalyses.* Paris: Kimé.

Taylor, E.W. (2000). Analyzing research on transformative learning theory. In J. Mezirow (Eds.), *Learning as transformation: Critical perspectives on a theory in progress* (pp.285–328). San Francisco: Jossey-Bass.

Chapter 11

The moment of emancipation and the rhythmic patterns of transgression

Exploring the movements, patterns and periodicities of emancipation

Through the previous chapters, a theoretical framework was established to describe and interpret the relationships among life, education's rhythmic features and the constraints and autonomy associated with them. It has also been suggested that a rhythm-centered perspective can be mobilized to enrich existing critical pedagogies and envision new educational approaches. At this stage, it seems relevant to explore how such a rhythmanalytical framework can be used in conjunction with biographical inquiry to interpret real-life experience and benefit from empirical facts. To illustrate the temporal heterogeneity and the rhythmicity constitutive of a process of emancipation, and to theorize further how emancipation relates to both everyday experiences and the biographical trajectory they belong to, this chapter is organized in three sections. The first one locates and introduces Lefebvre's theory of moments. This contribution appears as a critical resource to articulate the continuous and discontinuous features that characterize a process of emancipation, binding everyday experiences with dynamics that stretch over the life span. Accordingly, alienation and emancipation are conceived as 'moments' marked by their own rhythmic features. As we rarely refer to everyday experiences as 'emancipatory' ones, the second step of our exploration discusses the notion of transgression. Such a notion provides us indeed with a more tangible and concrete expression to exemplify casual episodes participating to a potential increase of autonomy. Inspired by Foucault's interpretation of the idea of transgression, the term is defined and then conceived – in congruence with the model developed previously – as an example of a generic pattern of emancipation. The third step of our inquiry brings us to locate and interpret the life history of a young adult, which appears as a particularly evocative example of an emancipatory path. Based on her narrative, we are going to illustrate how the movement of emancipation, the periodicities it relates to and the patterns it may display all may express the rhythms of emancipation as they unfold throughout one's existence.

Conceiving the moment of emancipation

The concept of moment

A moment is generally conceived as an interval in time, understood as a short duration in comparison with a total length, stressing the brevity of the experience of this duration (Ardoino, 2009, p. 14). The term 'moment' is often conceived as synonymous of instant, focusing on the *hic* and *nunc*, privileging a logical time, understood through a historical or chronological sequence: past, present and future. Traditional representations associated with this term, particularly in science, refer therefore to a flat understanding of time suggesting a chronological succession of moments (Ardoino, 2009, p. 14). The notion remains however polysemous. Hess (2009, pp. 6–9) highlights at least three distinct uses of this term: the "logical moment", the "historical moment" and the moment as "anthropological singularization" of a subject or a society. According to its etymology (*momentum*, affiliated with *movimentum*, meaning 'movement'), the term "moment" has been used since 1725 in physics to refer to a dynamic and to describe the rules of composition of concurring forces and the rotation of bodies; the concept was thus initially inscribed in a science of movement (Hess, 2009, pp. 6–7). This semantic background influenced Hegel's philosophy when he conceived his dialectical logic (Hess, 2009, pp. 6–7). For him, the dialectical moment is the force that leads from an idea to its opposite and then to a stage of progress in thought or in reality (Lalande, 1926/2002, p. 645). From a diachronic perspective, the idea of moment is used to describe every stage that can be assigned to any kind of development (e.g., material transformation, psychological or social process and dialectics) (Lalande, 1926/2002, p. 645). It refers therefore to a historical meaning. By distinction with the instant, which is ephemeral, the moment has a temporal consistency (Hess, 2009, p. 9). For Hegel, considering the history of philosophy, a historical moment described a specific time in the evolution of systematic thought. According to Lefebvre (1961/2002, pp. 343–344), the term "moment" receives special treatment in Hegel's philosophy:

> It designates the major figures of consciousness; each of them (e.g., the consciousness of the master and that of the slave in their mutual relations, the stoic or skeptical consciousness, the unhappy consciousness) is a moment in the dialectical ascent of self-consciousness.

According to Hess (2009, p. 8), Marx followed this use of the term to distinguish phases and stages in human history (e.g., slavery, serfdom, employment, and communism) or in human development (e.g., conception, birth, childhood and adulthood). Finally, a third meaning associated with the idea of moment emerged privileging an anthropological perspective. The moment appeared as an "anthropological singularization" of a subject or a society (Hess, 2009, p. 9). This definition was already present in Hegel's philosophy through the distinction between the moment of family, the moment of work, or the moment of the state. However, according to Hess (2009, p. 9), such an interpretation has mainly been developed by Lefebvre (1961/2002, 2009) in his theory of moments.

Lefebvre's theory of moments

Lefebvre's theory of moments emerged following the influence of Hegel's philosophy and in reaction to the psychological continuum advocated by Bergson. For Lefebvre, the experience of time can neither be reduced to linearity nor to discontinuities (Lefebvre, 2009). One finds within individual and collective consciousness some forms of "inner durations" (*durées intérieures*) that are formed and sustained for a lapse of time, without becoming fixed (Lefebvre, 2009, p. 226). A moment refers to some form of constancy within the course of time; it constitutes a common element shared by a series of instants, events, circumstances and dialectical movements (Lefebvre, 2009, p. 640). It tends to designate a 'structural' element that can be isolated or abstracted from the everyday life only through careful thinking. The term designates thus a "form", but this form is in each instance a specificity (Lefebvre, 2009, p. 640). The moment can be interpreted as an "emergence" (Alhadeff-Jones, in press) that relates to intertwined levels of organization (Lesourd, 2013). It appears as a "core" of the real-life experience that condensates what is scattered in everyday life through a unity, constituted by words, actions, situations or attitudes, feelings and representations (Lefebvre, 2009). Thus, the moment of contemplation, the moment of struggle, the moment of love, the moments of play and rest, the moments of justice, poetry or art (Lefebvre, 2009, pp. 226–227) repeat themselves in a lifetime. Each of those moments is built and emerges through the repetition of a specific pattern of activity. The moment can therefore be defined as "a higher form of repetition, renewal and reappearance" characterized by "the recognition of certain determinable relations with otherness (or the other) and with the self" (Lefebvre, 1961/2002, p. 344). The moment suggests a duration and, through its coexistence with other moments, generates a history; moments alternate and resonate with each other; they cover each other, emerge, last and disappear (Lefebvre, 2009). There is no way to draw up a complete list of moments because nothing prevents one inventing new moments (Lefebvre, 2009, p. 640). Among the criteria that define a moment, Lefebvre (1961/2002, pp. 344–347) highlights the following ones:

> (a) The moment is constituted by a choice which singles it out and separates it from a muddle or a confusion, i.e., from an initial ambiguity. . . . (b) The moment has a specific duration and its own duration. . . . (c) The moment has its memory. . . . (d) The moment has its content. . . . (e) Equally, the moment has its form: the rules of the game – the ceremony of love, its figures and rituals, and its symbolism. . . . (f) Every moment becomes an absolute. . . .

> Desalienating in regard of the triviality of everyday life . . . and in comparison with parceled activities it overcomes, the moment becomes alienation.

Designating a moment as such is a fundamental operation because it provides the person with a principle of coherence to organize and intensify the meaning of what would be otherwise experienced, either as a continuous repetition of everyday routines or as a discontinuous sum of unrelated experiences (Hess, 2009, p. 195). A moment is not a 'situation' because it results from a choice, an attempt to single a form of experience out. The moment creates and provokes situations; it condensates them by putting them in relations (Hess, 2009, p. 195). Conceived through the lens provided by a moment, everyday situations are no longer experienced passively through their banality; they are rather taken in charge as lived and they can become a matter of reflection and communication (Hess, 2009, p. 195). For Lefebvre (1961/2002), the relevance of this concept is inherent to his critical project aiming at favoring people's active appropriation of everyday life.

Alienating moments and the moment of emancipation

Within the context of our reflection, the relationship between moments and the experience of alienation is critical. For Lefebvre, the recognition of moments such as play, love, struggle, justice or art suggests that they represent some form of "absolute" (Lefebvre, 2009, p. 645). As such, their designation provides one the opportunity to conceive jointly the continuity and the discontinuity of specific life experiences. Becoming the subject of one's own moments constitutes a perpetual struggle against alienation. Freedom can be asserted through the constitution of moments, rooted in the reinterpretation of everyday experiences (Hess, 2009, p. 182). It is however when moments are experienced as an absolute that they also become alienating. Lefebvre (2009, p. 646) illustrates the case with the example of the moments of play and love; we could add eating or working as other examples. All represent casual activities; it is, nevertheless, when they are experienced as totalizing that they may become alienating. The compulsive gambler (or video game player), the obsessive lover, the person suffering from anorexia or bulimia and the workaholic all may experience some form of alienation because a specific moment tends to become hegemonic in the way they interpret and give meaning to their lives and their relationships with others. Such a predominance may appear as an individual feature; every moment finds nevertheless its roots within a social and cultural environment that enables it (Lefebvre, 2009, p. 643). Thus, the meaning taken by a moment constitutes a social construct shaped by the significations it takes within a collectivity (Lefebvre, 2009, p. 643). Whenever a moment becomes hegemonic in one's life, its rhythms and temporal constraints take over other temporalities. For the compulsive player, the temporal involvement of the game prevents one to participate to other activities; for the anorexic or the bulimic person, digestive rhythms are shortcut, and the rhythm of food ingestion becomes an omnipresent preoccupation; for the workaholic, professional time takes over all the other prominent rhythms of life and so on.

If the experience of a moment can become alienating, emancipating oneself can therefore be defined as the capacity to loose one's fondness (*se déprendre*) for a moment to change from one to another or to create a new moment (Lefebvre, 2009, p. 227). From this perspective, emancipation relates to the capacity to extract oneself from moments experienced as hegemonic. If we consider the moment of 'compulsion' (e.g., gambling, eating, consuming or working) as an example of an absolute form of experience, related to what could be otherwise conceived as a normal activity, then emancipation can be envisioned as the capacity to transition, move out, remove or extricate oneself from such experiences to create or reinvest other moments of one's existence.

Such a view also appears in congruence with the dual features (autonomy–dependence) previously associated with the idea of emancipation (cf. Chapter 8). Following Lefebvre's theory of moment, emancipation could thus be conceived as a moment in itself (or as a meta-moment), based on activities constitutive of a form of absolute, that relates to the human need for autonomy and freedom; as such, it may also be experienced as taking a hegemonic role within one's life. We could suppose that such a moment is particularly strong whenever someone's quest for autonomy becomes an end in itself (as it may be the case throughout one's adolescence). As much as it can feed a radical position, the moment of emancipation may also raise the risk for someone to become alienated by an ideal or by the means implemented to reach it. The relationships among the theory of moments, alienation and emancipation seems therefore characterized by the complementary, contradictory and antagonistic way those concepts relate with each other.

Transgression as a generic pattern of emancipation

Patterns of emancipation

From a temporal perspective, recognizing emancipation as a moment suggests that it involves, and evolves through, its own rhythms. The question appears then to establish what kind of rhythms are constitutive of an emancipatory process. Considering everyday life, how can we envision the casual rhythms that may contribute to someone's emancipation? How do they relate to temporal constraints? How are they inscribed within the broader temporalities of one's biography? To address such questions, we have to postulate that emancipation relies on specific discursive, corporeal and social schemes of activity (Michon, 2005). Depending on the theoretical framework mobilized to conceive emancipation, the main activity considered may differ; it may for instance relate to patterns of communication (e.g., Habermas's theory) or recognition (e.g., Honneth's contribution). Educational practices such as "life history" seminars (e.g., Dominicé, 2000) provide opportunities to identify various examples of activities that could be identified under the umbrella of the moment of emancipation. However, in the classroom, the word emancipation itself may not be used that often. It may rather be associated with specific situations, when increased freedom and autonomy appear as predominant features. Among those, episodes of 'transition' or 'transgression' regularly appear as specific times involved within a movement of extraction from perceived constraints (e.g., associated with culture, family, work or studies). In congruence with Lesourd's (2009, p. 221) comments around the formative role played by "rituals of transgression", such an observation contributes to the hypothesis according to which transgression may constitute one of the generic patterns constitutive of the moment of emancipation as it may lead – through its own repetition – to break through one's own limitations. It appears therefore relevant to consider experiences of transgression as an entry point to interpret and evaluate some of the rhythmic features of an emancipatory process, conceived through their movement, periodicities and specific patterns.

Defining transgression

The word transgression is usually connoted negatively as it is traditionally associated with the idea of violating orders, laws or divine commandments. The Latin etymology of the term opens up however a richer space of meaning; *trans-gredior* literally signifies "walking" or "moving through", "beyond", "above" or "on the other side" (Estellon, 2005, p. 151). Through the various meanings it carries, the term evokes exploratory aims, the qualities of insubordination or rebelliousness and some form of living curiosity related to secrecy as well (Estellon, 2005, p. 151). For Foucault (1963/1977, p. 35), the notion of transgression requires to be detached from its questionable association to ethics (e.g., the scandalous or the subversive) to be fully understood. As noticed by Estellon (2005, p. 151), fear, attraction for the unknown, morbid excitation and desire for discovery or exploration represent various states associated with the experience of transgression. From a psychoanalytical perspective, transgression can be interpreted as a way to challenge the distinction between the self and the other, characterizing identity troubles; the crisis of adolescence appears then as a paradigmatic figure (Roux, 2005, p. 7). For the psychoanalyst, the cure itself can be experienced as transgressive because it provides the individual with an opportunity to rediscover the gap between what is said and what is heard (Estellon, 2005, p. 152); sharing meanings that open a space for play (*jeu*) becomes therefore a matter of transgression. For the artist as well transgression may be generative as it produces the disequilibrium required to be creative. From the perspective of critical pedagogy, the notion also seems to evoke a core component of emancipatory education (e.g., hooks, 1994).

In his *Preface to Transgression* – an homage to George Bataille's work – Foucault (1963/1977, p. 33) explores the complexities of the notion:

> Transgression is an action which involves the limit, that narrow zone of a line where it displays the flash of its passage, but perhaps also its entire

trajectory, even its origin; it is likely that transgression has its entire space in the line it crosses.

The notion appears therefore through its temporality (i.e., its brevity), its repetitive nature and the tension it belongs to:

> The limit and transgression depend on each other for whatever density of being they possess: a limit could not exist if it were absolutely uncrossable and, reciprocally, transgression would be pointless if it merely crossed a limit composed of illusions and shadows.
> (Foucault, 1963/1977, p. 34)

Transgression and emancipation are related as they both suppose some forms of confinement to be conceived. However, for Foucault, transgression should not be reduced neither to violence nor a (revolutionary) victory over limits:

> [I]ts role is to measure the excessive distance that it opens at the heart of the limit and to trace the flashing line that causes the limit to arise. Transgression contains nothing negative, but affirms limited being – affirms the limitlessness into which it leaps as it opens this zone to existence for the first time.
> (Foucault, 1963/1977, p. 35)

If emancipation designates the opening of a space and time of rupture – as it has been suggested earlier – then transgression can be seen as a 'scheme' constitutive of the process of breaking through limitations. From a temporal perspective, if emancipation requires some duration to unfold, then transgression appears as one of the basic 'units' constitutive of its temporality. As suggested by Foucault (1963/1977, p. 35), transgression appears thus as a "flash of lightning in the night", an intense mark that requires to be repeated to continue existing as it does not subsist on its own. As a flash, transgression may be seen as the discontinuity that gives subjectification and emancipation their meanings. However, to remain meaningful and to carry on a movement of emancipation, transgression has to keep recurring until the limits that are imposed finally move or get redefined. From a temporal perspective, emancipation can therefore be interpreted as the moment of rupture emerging from the repetition of a pattern of transgression.

Ruth's life history: A tale of emancipation

Narrating one's own relationship to power and authority

To explore further what is at stake in the experience of emancipation – and in particular the transgressive dimension constitutive of this moment – the following section is based on the interpretation of a life narrative written by a young adult, Ruth (fictive name), who participated in one of the "life history" seminars I have been facilitating at the university (Alhadeff-Jones, 2010; Dominicé, 2000). When I met Ruth, the interpretation of her life history appeared to me as particularly relevant in regard to my own ongoing reflection around the theme of transgression. Her narrative expressed very clearly the double temporality – both irreversible and repetitive – that rhythms her experience of emancipation and, at the same time, the multiplicity of intertwined threads that characterize it. Such a theme was not however explicitly introduced in the presentation of the seminar. The course was organized around the theme 'leadership and self-development', and participants were required to share, orally at first, and then through a written narrative – submitted to the rest of the group for collective interpretation – significant life experiences related to ideas such as power, authority, control or mastery. The form as well as the type of experience described were freely chosen by each participant.[1]

Ruth's life history

Ruth was born at the end of the 1970s in a remote village in the Italian Alps. Her father migrated to the United States a few years before her birth, where he met her mother, a bi-national born and raised in North America, whose family originated from the same Italian town. After their wedding, the couple decided to go back to live there. The mother realized then that life in the village was very different from her expectations and that their conditions of living were more constraining than expected (e.g., no central heat, no hot water and no appliances). In addition, she was considered by her in-laws as a foreigner who was not particularly welcome. Living with her husband's family and working as a cashier for their butcher shop without any salary, she was expecting Ruth's birth as an opportunity "to fix some of this mess" (p. 1).[2] However, after the birth, nothing changed, and Ruth's mother, misunderstood and suffering from loneliness, started developing a depressive temper. As Ruth's father was working at the family butchery and spending most of his time with friends, her mother – in addition to her day time work – was in charge of the housekeeping and cooking for the family. Those two tasks were experienced as an everyday 'test' for her as she was continuously evaluated and judged by her husband's family. Early in her life, Ruth inherited the role allotted to women in her town: housekeeping and taking care of her younger brother. She was also invested as the one who could protect her mother from an environment perceived as hostile, even if that meant that she would suffer from the roughness of her own parents.

In many aspects, Ruth's narrative appears as a tale of emancipation – the emancipation of a young woman who was able, since her childhood, day after day, to learn to extract herself from her family, cultural, social, linguistic and geographic environment to finally leave and go study, first in Germany and later in the United States. Interrogating the experience of transgression leads first to the identification of the limits, the norms, the expectations and the situations that needed to be overcome. For Ruth, they appear through heterogeneous forms of material and symbolic forms of confinement: emotional confinement, as she was exposed in permanence to the anxiety and the depression of her mother, and the violence that was exerted on herself (e.g., getting hit); intellectual confinement, as she was experiencing the hermetic aspect of a world perceived as "very factual . . . made of things not thoughts" (p. 3), filled with the routines of daily household tasks; social confinement, as she was stuck with the roles, customs and codes imposed by gender stereotypes in a traditional society and the limitations of the financial resources of her family; cultural confinement, as she grew up in a family that did not value education; and physical confinement, as she was confronted to the narrowness of her hometown. It was also the linguistic captivity that she experienced, stuck between the dialect spoken by her father and the English spoken by her mother, two languages that prevented her as a child to think and express herself correctly and to acquire the official language (Italian) spoken at school. School difficulties and insolation emerged early on as core challenges. Later in her early adult life, additional limitations were experienced through the impossibility to have her boyfriend, a man from African descent and a Muslim, to be accepted and cohabit with her own family and to conjugate her desire for studying, traveling and the lack of financial support.

The evolution of the biographical movement of emancipation

The movement of Ruth's emancipation may be grasped, among others, through the evolution of her patterns of transgression. From a macro point of view, the moment of emancipation seems to have emerged in Ruth's life through a movement organized in three times: her initial exposure to transgressive models, her first experimentations of transgression and the reinforcement of her autonomy.

Initial exposure to transgressive models

The first period is characterized by her exposure to transgressive models. Before she turned one year old, Ruth's life was marked by the runaway of her mother, who brought her to the United States, where they stayed until her father decided – one year later – to join them and eventually convinced her mother to come back to Italy. Staying in a large city, Ruth discovered a horizon much larger than her hometown's:

> My first memory of Italy is in my grandmother's kitchen. . . . [S]he is lacing my sandals. She laces them too tight and I tell her 'they are too tight' and she answers 'they have to be tight otherwise you will lose them when you run'. That is how I felt about [the name of the town] from the very beginning: too tight.
>
> (p. 1)

When she was seven, her father refused to follow the recommendations of Ruth's teacher, who was asking for her to speak Italian at home (rather than the father's dialect or the mother's English) to help solve the learning issues she was experiencing at school:

> My father did not want Italian in the house and told me that my teacher could think what she wanted but that he was going to speak his language to me and nothing else. I sensed the tension between those two words [sic] and I saw from my father reaction that being against institutionalized authority was allowed.
>
> (p. 3)

Throughout anecdotic aspects of her everyday life, this first period of life brought Ruth to perceive herself as different from other children:

> I always felt different and I thought it was because [my mother] was not preparing for me the same snacks that my peers had, she dressed me with American clothes that my other grandmother sent, she could not help me with my school homework because she made orthographic mistakes.
>
> (p. 2)

In fifth grade, as she slowly started to express herself better in Italian, the attention provided by her new teacher eventually contributed to make her realize the role that education could play in her life: "I do not remember when I understood that school could be the way out of that town-tightness but I suspect it started with that teacher" (p. 4).

First experimentations of transgression

A second period started when Ruth was around 11 years old. The moment of emancipation may have emerged then, as she went through a period of experimentation and taking distance. During a visit to her mother's family in the United States, Ruth observed how relaxed her mother was there, and she experienced marks of affection she was not used to receiving in her hometown. Going back to Italy, she felt she was missing:

> all that explicit love, the love that [her American grand-parents] were not afraid to put in words and hugs. . . . I was eleven years old and determined to find a way out from [her hometown].
>
> (p. 4)

With the beginning of secondary education, studying in a middle school outside her town, Ruth discovered another social reality. Experiencing class and cultural differences, she started feeling ashamed of her parents' occupation. At that time, she decided to stop eating meat. She also chose to provoke her mother by stopping going to church. Then, she decided to withdraw herself to cook and eat alone. Doing so, Ruth was developing her capacity to take distance from her family and her parents' values:

> I started to feel ashamed about my father too because of his job. I thought it was not nice that he had to butcher animals and that he was always stained with blood. The first step I took to distance myself from them was to stop eating meat. This made my father furious of course. Then I stopped going to church, this mortify [sic] my mother and I was happy about it, after all she mortified constantly as a kid and giving some of that anger back made me somehow feel good. I could make some choices and they could not infer, I was trying to explore free will. . . . Not eating was for me also a way to prove to myself that I could take distance from a world that was made just of primary necessities (eat sleep) and objects without any embellishment.
>
> (p. 5)

Realizing the inequality of treatment between her and her brother, especially the privileges given regarding household duties, Ruth also took distance from him. Later, when she started her bachelor's degree, Ruth opted for a curriculum of study that was not proposed in the institution privileged by her father to register in a city located much farther away from her home. She experimented at that time the benefits of being away from her family and the possibility to study without the constraints of household duties imposed on her. At 21, she got a bursary to study in a major city in Germany. This was the opportunity to experiment with the unknown: she did not know anybody; she did not speak German; she did not know the culture. She finally got the opportunity to "grow out of [her] mold" (p. 6) without the fear of changing in front of people who would know her social origins. In spite of financial difficulties, Ruth was determined to get her diploma to prove to herself that she was an adult and to assert her differences in regard to her own parents:

> I was still attached to the idea of having a degree as a way to prove to myself that I was growing, becoming an adult. I also was thinking that I was different from my family and I needed a piece of paper to prove it.
>
> (p. 7)

At the same period, she introduced her boyfriend, a young man from African descent, to her parents. From there, her family refused to talk to her. Ruth was suffering from this breakup and from her parents' disavowal. She realized then the limits of her independence.

The reinforcement of autonomy

A third stage of her movement of emancipation emerged the following year with the reinforcement of her autonomy. Her partner lost his visa and became unemployed. Their couple life started to deteriorate economically and emotionally. Ruth was feeling prisoner of a situation she was no longer controlling. She decided then to quit her job, her partner, and her family to leave to the United States:

> I just wanted to find myself again. The only way I could think of doing it was by going away. Leaving a geographical place is the way I always dealt with suffering and discomfort in my live [sic].
>
> (p. 8)

Once she arrived in North America, Ruth worked at different places until she got hired to take care of children and be a housekeeper:

> The same job that my grandmother did when she migrated to the USA at the end of the '40s . . . I felt trapped in a cycle that I had not chosen, I could not identify what was keeping me in this caste of manual labor.
>
> (p. 9)

She decided then to start studying again and chose linguistics. She got accepted at a prestigious university. Throughout her life, Ruth suffered from not being able to express herself properly in any of the languages she was speaking: "I have an accent in every language I speak and I wanted to know why and if this meant that I could never express myself in anything I spoke" (p. 9). Through her studies, she started gaining self-confidence:

> I understood that multilingual speakers are not two or three monolingual speakers in the same head and that their language choices and ways of processing language is slightly different. I wish my teachers or my parents new [sic] this or that I could figure out this myself years ago.
>
> (p. 10)

The double periodicity of emancipation

The linearity adopted to restitute the emergence and the reinforcement through those three periods of the moment of emancipation should not occult the repetitions that characterize such a movement. Thus, the moment of emancipation seems to be articulated around heterogeneous rhythms that can be grouped under a double periodicity. On the one hand, Ruth's narrative suggests that the paces that shape the moment of emancipation vary according to the periodicity that marks the experience of temporal constraints experienced as alienating. On the other hand, it also displays the repetition of successive efforts to free herself from such constraints. For instance, throughout the everyday life of her childhood, the redundancy of household tasks, and the apprehension of the violence exerted on her, fed day after day Ruth's need to escape:

> [My mother] was really nervous about the housekeeping and cooking. . . . It was a situation in which we had to be always alert. My brother and I had specific duties for the house keeping and we would try to cheat as much as possible. She would get mad and hit us and tell us that we were not helping her.
> (p. 2)

The moment constituted around household duties (periodicity of temporal constraints) was thus anchored into a daily routine, which was occasionally challenged by the repeated attempts to 'cheat' (periodicity of transgression).

The periodicity of temporal constraints

Throughout her narrative, the periodicity of temporal constraints appears in reference to experiences or moments lived as *épreuves* that were particularly difficult to challenge and where transgressive strategies were difficult to implement. Thus, it was the school daily life that was feeding her recurring feeling of not being able to be understood, the isolation and the low self-esteem resulting from it: "In high school the refrain about me not being able to express myself started really soon, every teacher said I was not articulate" (p. 5). The incapacity to express herself verbally, according to the norm, was therefore locking Ruth within alienating discursive rhythms preventing the recognition of her intellectual capacity. Later, her working activity – either at home or through employment – and the succession of redundant work (e.g., cashier in a supermarket, waiter or housekeeper) raised another form of temporal constraints marked by the repetition of cadences perceived as alienating:

> [In Italy] I was not a brilliant student in high school but I managed to pass every year. I wanted to do better but I did not have time: I had to do housework after school and at night help my parents with the cleaning at the butcher shop. I started to think that my family was an obstacle to my achievement. . . . I kept helping with the housekeeping and helped my younger brother with his homework and helped at night in the store but I was an automaton.
> (p. 5)

The periodicity of transgression

During her childhood, with the experience of everyday dressing (wearing foreign clothes), the preparation of her daily snacks (different from Italian standards) and later through adolescence, the cooking of her own meals or the resistance to go to church, the repeated experience of 'micro-transgressions' (my word) participated first to the assertion of Ruth's own difference and later to her capacity to take distance from moments, such as family life. More distanced from each other, the repetition of her travels to America and the trips out of her hometown were also constitutive of some form of periodicity, providing Ruth with a resource to escape geographical confinement and to feed her desire to get away from the place where she was born. On a larger temporal scale, the repetition of situations characterized by a lack of language mastery (i.e., speaking Italian rather than her dialect at school and learning German when she studied abroad) brought her to adopt a transgressive strategy of study (in regard to the standard curriculum). Thus, as she was in Germany, she eventually developed her linguistic skills through night courses to accommodate temporal constraints:

> [In Germany] I felt more as a worker than a student. I started missing classes and by the end of the semester I found myself working 40 hours a week and going to night school to improve my German.
>
> (p. 7)

Individual and shared determinants of the patterns of emancipation

The temporalities that marked the development of Ruth's capacity to emancipate herself are as heterogeneous as the categories of experience within which it got exerted. As shown, the moment of emancipation expands through moments such as family life, school and studies, work, religion, travel and so on. Each of those moments is organized around rhythms that contributed to shape her experience of emancipation. Ruth's experience of emancipation is organized around heterogeneous rhythms that were shaped by both individual and collective temporal features. Thus, Ruth's development is at the same time singular, as it translates a movement characterizing the conjugation of repetitions and periodicities that are her own (as already illustrated), and at the same time it translates the influence of temporal constraints that go beyond her own individuality and that shape the patterns of her own individuation. The evolution of the moment of emancipation reveals therefore a dialogic between individual and collective dimensions as well as between chance and necessity. It is partly organized through the vicissitudes and the free will of Ruth's life, and at the same time it is inscribed in structures that translate predetermined temporal constraints.

Individual patterns of transgression and the singularity of emancipatory strategies

The patterns of transgression developed by Ruth throughout her life seem to have participated in the emergence of at least two distinct strategies of emancipation. The first one corresponds to a strategy of detachment; the second one appears as a strategy of (re)appropriation. The former emerges as a radical rupture; the latter rather appears through a sustained effort. The strategy of detachment appears the most clearly through the function played by geographical moves as expressions of physical transgression (here, the word is used almost literally as 'moving through') experienced when Ruth left her hometown to go study in another city, then went to Germany, and later moved to the United States. The pattern is repeated and, through its own repetition, gets more radical. If detachment appears geographically, it constitutes however an attempt to move away from symbolic, emotional and social ties: taking distance from her family, her partner, her gender-based household function, her culture and her class. Paradoxically, as much as it serves a purpose of detachment, it seems also rooted in her own mother's strategies of emancipation (e.g., her runaway to the United States 20 years earlier).

The strategy of (re)appropriation appears through Ruth's efforts to conquer the way she expresses herself verbally and relate to her experience of school and studies: challenging herself to study in Germany without speaking German and going to an American university to study linguistics to make sense of her childhood school difficulties. It is also intertwined with her attempt to overcome her experience of socioeconomic alienation, as it appears through her desire to escape her hometown and move beyond the repetitive jobs she finds herself condemned to repeat, wherever she lives. Here again, such a strategy seems to be anchored in family heritage. After all, her initial linguistic difficulties were embedded in her father's will to assert his dialect against the hegemony of Italian, a national language, and her struggle with employment repeats patterns already experienced by her grandmother when she migrated to America.

Based on Ruth's narrative, patterns of transgression and the strategies of emancipation they contribute to form appear as both distinct and intertwined. They are constitutive of specific moments, such as the moment of studies (actualized through her academic degree and her realization of how multilingual speakers process language choices) and the moment of traveling (actualized through her migration to the United States and her increased capacity to adjust to new places and new cultures). As reinforced and actualized moments, they demonstrate her capacity to emancipate herself. As moments, they carry the potential to become alienating, too. Their evolution – Ruth's self-development – questions therefore how one learns to keep such moments flowing. How does one learn to enrich existing moments with new emancipatory strategies? How does one learn to relate them to other moments of one's own existence?

Sociocultural and shared temporal constraints determining emancipatory strategies

Whether or not they participated in Ruth's emancipation, the actualization of specific patterns of transgression and emancipatory strategies remains embedded within sociocultural and shared temporal constraints. They are therefore inscribed not only in contingencies but also within a predetermined rhythmic environment. Three examples may illustrate this claim. First, the difficulties encountered by Ruth with language acquisition, and the strategies implemented to overcome them, cannot be reduced to tensions among institutional requirements, family preferences and her own perseverance. They are also, at the core, determined by cognitive processes inscribed within chronopsychological constraints that define how she could process language(s) at different stages of her life. They are bound from within her own organism. At another level, the geographical trajectory that led Ruth to leave her hometown to go to Germany, and later to the United States, was not strictly dependent on her capacity to be autonomous. It was also shaped by the temporal structure of the Italian curriculum of study and the way it was inscribed into European educational tracks. Such school and state policy provided her with entry and exit points to move away from her village, study in another country and eventually leave again to reenter a university on the other side of the ocean. In the same way, when she was in Germany, night courses provided her with a 'temporal buffer' (my word) to adjust with her employment schedule constraints. Finally, considering the role played by her gender in her experience of alienation, as a girl and later as a woman, the horizon of her own emancipation – beyond family dynamics – appears embedded within a dual history: on one side, the traditional community she came from, and the 'stage' of sociocultural development that characterizes it, which represent a clear limitation to the potential expression of her identity and the social roles she could assume, as long as she remained in her hometown; on the other side, the progressive values that characterize American culture at this time of history, and the appeal they may have represented in regard to her own emancipation.

From the moment of emancipation to the rhythms of emancipatory education

Inspired by Lefebvre's contribution, the first part of this chapter redefined the meaning of alienation, emancipation and their mutual relationships, considering them through the lenses provided by a theory of moments. Emancipation appeared as the capacity to extract oneself from moments experienced as alienating because of their totalizing dimensions and the prevalence of their own rhythms. Emancipation was defined as a moment, too: a moment related to human needs for autonomy and freedom; a moment characterized by its own rhythms; a moment that eventually could also reveal itself as potentially alienating. To envision emancipation from a temporal perspective, considering both its everyday manifestations and its inscription in the life span, the question was raised to determine how to study it, considering a real-life narrative. Inspired by the experience of life history seminars, and referring to Foucault's considerations on transgression, the hypothesis was then formulated that transgression may represent one of the generic patterns constitutive of the moment of emancipation as it may lead – through its own repetition – to break through limitations and confinements to redefine one's own autonomy.

To explore further the rhythmicity of the moment of emancipation, we turned to Ruth's life history. Through the interpretation of her narrative, we identified temporal features characterizing the way she evolved and was eventually able to emancipate herself from her family and her sociocultural background. Thus, her biographical movement of emancipation appeared as organized around three times: her initial exposure to transgressive models, her first experimentations of transgression and the reinforcement of her autonomy. Furthermore, the moment of emancipation appeared through the articulation of heterogeneous rhythms that could be grouped under a double periodicity: the periodicity of temporal constraints and the periodicity of transgression. Finally, the evolution of the moment of emancipation revealed a tension between individual and shared features, both determining its patterns: individual patterns of transgression and the singularity of Ruth's emancipatory strategies (detachment and (re)appropriation) on one hand; sociocultural and shared temporal constraints determining the unfolding of her emancipatory strategies on the other. Ruth's narrative evoked therefore a movement that is at the same time continuous and punctuated by ruptures. It is articulated around the irreversibility of a life organized around *épreuves* through which Ruth had to go to progressively conquer her own autonomy. It also expresses repetitions that organized the periodicity of activities and moments, experienced either as alienating or liberating. Finally, it displays patterns of transgression and strategies of emancipation, partly embedded in Ruth's origins and actualized through the contingencies of her own trajectory and partly related to collective and shared psychological, social and cultural temporal constraints determined by history.

Can we theorize the rhythmic dynamics of emancipation based on the interpretation of a single life history? Certainly not. It remains, however, that such an exercise displays features that would deserve to be explored more systematically and more broadly, both from a theoretical and an empirical perspective. It also raises questions regarding the way emancipatory education could be envisioned and defined. How does one influence the movement of emancipation? Is there such a thing as a 'pedagogy of transgression'? How does one learn to keep one's emancipatory strategies flowing to avoid being locked into one's patterns of transgression?

Notes

1 To study her narrative and preserve her anonymity, some changes have been made to the original text. The terms used to describe her experience have been either directly borrowed from her narrative or chosen carefully to remain very close to the meaning expressed in her writing. The content of my analysis and the chapter as a whole have been discussed with Ruth to make sure that the language used to qualify her experience was appropriate and that the interpretations were perceived as meaningful.
2 Page numbers refer to the original text written by Ruth.

References

Alhadeff-Jones, M. (2010, September). *Transformative learning, life history and the temporalities of learning*. Keynote lecture given at the Hellenic Adult Education Association 2010 Meeting, Athens, Greece. Retrieved from https://www.academia.edu/343377/Transformative_Learning_Life_History_and_the_Temporalities_of_Learning

Alhadeff-Jones, M. (in press). Rythmes et paradigme de la complexité: Perspectives moriniennes. In J. Lamy, & J.-J. Wunenburger (Eds.), *Rythmanalyse(s) et complexité*. Lyon: Jacques André Editeur.

Ardoino, J. (2009). Des moments et du temps. In R. Hess (Ed.), *Henri Lefebvre et la pensée du possible: Théorie des moments et construction de la personne* (pp.13–20). Paris: Economica-Anthropos.

Dominicé, P. (2000). *Learning from our lives: Using educational biographies with adults*. San Francisco: Jossey-Bass.

Estellon, V. (2005). Eloge de la transgression. *Champ Psychosomatique, 38*, 149–166.

Foucault, M. (1977). A preface to transgression. In D.F. Bouchard (Ed.), *Language, counter-memory, practice: Selected essays and interviews* (pp.29–52) (D.F. Bouchard, Trans.). New York: Cornell University Press. (Original work published 1963)

Hess, R. (2009). *Henri Lefebvre et la pensée du possible: Théorie des moments et construction de la personne*. Paris: Economica-Anthropos.

hooks, b. (1994). *Teaching to transgress*. New York: Routledge.

Lalande, A. (1926/2002). *Vocabulaire technique et critique de la philosophie*. Paris: Presses Universitaires de France.

Lefebvre, H. (2002). *Critique of everyday life (vol.2)* (J. Moore, Trans.). London: Verso. (Original work published 1961)

Lefebvre, H. (2009). *La somme et le reste*. Paris: Economica-Anthropos.

Lesourd, F. (2009). *L'homme en transition: Éducation et tournants de vie*. Paris: Economica-Anthropos.

Lesourd, F. (2013). 'Boucles étranges' et complexité des temporalités éducatives. In P. Roquet, M.J. Gonçalves, L. Roger, & A. Viana-Caetano (Eds.), *Temps, temporalités et complexité dans les activités éducatives et formatives* (pp.41–56). Paris: L'Harmattan.

Michon, P. (2005). *Rythmes, pouvoir, mondialisation*. Paris: Presses Universitaires de France.

Roux, A. (2005). Avant-propos. *Champ Psychosomatique, 38*, 7–11.

Chapter 12

The emergence of a rhythmological critique and the moment of theory in education

Modeling a rhythmanalytical approach to critical education

The reflection conducted in this book started with the observation that the idea of time – as discussed for instance in philosophy, physics, biology or human sciences but also in the arts and religions – reveals both an impressive amount of attempts to reduce it to something that can be grasped by the human mind and the unavoidable confusion associated with the heterogeneity of phenomena they relate to. One of the underlying assumptions framing our reflection was that to conceive both the orders and the disorders inherent to the experience and the study of time, one must question the ways they are – or could be – organized. What appears through the successive chapters is that such modalities of organization constitute a theoretical issue as much as it represents a practical and existential one. Learning to think and conceptualize the idea of time cannot be conceived without questioning how we experience it, in the everyday life, throughout the life span and through history. Moreover, conceiving the heterogeneity of temporalities that shape education raises issues related to their mutual relationships: how do they interact or influence each other? How do they evolve? Such questions brought us to explore temporal constraints and the ways they confine, bind, restrict or put into tension the rhythmic features that characterize educational phenomena, such as individual or collective learning, transformation or development. We have then explored the evolution of the social imaginary of time, the exercise of temporal discipline, the tensions between conflicting rhythmic ideals, their internalization and the ubiquity of the experience of discontinuity as phenomena that affect both the practice and the meaning of education throughout history. From the study of temporal constraints and their impact on autonomy, we moved to the idea of emancipation, conceived as a rhythmic phenomenon related to a temporal environment experienced as alienating. It brought us to consider how the development of autonomy relates to rhythmic patterns, periodicities and movements that may be experienced as constraining or even alienating. We have then started envisioning what may be at stake in the development of rhythmanalytical approaches to critical education. Finally, we explored how the movement of emancipation itself expresses rhythmic features that can be conceptualized. As a way to summarize some key aspects developed in this book, and to open up this reflection, this conclusive chapter suggests six core issues to consider to develop further the elaboration of a rhythmic theory of emancipatory education and the praxis it may involve. Adopting a recursive position, it concludes with a reflection around the specific rhythms of educational theory and some of their critical functions.

Questioning the rhythms of emancipatory education

The aim of the following sections is neither to make prescriptions nor to reduce the complexity of the matter to a finite set of problems. The intent is rather to formulate intuitions fed by the reflections conducted throughout this book to organize – between the order provided by theoretical constructs and the disorder of the praxis – the functions that may be constitutive of the 'moment of rhythmological critique', whether conceived from the perspective of educational theory or praxis. To proceed, this section is organized around six logics, identified in previous research (Alhadeff-Jones, 2007) as key aspects organizing the finalities and the functions associated with the idea of critique in education.

Discriminating rhythms

The term "discrimination" refers to the conscious or unconscious activity of differentiating and distinguishing elements from each other to process them according to specific treatments (e.g., establishing similarities and differences, identities and otherness, equalities and inequalities, etc.) (Alhadeff-Jones, 2007, 2013). Some temporalities are obvious (e.g., circadian and seasonal) due to the prevalence of the changes that constitute them or their specific pace. Others remain subtler either because their periodicities are too long or too short to be discriminated (e.g., a young child cannot conceive what a 'year' represents and under a tenth of second, the brain cannot perceive discontinuities) (Sauvanet, 2000, p. 180) or because their patterns involve changes that occur without being noticed (e.g., being too casual). Perceiving a rhythm is a matter of education. Recognizing the presence of multiple and heterogeneous temporalities questions therefore the way one learns to discriminate – purposefully or not – the succession of lived or observed changes and repetitions as well as the rhythms they may express. From a critical perspective, the first function of a rhythmic education may be therefore to interrogate how one learns to identify and distinguish specific physical, biological or sociocultural rhythms, such as those expressed through discourse, body and sociality. Considering the fact that "[w]e are only conscious of most of our rhythms when we begin to suffer from some irregularity" (Lefebvre, 1992/2004, p. 77), paying attention to irregularities experienced in the quotidian (e.g., breakdown, dysfunction or sickness), or taking advantage of the resistances offered by a specific medium (e.g., reading or urban space), may constitute privileged ways to trigger the detachment required to identify and distinguish rhythmic patterns, periodicities and movements remaining otherwise taken for granted or unchallenged. From an educational perspective, such phenomena question how to promote some form of 'exochrony' (from the Greek: *exo-*, meaning 'outside, outer' and *chronos*, time) as a capacity to detach oneself from a familiar experience of time.[1]

Interpreting rhythmic phenomena

Interpretation refers to at least two operations constitutive of the process of meaning making. The first one is a matter of translation, which implies transforming what is discriminated to assimilate it according to a set of invariants (e.g., perceptive, linguistic, conceptual, anthropological, etc.) (Alhadeff-Jones, 2007, 2013). Once discriminated, a rhythm typically requires symbols to be described. As discussed around the meaning of *rhuthmos* in Greek philosophy (cf. Chapter 4), one key aspect is for instance to determine whether a rhythmic phenomenon is interpreted through quantitative or qualitative features. The second interpretive operation is to attribute meaning to what is discriminated, according to a specific language. The history of education shows that such language may come from any 'branch' of human activity (e.g., arts, biology, economy, mathematics, philosophy, physics, psychology or religion) and that it is usually disciplinary, doctrine or theory based. Thus, for Plato, conceiving rhythms through their arithmetic measure served his doctrine and brought him to establish specific forms of order to describe how moral and esthetic education are related. More broadly, what is at stake is to identify what kind of discourse may serve the purpose of giving meaning to a rhythmic phenomenon and according to which logics does it proceed. From an educational perspective, the assumption is that educational phenomena may require the development of a specific vocabulary to interpret the temporalities expressed through learning, transformational or developmental dynamics. As discussed in Chapters 8 and 9, envisioning the rhythmic nuances of educational praxis requires a gamut of expressions that goes beyond 'fast' and 'slow'. In addition, as illustrated by Ruth's biography (cf. Chapter 11), resources mobilized to interpret one's temporal experience are also produced through one's life history; they borrow from any aspect and any period of one's trajectory to give coherence to and articulate one's past, present and future.

Examining rhythms' values and their normative features

Examination supposes the capacity to evaluate a phenomenon to better appreciate, know or understand it. Beyond discrimination and interpretation, examination involves the adoption of a system of values, norms and standards to compare the object of study with a scale, a referential or a system and determine its value

(Alhadeff-Jones, 2007, 2013). Reducing a rhythm to the measurement of some of its features (e.g., periodicity) is convenient because it provides an easy way to examine and evaluate it. In education however, most rhythmic phenomena cannot – or should not – be reduced to a metric. A critical matter is therefore to determine according to which values educational patterns, periodicities and movement are appreciated and evaluated. As illustrated in Chapter 4, the adoption of a specific system of rhythmic value remains a normative choice embedded within social and historical dynamics. As discussed in Chapter 5, the development of an abstract and quantified conception of time in education contributed to reproduce the principles carried on by the industrialization of society and the rise of capitalism. It also led to the emergence of innovative educational methods contesting such standards and valorizing other referentials (e.g., artistic, embodied and spiritual) to appreciate empowering rhythmic experiences. The reflections around temporal double binds (cf. Chapter 6) and schizochrony (cf. Chapter 7) also illustrate how conflicting temporal standards (e.g., efficiency vs. equity or family vs. work) may be internalized and become a source of suffering. The choice of criteria used not only to qualify but to appreciate educational experiences is a critical matter. As discussed in Chapter 8, referring to slowness is not enough to build up a rational critique of temporal alienation. It seems that the vocabulary is still missing in education to assess the heterogeneity of temporal experience. It appears therefore critical to determine how one learns to define, organize and hierarchize the values attributed to the rhythms of one's existence.

Arguing about the evidences and the logics of rhythmic influences

From an educational and critical perspective as well, one of the key questions remains to determine the nature of the influence between heterogeneous rhythms (e.g., physical, discursive, corporeal, social, individual and collective) and the ways they eventually synchronize with each other. As discussed through the limitations of rhythmic contributions to educational theories developed in the early 20th century, establishing rational connections among environmental, social, cultural and psychological rhythms raises difficulties (cf. Chapter 5). As an activity, argumentation refers to at least three operations that contribute respectively to establish evidence, deliberate and communicate around the legitimacy of the way a phenomenon is interpreted and examined. Argumentation is based on the way one pays attention to evidence that is produced (e.g., observations, recording, transcript and measurement) and the logics that frame the discourses through which such evidence is elaborated (e.g., forms of rationality, logics, calculus, rules of argumentation, rhetoric, etc.) (Alhadeff-Jones, 2007, 2013). From an educational perspective, it seems critical to determine how one establishes the nature of rhythmic influences (whether or not experienced as constraining, liberating or both). It seems equally decisive to establish what rationale may express or explain why and how temporal constraints occur.

Considering phenomena of synchronization from a sociological perspective, the reflections conducted in Chapter 3 discussed both the functional and symbolic dimensions associated with the influence of temporal norms. Exploring the evolution of traditional education, the examples provided in Chapter 4 illustrate how temporal discipline is exercised through heterogeneous influences occurring at the level of discourse, corporeity and sociality. Some of the examples of rhythmic theories provided in Chapter 5 also illustrate the issues raised by esoteric or analogical modes of argumentation, establishing pseudo-rational connections among language, body and social change. With the interpretation of Ruth's narrative (cf. Chapter 11), we have tried to demonstrate how discursive rhythms (e.g., linguistic dynamics), social rhythms (e.g., family dynamics, curriculum organization and historical context) and corporeal rhythms (e.g., travels) were influenced by each other. As suggested with the references to life histories (cf. Chapters 7 and 11), the capacity to elaborate a narrative plays a critical role in such an interpretive process. Beyond explanation, the capacity to argue and communicate around the evidence and the logic of rhythmic influence raises an additional question: how does one learn to build up a sense of rhythmic cohesion, not only from a rational and scientific perspective but also, and more deeply, from an existential one, taking into consideration the heterogeneous determinants that organize one's experience of time?

Judging and balancing rhythmic features

Formulating a judgment is closely intertwined with activities such as discriminating, interpreting, examining and arguing; it involves however an additional critical function. Through the formulation of an opinion, a judgment establishes some form of authority (acknowledged or not) involving the adoption of a set of principles that define what is right or wrong, fair or unfair and balanced or unbalanced. Establishing a judgment questions the underlying principles of justice (e.g., Boltanski & Thévenot, 1991/2006) that may be mobilized when one tries to justify the formulation of a critique or solve a situation experienced as an *épreuve*. More fundamentally, an act of judgment involves a process of equilibration aimed at resolving a state of unbalance (Alhadeff-Jones, 2007, 2013). Because there are no emancipatory or alienating rhythms per se, uncertainty can only remain regarding what constitutes a 'good' rhythm or a 'legitimate' rhythmic influence. From an educational perspective, it seems nevertheless critical to interrogate how one judges, for oneself or for others, what constitutes the 'right' temporal experience. How does one learn to (re)establish balance, whether considered symbolically as an expression of justice and equity, and physiologically, psychologically and socially, as an expression of individual and collective well-being? Considerations developed in Chapter 9 around the rhythmic features of temporal constraints (patterns, periodicities and movements) provide criteria to carry a judgment in relation to rhythmic experiences. Judging the temporal relevance of phenomena such as learning, teaching, change or development, from the perspective of rhythmic balance, brings one to question the equilibrium between continuity and discontinuity within a rhythmic movement or between the different paces of change constitutive of periodic phenomena. It also interrogates the balance found between the rigidity and the fluidity of rhythmic patterns, including those that may organize one's own process of emancipation (cf. Chapter 11).

Challenging rhythms

Discriminating, interpreting, examining, arguing and judging the experience of time involve activities that contribute to alter, change and modify, but also challenge and put into question, the way rhythms are experienced and conceived. They may also trigger a crisis or lead to a significant transformation, whether individual or collective. To some extent, it may be one of the main functions of emancipatory education (Alhadeff-Jones, 2007, 2013). Challenging rhythms involves disturbance and tensions and may eventually lead to ruptures within a temporal order, characterized until then by the relative stability of a moment's rhythms. As discussed in Chapter 7, the recent history of education illustrates well the role played by discontinuities within learning activities, in settings such as dual education, through the evolving relationship between formal and informal education or considering the continuum of one's own biography. The experience of discontinuity is critical because it challenges the rhythms that characterize a specific moment through the introduction of a differential of durations, what Sauvanet (2000) describes through the notion of syncope (cf. Chapter 9). As suggested in Chapter 11, if alienation is conceived as the expression of the hegemony of a specific moment in one's life, then emancipation appears through the capacity to move out, transition or extract oneself from its activities. It may involve a capacity of transgression.

From an educational perspective, what is at stake is to determine what may be the educational effects associated with the modification of a rhythmic equilibrium, whether or not it can be incremental, and how it can be managed. As it appears through the interpretation of Ruth's narrative (cf. Chapter 11), transgressing the rhythms of a moment may constitute one of the generic patterns of emancipation and lead to the development of specific strategies of autonomization. We may assume that the consequences of the efforts implemented to extract oneself from a moment is proportional to the intensity of the disruption affecting the rhythmic pattern that organize its activities, the flow of their movement or the modulation of their periodicity. However, beyond the intensity of the tensions it provokes, a transgression seems to carry meaningful effects only if it occurs at the right time.

The *kairos* of transgression plays therefore a critical role. When considering the relationship between individual changes and social transformation, a contribution such as Archer's (1979) morphogenetic theory suggests indeed that the nature of the timing between decisions made at the level of individuals, on the one hand, and the windows of opportunity provided by changes occurring at the level of culture and social structures, on the other hand, constitutes a critical aspect of social transformations. From a rhythmic perspective, the challenging function of emancipatory education appears therefore through the capacity to identify the opportune time (Galvani, 2011), the *kairos*, through which individual agency may effectively influence collective changes. It finally questions how one develops the capacity to discriminate, interpret, examine, argue and judge what may be the 'right' timing to alter and transform both individual and collective experiences of temporal constraints.

The moment of theory as a time of rhythmic transgression

Conceived through the lens of rhythmanalysis, educational theory represents a moment characterized by its own history and defined by the rhythms of the moments it relates to (e.g., reading, reflecting, writing, discussing, sharing or resting). It can also be conceived as being part of larger moments, such as the moment of education and the moment of theory. The reflection conducted in this book aims at renewing those moments. When considering the importance of questioning temporal constraints and temporal alienation, at this specific time of our history, it seems not only relevant but particularly opportune to envision how a rhythmological critique can enrich and be enriched by the work of those who dedicate themselves to both education and research. Because a moment tends to become an absolute, it is relatively easy to conceive that educational theory may become alienating, locking those who embrace it within a space and time disconnected from other moments of existence. As a matter of fact, during those two past years, how many days, weeks or months did I spend on my own, distant from my wife, my children, my family, my friends and my colleagues, to experience, nourish and be fed by this moment? However, its emancipatory value only takes its worth from the nature and the intensity of its connections to the other moments of one's life.

To nurture the critical and emancipatory function of educational theory, this moment has to remain connected to other educational moments. It has to be conceived in relation with the individual experience of *auto-formation* (self-development) and the shared experience of *hétéro-formation* (learning with and through the other). It must rely on *éco-formation* as an opportunity to learn with and through one's environment (Pineau, 2000). It has to be related to the collective experience of school time, higher education, vocational training, *éducation permanente* and lifelong learning. It cannot be separated from the management of educational organizations or the negotiation of educational policies. For the moment of educational theory to enrich and be enriched by those moments, it has to remain articulated with them. Many reasons can be formulated to justify the relevance of educational theory or denounce its irrelevance (Biesta, Allan, & Edwards, 2014). Among the arguments often cited, one finds the specificity of the discourses educational theory can produce about education. At this stage of the reflection, my conviction is that the value of this moment has to do with its content, its features, as much as it relates to the processes it involves. Theory is the product of a rhythmic activity, mostly discursive and definitely social but nevertheless embodied. As such, it is inscribed in a specific time. It seems therefore reasonable to believe that the critical value of educational theory is found within the rhythms it sustains and perpetuates.

The relevance of educational theory is a matter of time and timing, rhythms and synchronization. It expresses patterns, periodicities and movements. The content of educational theory is important. But beyond, educational theory is precious because of the specific values of the rhythms that configure and organize such a discursivity. Through their fundamental heterogeneity, the rhythms through which educational theory is produced participate in the time of the world. They may look similar to other rhythms contributing to the social organization of science. But in fact, they have their own idiorhythmy. Therefore, theorizing the rhythms of emancipatory education constitutes a critical endeavor, not only because it provides a theoretical framework to discriminate, interpret, examine, argue, judge and challenge the temporal constraints that shape education. Its critical and emancipatory value also comes from what it demonstrates, its *rhuthmos*: the patterns, periodicities and movements that characterize a specific way to relate to the world and to the way, every day, we try to nurture what makes us be more human. In comparison with the environment within which it evolves, the moment of educational theory may constitute a rupture. Theorizing the rhythms of emancipatory education is an activity that is critical, not only because of the knowledge it may produce but because it leads one to challenge the temporal standards that constrain the educational phenomena it relates to. At the core, entering into the activity of theorization constitutes therefore an invitation to transgress. Whether such a transgression is valuable to extract oneself from moments experienced as alienating remains a feature that cannot be generalized or abstracted. My personal experience is that it may lead to detachment, as well as it may participate in a (re)appropriation of the world I am living in and the time I am living through. But above all, it may be emancipating because, as a transgressive moment desired and freely chosen, it provides resources to create rhythms through which one can relate to the world, to others and to oneself . . . at one's own pace.

Note

1 See also Baudouin's (2009) use of the notion of *exotopie*, borrowed from Bakhtine. In the context of biographical research, the notion refers to the experience of spaces that are distant from the adult learner's proximal environment and that challenge one's own points of reference.

References

Alhadeff-Jones, M. (2007). *Education, critique et complexité: Modèle et expérience de conception d'une approche multiréférentielle de la critique en sciences de l'éducation*. Lille, France: Atelier National de Reproduction des Thèses.

Alhadeff-Jones, M. (2013). Complexity, methodology and method: Crafting a critical process of research. *Complicity: An International Journal of Complexity and Education, 10*(1/2), 19–44.
Archer, M.S. (1979). *Social origins of educational systems*. London: Sage.
Baudouin, J.-M. (2009). L'autobiographie à l'épreuve du texte: La formation comme exotopie. In D. Bachelart, & G. Pineau (Eds.), *Le biographique, la réflexivité et les temporalités: Articuler langues, cultures et formation* (pp. 97–108). Paris: L'Harmattan.
Biesta, G., Allan, J., & Edwards, R. (Eds.). (2014). *Making a difference in theory: The theory question in education and the education question in theory*. London: Routledge.
Boltanski, L., & Thévenot, L. (2006). *On justification: Economies of worth* (C. Porter, Trans.). Princeton: Princeton University Press. (Original work published 1991)
Galvani, P. (2011). Moments d'autoformation, kaïros de mise en forme et en sens de soi. In P. Galvani, D. Nolin, Y. de Champlain, & G. Dubé (Eds.), *Moments de formation et mise en sens de soi* (pp. 69–96). Paris: L'Harmattan.
Lefebvre, H. (2004). *Rhythmanalysis: Space, time and everyday life* (S. Elden & G. Moore, Trans.). London: Continuum. (Original work published 1992)
Pineau, G. (2000). *Temporalités en formation: Vers de nouveaux synchroniseurs*. Paris: Anthropos.
Sauvanet, P. (2000). *Le rythme et la raison (vol. 1): Rythmologiques*. Paris: Kimé.

Index

academic learning time (ALT) *see* instructional time
accelerated learning programs 1, 9, 142, 152, 153–4, 165; accelerated/intensive courses 152; and adult education 152; and classroom boredom 165; as commodification of learning 152; and higher education 152; origins of 155n1
Adam, B. 20–2, 26, 29, 44–5
agency 9, 50, 51, 127, 132, 134, 160, 161, 166, 215; *see also* autonomy
Alheit, P. 133; and biographicity 133
alienation 4, 9, 10, 51, 56, 59, 97, 146, 147–8, 149, 158, 164–5, 167, 168, 169, 181, 194; and arrhythmic behaviors 167, 169; definition of 206; and discontinuities 170, 185; as hegemonic moment 214; and institutional autonomization 151; as moment 191, 194–5, 214, 216; and periodicity 164; and quotidian rhythms 181; and repetition 164–5; socioeconomic 205; temporal 3, 5, 9, 136, 141–2, 148–9, 151, 155, 188n1, 212, 215
alternance 8, 17, 38, 43, 64, 92, 113–14, 118n3, 121, 124, 125–8, 130, 136, 147, 160, 162, 163, 164, 184; associative 127; copulative 127; juxtapositive 126–7; temporal 70; and vocational training 164
anthroposophy 8, 86, 101; anthroposophic society 98
Archer, M. 159–60, 214; morphogenetic theory of 214
Ardoino, J. 45, 59–60; *Education et Politique* 54
Aristotle 17–19, 75–6, 77, 143, 146; *Physics* 17; and rhythm 92, 98
Aristoxenus 75–6
arrhythmia 92, 93, 167, 169, 182; *see also* rhythm

Attali, J. 53, 70, 79–80
Augustine 17–19; *Confessions* 17–18; and phenomenological approach to time 18–19
auto-formation 127, 130, 183–4, 186, 187, 215; vs. *éco-formation* 183, 215; vs. *hétéro-formation* 183–4, 187, 215; rhythmicity of 188
autonomy 6, 7–9, 10, 25, 47, 50, 51, 52, 56, 78, 84, 92, 95, 98, 104, 108–10, 125, 127–9, 141–7, 149, 154–5, 158–64, 166–7, 169–70, 178, 183, 186–8, 191, 195–6, 199, 202, 206–7, 209; and auto-formation 186, 187; autonomy-dependence principle 145, 195; vs. dependence 144–5, 146–7, 155, 160–1, 169, 183; individual 187; and movement(s) 169, 170, 187, 209; and patterns 187, 209; and periodicities 187, 209; and repetition 164; rhythmic 145, 187, 191; as self-determination 149; vs. social acceleration 149; vs. social constraints 162; strategies of 214; of students 108, 125, 127–8, 162, 178; of teachers 108, 109; temporal 8, 118; and temporal constraints 141, 145, 155, 209; and transgression 191, 206–7; of workers 129

Bachelard, G. 5, 9, 93, 122–3, 136, 137, 172, 180–2, 187–8; and formation 123; philosophy of instant 180–1; *see also* rhythmanalysis; temporal discontinuity
balance 93, 94, 98, 99, 100, 111, 122, 123, 168, 170, 181, 183, 213; rhythmic 214
Barthes, R. 5
Batencour, J. de 82
Benveniste, E. 5, 75, 165

Bergson, H. 18, 93, 122–3, 180, 193; theory of time 180; *see also* duration; temporal continuity
biographicity 133; biographical inquiry 191
biological time 24–7, 37, 41, 59; environmental factors 114; epigenetic rates of change 24–6; evolutionary rates of change 24–6, 27; metabolic rates of change 24–6
Bloom, B. S. 105–7
Bode, R. 8, 86, 97–8, 100, 162, 165, 182; and *Koerperkultur* 97; and national socialism 98; and rhythmic gymnastics 97–8; rhythmic methods of 182; and synchronicity 98
Bourgeon, G. 126–7
Bücher, K. 92–3

Carroll, J. 105–7
Castoriadis, C. 4, 54–6, 63, 151
Chopin, M.-P. 107–8
Christian Church 77, 79, 162; hegemony of 84
chronobiology 25, 34, 113–14, 115–16, 183; concept of synchronization 183; *see also* biological time; rhythm(s)
chronography/chronographical approach 32, 33, 34–5; and chronicles 34–5; and narratives 35, 40; and stories/tales 35
chronology/chronological approach 32, 33, 35, 59, 60, 61, 62, 134, 160, 192; and the past 35
chronometry/chronometrical approach 32, 33–4, 35, 59; and time management 34; and time shortage 34
chronopsychology 8, 34, 104, 113, 114–16, 206; and psychology of time 114
chronosophy 32, 33, 35–6, 175; ascending 48n1; and astrology 36; and clairvoyance 36; cyclical 48n1; definition of 35–6; descending 48n1; and divination 36; and the future 36; linear 48n1; and pedagogy of the oppressed 174; pluralist 36–7, 44; stationary 48n1
complexity, paradigm of 6, 16
complexivist epistemology 6, 16, 20
complexivist understanding/perspective 26, 27, 30, 144–5
compulsory education 87, 88, 128, 167; and idiorhythmy 167; laws about 87
cooperative teaching *see* team teaching
corporeity 147, 158–9, 161–2, 169, 170, 187, 213; corporeal rhythms 162, 167, 210, 213; features of 166; patterns of 163; schemes of activity 195; and temporal discipline 213
Csikszentmihalyi, M. 186; concept of flow 186

Démia, C. 82
Democritus 75
dependence 164, 166; vs. autonomy 9, 141, 144–7, 154–5, 160–1, 164, 166, 169, 183, 195
Dewey, J. 110; educational theory of 163–4
differentiated staffing 110
discontinuity *see* temporal discontinuity(-ies)
discrimination 3, 61–2, 210, 211; ageism 61
discursivity 147, 158–9, 169, 170, 187, 216; discursive flow 168; discursive rhythms 161, 167, 203, 210, 213; features of 166; patterns of 163; schemes of activity 195; and temporal discipline 213
disjunction: principle of 26; principle of absolute 23
distinction, principle of 26
division of labor, principle of 87, 111, 128
dos Santos, Pinheiro 180; and rhythmanalysis 180
double bind, concept of 8, 104, 116–18, 141, 212; and formal education 117–18; temporal 8, 141, 212
"double loop learning" theory 164
duration 25, 27, 28–9, 57–9, 64, 70, 93, 122, 123, 128, 130, 134, 152, 159, 174, 177, 180, 184, 188n3, 192, 193, 197, 214; experienced 18, 122; philosophy of 123; *see also* moment
Durkheim, E. 28, 53, 93

Early Modern period 1, 7, 50, 69, 77, 80, 83, 84, 162; economic influence 82, 84, 162; educational compartmentalization in 82; educational standardization in 82, 162; efficiency of students/teachers 83, 84; elementary schools in 82–3; measurement of learning 83; obedience of students 83, 84, 162; school schedules 82–3, 84
education: adult 2, 35, 130, 132, 161, 166, 172, 183, 185; conservative function of 164; definition of 42; dual 39, 160, 163, 214; evolutionary process of 164; formal 2, 8, 57, 61, 62, 72, 90, 104, 113, 117–18, 125, 128, 130, 160, 176, 184, 214; higher 1, 10, 10n1, 60, 152, 172, 183, 185, 215; informal 8, 65, 118, 121,

128, 130, 184, 214; and instituted time 56–63; nonformal 184; permanent 132; political dimensions of 54; and repetition 165; rhythmic 8, 86, 94, 96, 98, 101, 118, 154, 162, 210; rhythmic movement of 170, 172, 191; sciences of 42–4; and social organization 163; and social time 53–4; *see also* compulsory education; emancipatory education; Greek education; home education; rhythmic theory of education; traditional education; vocational education
educational psychology 105, 155n1
educational rhythm(s) 8, 9, 127, 158, 169, 179; periodicity of 9
educational temporality(-ies) 6, 7, 27, 29–30, 32, 37, 39–41, 43, 47, 63, 86, 104, 109, 115–16, 125, 136, 158–9, 162, 179, 183; heterogeneity of 209; *see also* temporal experience
educational theory 5, 6, 9, 10, 29, 32, 37, 42, 43, 45–6, 84, 86, 90, 97, 99, 100, 116, 124, 152, 163, 172, 180, 182, 183, 210, 215–16; as alienating 215; critical function of 215; emancipatory function of 215; and idiorhythmy 216; moment of 215–16; relevance of 216; as transgressive 216
educational third-time 131
educational time 6, 7, 23, 27, 69, 109, 130–1, 155n2; directionality of 23; irreversibility of 23; as linear 23–4; non- 130
educational tracking/tracks 57, 61, 206
éducation permanente 59, 126, 128, 129–30, 183, 215; *see also* lifelong learning
Einstein, A. 21–2; *Eigenzeit* 21; theories of relativity 21
Elias, N. 20, 29, 44, 146
emancipation 3, 5, 6, 7, 9–10, 47, 50, 51, 96, 141–7, 149, 151, 154–5, 158, 159, 162, 163, 169, 172, 188; vs. alienation 146; and auto-formation 186; and biographical trajectory 191; definition of 142, 206; and duration 197; and everyday experiences 191, 195; from hegemonic moments 195; through history 142; as irreversible discontinuity 174; and kairos 186; as meta-moment 195; modernist idea of 149; as moment 191, 195–6, 197, 202, 204, 205, 206–7; and movement 166, 168–9, 191, 196, 210; patterns of 177, 179, 191, 196, 204; and periodicity 164, 179, 191, 196, 202; and privileged moments 186; and quotidian rhythms 181; and repetition 164; and resonance 151; and rhythm 96, 167, 187, 195; rhythmic features of 10, 170; rhythmicity of 10, 158, 170, 188, 191, 209; and rhythmic patterns 169, 214; as rupture 169–70, 197, 205, 207; strategies of 204–6, 207; as subjectification 175, 197; and syncope 167–8; temporal heterogeneity of 191; as transgressive act 175, 196, 197, 206–7, 214; as transition 196, 214; *see also* autonomy; individuation
emancipatory education 10, 30, 41, 51, 52, 65, 118, 125, 136, 141, 144, 147, 151, 155, 166, 167, 175, 178, 180, 182, 196, 207, 210, 214–16; definition of 207; functions of 214, 215; and movement 166, 167; paradox of 125, 143–4, 146; rhythmic dimensions of 147, 155, 166, 180; rhythmic theory of 210, 216; rhythmoformation and 182; transgression and 196
Enlightenment 91, 143
eurhythmics 8, 86, 95–8, 101
eurhythmy 100
Evans-Pritchard, E. E. 69–70
everyday life 2, 4, 9, 47, 56, 65, 114, 117, 129, 133, 148, 150–1, 155, 160, 163, 164, 169, 178–9, 181, 183–5, 193–5, 200, 203, 209
exochrony 211
expression, idiosyncrasies of 167, 168; as arrhythmic behaviors 167

Feuerbach, L.: on religious alienation 148
First World War 87, 88, 101, 128
Ford 87; assembly line 87, 97, 164
formal education: defragmentation of 8, 118; *see also* education
formation 3, 123; *parcours de* 110; *see also* auto-formation
Foucault, M. 82–3, 191; on transgression 191, 196–7, 206
France 82, 93, 131, 159, 182–3, 188n2; and *éducation permanente* 128, 129–30; study of education in 41, 108, 110, 115; vocational training in 126
Fraser, J. T. 44
Freire, P. 9, 172, 173–4, 176, 177, 178, 179; pedagogy of the oppressed 172–4
Freud, S. 180; Freudian slip 60; psychoanalytical theory 180

Galvani, P. 172, 186, 187, 188; on kairos 186; on moments of auto-formation 186
German Enlightenment 91; and rhythm 91–3
Germany 91, 93, 98, 198, 201, 204, 205, 206; apprenticeship in 126; gymnastics in 97; study of education in 41, 94
Goethe, J. 92
Greek education 72, 73–4, 84; Homeric education 74; and rote repetition 73; and separation of subjects 73; *see also* Hellenic musical education; Spartan musical education
Greek mythology 186, 188n3; Aion 188n3; Chronos 188n3; Kairos 188n3
Gurvitch, G. 29

Habermas, J. 178, 195
Halbwachs, M. 28
Hargreaves, A. 112
Hegel, G. W. F.: on alienation 147–8; and dialectical moment 192; on moments 192–3
Heidegger, M. 19–20; *Dasein* 19; *Geschichtlichkeit* 19; *Innerzeitlichkeit* 19; levels of temporization 19; *Zeitlichkeit* 19
Hellenic musical education 7, 69, 75–7; and moral values 84
Hess, R. 172, 182–3, 184, 187, 188, 192, 193; concept of moment 182, 184–5, 192; on Marx 192
Hölderlin, F. 92
holisitic assessment practices 110
home education 167; and autonomy 167
human machine metaphor 118–19n4
Husserl, E. 18–19

idiorrhythmy 78, 162, 167, 216
individualization 110, 129, 131, 175; and *épreuve* 135, 164, 203, 207, 213; and narrative identity 133; *see also* individuation
individualized instruction 110, 131
individuation 93, 146–7, 158, 204; and corporeity 147; and discursivity 147, 161; and sociality 147
Industrial Age 118–19n4
Industrial Revolution 1, 8, 77, 86–8, 90, 162; effect on education/schools 87–8, 91, 100–1; and idleness 87; and saving time 87; and temporal framework 148; and time clock 87; and time management 87; and training schools 126; and value of efficiency 87, 91; and working time 80, 86–7, 91; and work/rest schedules 87
institution: definition of 54–5; and otherness-alteration time 55–6, 59; and symbols 54–5
instructional time 8, 34, 81–2, 86–90, 101, 105, 108–9, 117, 130, 153, 160; academic learning time (ALT) 34, 89, 105, 106–7, 108–9, 183; and achievement 105; allocated time 89, 106, 107; and aptitude 89, 105, 106; commodification of 90; didactic 104, 108–9; engaged time/attention 89, 106; and "identical presents" 90; and opportunity to learn 105; and perseverance/pace 89, 105, 106; time on task 26, 89, 105, 106; transition time 89, 106, 130; waiting time 89, 106
International Society for the Study of Time 30n1
invariant 17, 21, 25, 33, 184, 211

Jacotot, J. 176
Jankélévitch, V. 186
Jaques-Dalcroze, E. 8, 86, 94, 96, 97, 98, 99, 162, 165; and musical education 94–5; and rhythm 95, 96, 100, 182; *see also* eurhythmics
Jewish education 7, 69, 70–4, 83–4; and absence of books 73; and absence of vowels 73, 161; ancient history of 71–2, 118n1; and cantillation 74; and circadian rhythm 72; and elementary school 71–3; and memorization 73; and Oral Law 71, 72, 73; and oral tradition 161; and the Pentateuch 72–3; and rote repetition 73; and scripture 72, 73; and social/political order 83; during Talmudic period 72

kairos 4, 167, 168, 170, 186, 214, 215; *see also* Greek mythology; opportune time
Kant, E. 18–19, 143; and emancipation 143; and temporal schemes 18–19, 122
Kierkegaard, S. 168; notion of leap 168

Laban, R. 94–5, 97; and dance education 94–5
La Salle, J.-B. de 82
learning: cycle(s) 8, 104, 109, 110, 111, 113, 160; everyday 130; outcomes 109–10; *see also* lifelong learning
Lefebvre, H. 5, 9, 10, 164, 172, 180, 181–2, 184, 188, 191, 206; on Hegel 192; on moment 184–5, 187; and quotidian

rhythms 181; and rhythmanalysis 181–2, 187; theory of moments 191, 193–5, 206; *see also* moment
Lesourd, F. 172, 185–6, 187, 188; on privileged moments 185–6, 187; on rituals of transgression 196
lifelong learning 3, 8, 59, 62, 121, 128, 129–30, 132, 215; and agency 161; and idea of adulthood 132; and life history and biographical methodologies 132–3, 136, 161, 183, 187, 197–207, 211, 213; *see also éducation permanente*
linear causality, principle of 23

Mandelstam, O. 96; and cadence 96; and eurhythmics 96; and rhythmic education 96; rhythmic methods of 182
Marx, K.: on alienation 148; on human history and development 192; and oppression 173; perspectives on work 150, 151
Marxist 97, 173; anti- 98
mastery learning model 106
Mauss, M. 5, 28, 69–70, 93, 146–7
Mead, G. H. 28
mechanics: and time 21, 25
medieval period 77; anchorites 78; asceticism in 78; autarky in 78; collective life 79; and control of rhythms 84; "fight" against idiorhythmy 78, 162, 167; and "God's time" 80; hermits 78; monasteries 79, 80; monastic education 7, 69, 78–9, 161, 162; monasticism 78; and obedience 79, 167
Meschonnic, H. 5, 146
Mezirow, J. 9, 172, 177–8, 179; and domains of learning 178; on emancipatory and transformative learning 172, 177–8, 183; transformative learning theory of 177–9, 186
Michon, P. 5, 63, 70, 88, 96, 146–7, 158, 161
Middle Ages 80; and "merchants" time 80; and working day 80
moment(s): as absolute 194; as alienation/alienating 194–5, 206; as anthropological singularization 192–3; of compulsion 195; definition of 192, 193; of education 215; hegemonic 194–5; historical 192; vs. instant 192; logical 192; in physics 192; theory of 10, 185, 193, 195, 206, 215; transgressive 216
Montessori, M. 110
Morin, E. 6, 16, 30, 145, 147, 151; *Method* 144; paradigm 30

Moritz, K. P. 92
movement(s) 4, 9, 18, 23, 28, 39, 42, 59, 75, 76, 81, 90, 92–3, 98, 123, 158, 163, 165–8, 170, 173, 176, 183, 187, 196, 204, 209, 211, 212, 213, 214, 216; of autonomy 188; biographical 10, 170, 207; of the body 95, 99–100, 147, 162; celestial 17, 21, 99; continuity or discontinuity of 170, 214; dialectical 193; double 15; educational 43, 88, 97, 104, 118, 130, 136–7, 170, 212; of educational theory 216; of emancipation 142, 146, 168–9, 179, 191, 197, 199, 202, 207, 210; of history 83–4; and moment 192; science of 192; subatomic 22; of transformation 179
multiage classroom/pupil grouping 106, 110
multigraded pupil grouping *see* multiage pupil grouping
multireferentiality 45–6, 47, 69

Newton, Isaac 21–3; on absolute time 21; mechanics 25; on physical time 37; *Principia* 21; on relative time 21
Nietzsche, F. 92
nongraded schools 109, 111, 113; Dewey's Laboratory School 110; elementary 110; Stoddard's Dual Progress Plan 110
Nowotny, H. 53, 129

opportune time 188n3, 215
Organization for Economic Cooperation and Development's (OECD) 126, 130

pattern(s) 4, 10, 25, 61, 110, 163, 168, 173, 175, 187–8, 193, 209, 210, 211, 213, 216; and chronosophy 48n1; communication 117, 195; of duality 181; educational 125, 164, 174, 177, 212; of educational theory 216; of emancipation 177–9, 191, 196, 206; of freedom 124; of individuation 204; learning 179; periodic 39; rhythmic 118, 128, 158–62, 165, 167, 169–70, 214, 216; social 57; temporal 27, 57, 115, 136, 149, 163; of transgression 197, 199, 204–5, 207; work 115
pedagogy of the oppressed 172, 173–5; and chronosophy 174, 175
periodicity(-ies) 4, 9, 10, 25, 27, 75, 83, 116, 124, 125, 128, 136, 158, 166, 168, 173, 187, 209, 210, 211, 212, 213, 214, 216; circadian 181; double 202, 207; educational 162–5, 169, 212; of educational theory 216; of emancipation

170, 179, 188, 191, 196, 202; of temporal constraints 203, 204, 207; of transgression 203, 204, 207
Pestalozzi, J. H. 95
Piagetian theory 127
Pineau, G. 3, 20, 130, 134, 172, 182–4, 185, 187, 188; chronoformation 182, 183; educational theory of 183–4; rhythmoformation 182, 183, 185
Plato 2, 17, 75–7, 84, 146; and moral values 84, 161; *The Republic* 2, 76; and rhythm 92, 95, 98, 101, 116, 161, 211
Pomian, K. 33, 35, 37, 39, 44, 45, 48n1
Prussian school system 87
psychic being 146–7
Pythagorean concept 75, 122

quantum physics 122; and time 21–2

Rancière, J. 9, 144, 172, 175, 178, 179; on education 176–7; on emancipation 172, 175–6; on equality 175–6; on pedagogical practice 172, 176–7; *see also* subjectification
recurring education *see* lifelong learning
Reformation 81
Renaissance 69, 77, 81, 84; and Greek classics 81; and 'the order of reading' 81, 161; and school schedules 81
repetition 25, 27, 33, 55, 56, 64, 70, 71, 75, 86, 90, 97, 117, 123–5, 128, 136, 158, 162–9, 173, 174, 177, 179, 181, 184–5, 186, 193, 194, 196, 197, 202–5, 207, 210; and alienation 164–5; rhythmic 34; rote 73
rhuthmos 75–6, 78, 92, 146, 154, 165, 167, 170, 211, 216
rhythm(s) 51, 63–6, 86; anthropological 64; arrhythmic behaviors 167, 169; biological 24–6, 37, 39, 46, 60, 64, 113–14, 116, 134, 162, 183; of the body 93, 113–14; collective 84, 96, 167, 182, 212; concept of 187; corporeal 162, 167, 187, 212, 213; cosmic/cosmological 64, 181, 183; definition of 158; discursive 161, 167, 187, 203, 212, 213; duplicity of 76; as economic principle 92–3; and education 121; etymology of 75, 78; external 84, 98, 114, 182, 183; heterogeneity of 212, 216; idiorhythmy 78, 162, 167, 216; individual 212; internal 98, 99, 134, 167, 183; of language 93; movement(s) of 166, 187, 211, 214, 216; natural 57, 76, 97, 98, 99; and pattern(s) 159, 187, 211, 214, 216; and periodicity(-ies) 162–3, 165, 187, 211, 214, 216; phenomenology of 180; physical 212; as political utopia 96; and power 83; psychological 60, 212; school 34, 115, 118n3; social 28, 57, 93, 98, 134, 158, 183, 187, 212, 213; and structure 159; synchronization of 2, 28, 34, 44, 115, 183, 212; and syncope 167–8, 170, 214; and time 64–5; *see also* Aristotle; eurhythmics; Plato; rhythmic education; rhythmic experiences; rhythmic phenomena
rhythmanalysis 9–10, 93, 123, 137, 164–5, 170, 172, 180–2, 187–8, 215; and critical education 209–10; emancipatory aim of 181; framework for 191; and patterns of duality 181; and quotidian rhythms 181
rhythmic cohesion 213
rhythmic constraints 97, 128
rhythmic discontinuities 52
rhythmic dissonance 1
rhythmic education 8, 86, 94, 96, 98, 101, 118, 154, 162; functions of 210
rhythmic equilibrium 214
rhythmic experience(s) 101, 167, 212, 213; embodied 8; and introspection 181; *see also* Bachelard; rhythmanalysis
rhythmic gymnastics 8, 86, 97–8, 101
rhythmic harmony 8, 52
rhythmicity 9, 10, 57, 72, 73, 91, 92, 97, 100, 118n3, 122, 136, 146, 155, 158, 159, 163, 184, 191; of emancipation 170, 188, 207; natural 57; social 57
rhythmic movement 136–7, 167, 170, 214
rhythmic phenomena 5, 76, 101, 116, 159, 162, 165, 178, 212; criteria for 158; interpretation of 211–14; *see also* movement; pattern; periodicity
rhythmic theory of education 121, 124, 125, 136, 164
rhythmoformation 182, 183, 185
rhythmological: critique 210, 215; moment of 210; perspective 169, 172, 180
rhythmological theory of emancipatory education 10
Ricoeur, P. 17–20, 133; aporetics of time 20
Roman empire 77, 79
Romanticism 91, 125
Rousseau, J.-J. 2, 95, 153; on alienation 147–8; *Emile* 2, 153

Sauvanet, P. 5, 64–5, 158–9, 162, 165, 167, 181, 214; and *rhuthmos* 75
Schiller, F. 92; on education 94
schizochrony 121, 134, 136, 141, 183, 212
Schlegel, A. W. 92
school time 87, 130–2, 215; differentiated 110–11, 117
Second World War 86, 88, 101, 110, 113, 128
segmentation 26, 55, 90
self-directed learning 130
slow movement 153, 168; market of slowness 174; slowness 212; *see also* slow school movement
slow school movement 2, 153, 165; vs. school deregulation 153; slow education 9, 142, 153–4, 155n2
social acceleration 142, 148–9, 151, 152, 154, 174; and alienation 165; vs. autonomy 149; of the pace of life 149; of social change 149; technical 149; and temporal alienation 148–50; as totalitarian phenomenon 150; *see also* accelerated learning programs
social being 28, 46, 146–7
social imaginary 51, 55, 56: of human rhythms 118–19n4; of time 60, 63, 65, 116, 121, 209
sociality 70, 147, 153, 158–9, 167, 169, 170, 187, 213; features of 166; patterns of 163; schemes of activity 195; social rhythms 28, 210; and temporal discipline 213
sociology of time 28, 51
Socrates 143, 176
Sorokin, P. A. 28
Spartan musical education 7, 69, 74–5; and discipline 75, 162; and gymnastic 74; and moral values 84; and poetry 74; and religious festivals 75
speed 6, 9, 80, 83, 87, 91, 141, 148–54, 162, 165, 169; of light 22
standardization: of education 2, 10n1; of learning 153; of life course 160; of social behavior 53; of work 88
state educational systems: centralized 159; decentralized 160
Steiner, R. 8, 86, 98–9, 165; and Waldorf education 99–100; *see also* eurhythmy
structure *see* pattern
subjectification 143, 145, 175, 177, 197
Sue, R. 53, 131

symbolism: definition of 55
synchronization 134, 213; of rhythm 2, 28, 34, 44, 115, 183, 212
syncope 167–8, 170, 214

Taylor, F. 87, 151, 179; taylorization of learning and teaching 90
team teaching 110
temporal alienation *see* alienation
temporal cohesion 8, 137
temporal constraint(s) 1, 7–10, 50–2, 64, 65, 65n1, 116, 128, 134, 151, 158, 162, 174, 180, 191, 194, 195, 212, 215; alienating 202; vs. autonomy 141, 145, 159, 160, 209; collective 215; definition of 52; and discipline 82; as double bind 118; and education 69, 71, 84, 104, 108–9, 113, 117, 209, 216; and emancipation 154–5, 195; forms of 160; generational 61–2; individual 215; and individuation 204; institutionalist perspective on 54–63; movement(s) of 213; pattern(s) of 213; periodicity(-ies) of 169, 202–3, 207, 213; and power 82; shared 205–6, 207; *see also* temporal discontinuity(-ies)
temporal continuity(-ies) 112, 121, 122, 128, 132
temporal contradictions 52, 117
temporal discipline 3, 8, 9, 52, 101, 128, 141, 209, 213
temporal discontinuity(-ies) 118, 121–3, 127, 128, 129, 131, 132, 133, 136–7, 141, 158, 166, 168, 210; and double belonging 133–4; and education 209, 214; as epiphany(-ies) 121, 134–5, 136, 164; as *épreuve(s)* 121, 134–5, 136, 164, 168, 203, 207, 213; experience of 8, 9, 214; and fragmentation 133–4, 136, 141, 164; irreversible 174; vs. reliance 151
temporal efficiency 52
temporal exile 134
temporal experience(s) 5, 7, 50, 53, 65, 101, 109, 112, 134, 152, 169, 174, 211, 212, 213; of administrators 112; "changeability" 174; "despair" 174; "existential insecurity" 174; heterogeneity of 212; "non-progressiveness" 174; "presenteism" 174; 'right' 213; of teachers 112
temporal inequalities 91
temporal norms 7, 9, 50, 53, 65, 84, 90, 104, 118, 141, 149, 151, 213

temporal pressures/tensions/conflicts 1, 81, 109, 112, 149, 150, 174–5; between administrators and teachers 112, 118; efficiency vs. fairness 113, 117; between students and teachers 112
temporal regularity 57–9
temporal units 127, 162
thermodynamics 21–2, 23; dissipative structures in 22, 27; and entropy 22; and time 21, 22
tiers-temps scolaire 121, 160, 164; *see also éducation permanente;* lifelong learning
time: absolute 22–3; abstract 109; of action and production 125; of auto-formation 127, 130; biological 24–6, 37, 41, 59, 210; calendar 55; and change 37–9; of classical physics 55; and clocks 2, 19, 23, 33, 37, 38, 53, 56, 58, 79–80, 87, 115; as *Dasein* 19; definition of 2–3, 16, 64; and dissipative structures 22; beyond dualistic views of 20–1; and entropy 22; as eternal/external 17, 19, 33–4, 43, 109, 134; as experienced duration 18, 122, 130, 134; free 2, 129, 131; of the future (expectation) 18; heterogeneity of 209; horizons of 18; of human experience 55; identitary 55; imaginary 55–6; industrial 128, 212; instituted 55, 59, 60; instructional 8, 34, 81–2, 86–90, 101, 105–6, 108–9, 117, 130, 153, 160; as internal 17, 43; as irreversible 22, 169; as language 19; legal 108; leisure 105, 128; levels of temporization of 19; as linear 22, 23–4; measurable 109; as natural 29, 43, 109; opportune 188n3, 215; of the past (memory) 18; as perceived 18; phenomenological approach to 19; physical 37, 38, 41, 134, 210; plurality of 36, 44–5; and power 52–3; of the present (consideration) 18; private 90–1; processual 107–8, 109; 'proper' 90–1, 129, 155n2; as psychological experience 43, 59; public 90–1; as a quality 43, 148, 151; as a quantity/quantifiable 21, 43, 109, 148, 151; as relationship 39; as reversible 21; and rhythms 64; sacred 70, 83; singular collective of 18; social 28–9, 40, 41, 43, 50, 53, 56, 59, 65, 93, 116, 134, 150, 181, 184; as social construct/construction 4, 7, 23, 28, 29, 34, 35, 37, 40, 43, 51, 53, 194; sociocultural 28–9, 210; spatialization of 93; of study and the mind 125; transcendental approach to 19; tyranny of 148; universal 22–3; working 53, 59, 80, 86, 87, 104, 129, 148; *see also* biological time; educational time; Heidegger; institution; instructional time; opportune time; school time; social imaginary of time
time-levels of existence 44–5
traditional education 69, 70–1, 74, 83, 100, 161, 183, 213; ethical 71; technical 71
transgression 10, 130, 175, 191, 196–7, 214, 216; definition of 196; and emancipation 197; examples of 198–207; *kairos* of 214; patterns of 204–6; pedagogy of 207; periodicity of 203–4, 207; physical 205
transgressive models 199–202, 207

United Kingdom 62, 93
United Nations Educational, Scientific and Cultural Organization (UNESCO) 130
United States 87, 198, 200, 202, 205, 206; and academic learning time 106–7; and education of the "gifted and talented" 155n1; and "graded school" system 87–8; National Educational Commission on Time and Learning (NECTL) 107; and nongraded schools 110, 111; study of instructional time in 88–90, 105, 107; *see also* instructional time
urgency, experience of 3, 9, 141, 142, 148–9, 150–2; and alienation 165; vs. freedom 150; and the time-urgent personality 150

vocational education/training 53, 74, 80, 121, 125, 128, 160, 215; and alternance 121, 125–7, 164; and apprenticeship 125–6; and mentorship 125

Wagner, R. 92
Whitehead, A. N. 5, 93, 121, 122, 123–4; and process 124; and rhythmic theory of education 124–5, 136, 164; and threefold cycle 124–5, 161

Zerubavel, E. 57–8